Comparative Economic Systems

An Inquiry Approach

Holt Social Studies Curriculum
GENERAL EDITOR EDWIN FENTON

Comparative Economic Systems

An Inquiry Approach

JOHN R. COLEMAN
President, Haverford College
Formerly Dean, Division of Humanities and Social Sciences,
and Professor of Economics, Carnegie-Mellon University

Holt, Rinehart and Winston, Inc.
New York, Toronto, London

For John, Nancy, Patty, Paul, and Stephen

Printed in the United States of America
03–065170–0
0123 19 98765

Contents

To the Student

This is a new kind of textbook. Most social studies texts you have read in the past contained information about a particular subject, like American history or geography. The texts were written by one or two authors who organized their material into chapters, each with an important theme. There were numerous illustrations in the form of pictures, graphs, tables, and charts. You read or examined this material to learn the facts and generalizations it contained.

Instead of twenty or thirty chapters written by one or two authors, this text has sixty readings. Each reading contains an article, or at least one piece of source material taken from a newspaper, magazine, book, government document, or other publication. An introduction—which links one reading with another—and study questions—which will alert you to important points and issues—precede the article or the source material.

You will not find many pictures in this text, but filmstrips, a recording, and transparencies for the overhead projector have been provided for use with many of the readings.

Both the written and the audio-visual materials have been designed so that instead of merely memorizing facts and generalizations, you will identify problems, develop hypotheses—or tentative answers to questions—and draw your own conclusions from factual evidence. Throughout this course in Comparative Economic Systems, you will be challenged to think for yourself and to make up your own mind.

Most students are able to study one reading in this text for each night's homework assignment. Because most classes meet from seventy-five to eighty-five times a semester and there are only sixty readings in all, there will be days when no readings from this book are assigned. On these days, your teacher may wish to give tests, to assign supplementary readings, to analyze the local or state economy, to study current events, or to hold individual conferences with students.

During mankind's history, three main types of economic systems have developed: the traditional economy, the market economy, and the command economy. This course examines the predominantly traditional economy of primitive tribes, the predominantly market economy of the United

States, and the predominantly command economy of the Soviet Union. No economy, however, is purely any one of the three types. Each society has developed its own variations. In a semester, there is not time to study every society's economic system. But you can learn how to approach the study of an economic system and can develop the tools you will need to analyze any economic system at any time or in any part of the world.

We welcome you to a fascinating subject, as complicated as man himself: the ways in which different societies solve similar economic problems.

Edwin Fenton
General Editor
Holt Social Studies Curriculum

How To Use This Book

The text of *Comparative Economic Systems* consists of sixty readings which have been edited from published works or written especially for this course. Each day's assignment follows a common pattern:

1. *An introduction* giving background information and relating the reading to other readings in the same chapter.
2. *Study questions* stressing key points which you should think about to prepare for class discussion.
3. *An article written especially for this course, or a piece of source material* such as a newspaper article, a speech, or an excerpt from a book.

Before coming to class, read the lesson and take notes. Since your teacher will distribute dittoed material from time to time, you should have a three-ring looseleaf notebook which can hold both the material which will be distributed and your homework and classroom notes. Note-taking helps you to remember what the lesson is about, and thus prepares you for class discussion. There are many methods of note-taking. But unless you find from experience that a different method works better, use the following one:

1. *Write the reading number and the title of the reading at the top of a piece of paper.*
2. *Skim the entire reading.* Read the topic sentences of the introduction. Next, read the study questions and fix them in your mind. Then read the topic sentences of the article itself. When you have finished, state in your own words what the reading is about. All this should take no more than two or three minutes.

3. *Read the introduction and take notes as you read.* Pick out the major ideas and necessary information to support those ideas. It will save time if you develop your own method of shorthand, instead of using complete sentences. But remember that you may wish to study from the notes several months later, so take down enough information to make the notes meaningful. Do not underline or mark the text.
4. *Read the article or source material carefully and take notes as you read.* Put any conclusions you draw in parentheses as a reminder that they are your ideas. Do not underline or mark the text.
5. *Go over your notes, underlining key words or ideas.* This will help you to learn the information in the reading, and prepare for class discussion.
6. *Try to answer the study questions for yourself.* Do not write your answers out. Simply think about them and be prepared to present and defend your answers in class.
7. *Keep a vocabulary list of new words and their definitions.*

It will also help to keep your class notes and your reading notes together in your notebook, so that you can review without flipping through a mass of paper to find material which goes together.

If you have trouble with this note-taking method, or if it takes too long, ask your teacher for help. Because some lessons are based on charts or tables, the note-taking technique we have suggested cannot always be used. In such cases, your teacher will give you supplementary instructions.

Supplementary Reading Material

At the end of each of the first six units, you will find a list of selections from paperback books and pamphlets suggested for supplementary reading. In some cases, teachers may add items to the supplementary reading list in order to cover topics of special interest to students in a particular part of the country. Your teacher may have placed these books in the library or in your classroom. He may require you to read some of them or may assign some for extra credit.

Beneath each of the book or pamphlet titles, you will find a study question. These questions should help you to decide which item you want to read. You may also want to leaf through a number of the items suggested, to get a better idea of what they are like. Some of the items are easier to read than others. You should choose which to read on the basis of your own interests and reading skill.

Your teacher may wish to make special rules and regulations about the supplementary reading material. Some teachers may choose not to use them at all. Others may ask you to submit short papers or book reports based on the volume you select.

The list below includes all paperback books and pamphlets cited in the supplementary reading lists at the ends of the first six units:

COMMITTEE FOR ECONOMIC DEVELOPMENT, *An Adaptive Program for Agriculture.* New York: Committee for Economic Development, 1962.

____________, *Raising Low Incomes Through Improved Education.* New York: Committee for Economic Development, 1965.

DAUGHERTY, MARION, *Understanding Economic Growth.* Glenview, Ill.: Scott, Foresman and Company, 1961.

DUNBAR, ROBERT G., *The Farmer and the American Way.* New York: Oxford Book Company, 1956.

FEDERAL RESERVE BANK OF NEW YORK, *Money: Master or Servant?* New York: Federal Reserve Bank of New York, 1966.

____________, *The Story of Checks.* New York: Federal Reserve Bank of New York, 1966.

FEDERAL RESERVE BANK OF PHILADELPHIA, *Automation; Inflation and/or Unemployment; The Mystery of Economic Growth; The National Debt; The New Poverty; The Price System; Unemployment in Prosperity: Why?* Philadelphia: Federal Reserve Bank of Philadelphia.

HEILBRONER, ROBERT L., *The Worldly Philosophers.* New York: Simon and Schuster, Inc., 1967.

INDUSTRIAL RELATIONS CENTER, UNIVERSITY OF CHICAGO, *Capital: Key to Progress.* Chicago: Industrial Relations Center, University of Chicago, 1952.

____________, *Competitive Prices in Action.* Chicago: Industrial Relations Center, University of Chicago, 1958.

____________, *Profits at Work.* Chicago: Industrial Relations Center, University of Chicago, 1961.

KOREY, EDWARD L., "Business in a Changing World," *Business and the American Way.* New York: Oxford Book Company, 1961.

KOSTER-DANA CORPORATION, *Inside the Modern Corporation,* New York: Koster-Dana Corporation.

LISITZKY, GENE, *Four Ways of Being Human.* New York: The Viking Press, 1962.

RIEBER, ALFRED J. and ROBERT C. NELSON, editors, *The USSR and Communism: Source Readings and Interpretations.* Glenview, Ill.: Scott, Foresman and Company, 1964.

SCHWARTZ, HARRY, editor, *The Many Faces of Communism.* New York: Berkley Publishing Corporation, 1962.

SENESH, LAWRENCE and BARBARA WARNE NEWELL, *Our Labor Force.* Glenview, Ill.: Scott, Foresman and Company, 1961.

THEOBALD, ROBERT, *The Rich and the Poor.* New York: New American Library, 1961.

WAGNER, LEWIS E., *What Are Economic Problems?* Iowa City: Bureau of Business and Economic Research, University of Iowa, 1966.

Unit One

Introduction to Comparative Economic Systems

EVERY GROUP OF PEOPLE—from the smallest family to the largest nation—produces and consumes goods and services. Those goods may range from steel mills to diapers; the services may range from heart surgery to housekeeping. Every group of people must therefore decide what goods and services to produce, how to go about producing them, and how to distribute what is produced. For that reason, every group of people has an economic system—a way of deciding how to use its time and resources.

In this course, we will examine and compare some major types of economic systems. We will observe the great variety of economic systems that have grown up in the world. But we will also see that all economic systems share much in common, for all must answer the ever-present questions of what to produce, how to produce it, and for whom to produce it.

Chapter 1

Values and Economics

STATING THE ISSUE Every society carries a host of traditions, ideals, preferences, and goals that profoundly influence its economic decisions. Sometimes those values are unspoken. Americans, for example, believe that a rising standard of living is a wise goal. That value is so much a part of our culture, however, that Americans rarely feel it necessary to state their belief in a rising standard of living. Other values are openly discussed. The goal of eliminating poverty, for instance, is a frequent theme in the speeches of American leaders.

Many of us take American economic values for granted. We often assume that all people share our values, simply because they are human beings. The history of the world shows otherwise, however. Some societies have not even valued progress, for example. For them many of the economic policies of the United States would make no sense at all.

Our comparison of economic systems therefore begins with a comparison of the values that stand behind those systems. Later in the course we will analyze specific economic policies of Eskimo tribes, the United States, and the Soviet Union. And even in readings in which values are not openly discussed, their influence should not be forgotten. Economic decisions that take no account of the values of a society are doomed to distortion or total failure. Economics is part of a society's way of life. No economic system can be understood without awareness of the values of the society in which it exists.

In Chapter 1, we will examine the values of three societies—an unusual Indian tribe, the United States, and the Soviet Union. We will not, of course, try to understand the entire economic systems of those three societies in this chapter. Rather, we will look for underlying values that will form the basis for understanding the rest of the course.

1 What Difference Do Values Make?

A recurring theme throughout economics is the necessity of making choices. Indeed, one short but useful definition of economics is "the study of how man, at different times and in different places, goes about choosing how to use his resources."

Man must always choose because of one unchanging fact: There is never enough of everything to go around. The poor man's choices may be particularly harsh and desperate: Should he spend his last dollar on bread or on shelter? But the rich man also must choose, even if his choice is between a Rolls Royce and a Cadillac. However large or small his resources, a man must decide how to use them. Few men's desires are smaller than their resources.

We will come back to this problem of choice again and again. Here we want only to point out that the problem exists, and that it appears in different forms to different men. Today's reading is concerned with the ways in which people solve the problem of choice—that is, how they decide that one choice is preferable to the alternative choices.

The key word for this reading is *values*. Of the several meanings of value, the one that best fits our present purpose is the estimate of the usefulness, worth, or importance of one thing compared to other things.

A man's values tell us what things he considers most important to himself. A man may value material things such as food or shelter. But men also value abstract ideas and feelings such as security, freedom, beauty, and just plain fun. Different men and different societies rank their values differently. Largely because of those differences in values, each society has its own economic system.

As you read today's lesson, keep these questions in mind:

1. What are some observable differences in values among the students in your class?
2. How do the values of Messrs. A, B, and C conflict? How do they agree?

"One Man's Meat Is Another Man's Poison"

If you spend long enough with a list of popular proverbs, you probably will find that every one, however right it sounds, has an opposite that also sounds right. Thus, if it's wise to "Look before you leap," it's also wise "Never to put off till tomorrow what you can do today." And, though "A stitch in time saves nine," "Haste makes waste." "A bird in the hand is worth two in the bush," but then "Nothing ventured, nothing gained." So it is a dangerous business to accept any one proverb as the sum of man's wisdom. Nevertheless, if economists had to choose a single proverb for their work, they would probably reject "What's sauce for the goose is sauce for the gander" in favor of its opposite, "One man's meat is another man's poison."

"Meat" and "poison" may put the matter too bluntly. But people do differ in the things they value. Jack Sprat liked leaner meat than Mrs. Sprat did. Few Rhode Islanders share a Georgian's enthusiasm for grits. When Europeans see us eating corn on the cob, they worry about the state of American civilization.

The case is the same when we talk about abstract values as when we talk about food. A teen-ager's desire for freedom from parental control often conflicts with his parents' desire to see their child grow up in a certain way. People in one neighborhood may prefer a progressive school system, while those in another neighborhood may wish the schools to teach by traditional methods. One society talks constantly of growth and change; another wants to keep things as they have been for centuries.

The economist has little to say about why people's values differ. That is the job of anthropologists, sociologists, and psychologists. But the economist must recognize that such differences exist, for they will have great influence on the success of his proposals. Whether a particular economic policy is good or bad depends on the values of the people who will be affected by that policy. Building an airport for people who simply want to be left alone is a poor economic policy. A decision to tax the poor more heavily than the rich is a bad decision for a society which believes that all people should have equal incomes.

To illustrate how values affect economic choices, we will examine summaries of the economic values of three men, drawn from their own writings. All three of these men actually lived; all three were famous; and all three had profound impacts on their times. We are omitting their names in order to concentrate solely on the values the statements express.

1. The Economic Creed of Mr. A. (as paraphrased from his writings):

Remember that time is money. He who can earn ten dollars a day by his labor, but sits idle one half of that day, though he spend but fifty cents during his idleness, ought not to reckon that fifty cents his only expense. He has really spent, or rather thrown away, five dollars besides.

Remember that credit is money. If a man lets his money lie in my hands after it is due, he gives me the interest, or as much as I can make of it during that time.

Remember that money can beget money, and its offspring can beget more, and so on. The more there is of it, the more it produces at every turning, so that the profits rise quicker and quicker.

2. The Economic Creed of Mr. B. (as paraphrased from his writings):

Our theory can be summed up in a single phrase: abolition of private property.

You are horrified at our intending to do away with private property. But in your existing society, private property is already done away with for nine tenths of the population. Its existence for the few is solely due to its non-existence in the hands of the nine tenths.

The first step is to raise the workers to the position of ruling class. Workers will use their political supremacy to seize all property from today's wealthy, to centralize production in the hands of the state, and to increase the total productive resources as soon as possible.

3. The Economic Creed of Mr. C. (as paraphrased from his writings):

We have to change the current standards. We promise you no earthly careers. We want ideal laborers in the country's cause. They will not bother about what food they get or what comforts they are assured by those whom they serve. They will trust to God for whatever they need and will exult in the trials or tribulations they might have to undergo.

I do not think there need be any clash between capital and labor. Each is dependent upon the other. In my opinion, the mill hands are as much the owners of the mills as the stockholders, and when the mill owners realize this, there will be no quarrel between them. But there is no right in the world that does not presuppose a duty. Fight if you must on the path of righteousness, and God will be with you. There is no royal road, I repeat, to gaining your rights except self-purification and suffering.

★ ★ ★

Now let's put our three men into a situation involving economic choices. We will put them into two additional situations in class when we discuss this reading. Solely on the basis of the values presented in the statements you have just read, decide how each of the three men would probably choose between the alternatives in the case below. A "can't tell" answer is acceptable for any of the three if his statement of values gives no clue to what choice he might make.

> A professional basketball star wants a higher salary for next season. His choices: appeal to the club owner's fairness and generosity, or try to persuade his teammates to form a labor union in order to demand higher pay for all.

2 The Kwakiutl's Values

Today's lesson begins a study of how the values of different societies affect their economic systems and beliefs. It focuses on the Kwakiutl (kwah-kee-*you*-t'l) Indians of the nineteenth century. The next two lessons look at the values of a modern American and a modern Soviet Communist. Our key questions for each of the three societies are the same: What does it regard as good and desirable? How do these value choices affect its economic systems and beliefs? We are not now trying to decide whether we agree or disagree with the Kwakiutl's values. We want solely to understand his view of the world around him.

As you read today's assignment, keep the following questions in mind:

1. How was the economy of the Kwakiutls organized? What goods were produced? Why these and not others? How were they produced? How were goods distributed?
2. As far as we know, the amount of goods produced per man by the Kwakiutls did not increase over time. Why?
3. How might a Kwakiutl regard an American's desire to own a $75,000 home? How might he regard an American's pleasure in making a large public donation to charity?

1. The Kwakiutls

For centuries men lived primitively in parts of the world that today teem with gigantic industries. Settled comfortably in traditional societies, these people rarely challenged the customs of their forefathers. Close at hand were abundant natural resources. Where food could be gathered easily, there was abundant surplus labor which could have been devoted to making the tools needed for increased production. Often, primitive societies also had the group coordination necessary for major economic undertakings. But they lacked a necessary ingredient: the desire to take advantage of their economic opportunities.

The Kwakiutl Indians who lived on the narrow strip of land between the Rockies and the Pacific Ocean, from Alaska to Puget Sound, can serve as an example of a traditional society. As traditional societies go, the Kwakiutls were wealthy. From rivers and the ocean, the men could easily harvest enough salmon and other fish to feed their families. Thus, the Kwakiutls did not have to farm. From the cedar trees that grew along the coast, the men made ocean-going canoes, totem poles, and boards for houses and storage boxes.

Along with rich natural resources, the Kwakiutls had a well-developed system of private property. Family groups "owned" hunting territories and fishing areas. There was also another sort of private property. This property was evidence of rank or status in society. Some of it was made of material objects, such as decorated spoons or posts around which houses were built. Like the Cadillac in the United States, these things were signs of social standing. But the most important property of all was immaterial. Above all else, the Kwakiutls valued titles, names, and privileges.

Each family had rights to a group of titles of nobility. When a family member was given one of those titles, he was believed to inherit the greatness of his ancestors who had held that same title. Titles were passed on from father to eldest son, in elaborate ceremonies known as *potlatches.* To assume a title, the eldest son had to show his worth by distributing great quantities of wealth. To prepare for potlatch ceremonies, the women of his family made mats, blankets, and cedar-bark blankets. The men made canoes and shell-money. They also fashioned etched sheets of copper, which were valued according to the amount that had been paid for them when they last changed hands. These copper sheets, which were often given names, were valued as high as ten thousand cedar-bark blankets. Thus, the Kwakiutls spent much of their time making goods to be given away in ceremonies in which men acquired new titles.

A Kwakiutl's social standing was always open to challenge in contests in which rivals tried to shame each other by generosity. When a Kwakiutl presented a gift to a rival, the rival was expected to return an even larger gift in return. If he could not, he would lose "face" and status, and the original gift-giver's status would grow. A man could also win a victory by destroying more property than his rival could destroy.

The following story of two Kwakiutl chiefs, recorded by an anthropologist, describes a series of potlatch feasts. It shows how far Kwakiutl competition could go.

2. Potlatch

RUTH BENEDICT

From Patterns of Culture. *Boston: Houghton Mifflin Company, 1934, pp. 197–201. Copyright © by Ruth Benedict. Reprinted with permission of the publisher. British rights controlled by Routledge & Kegan Paul, Ltd.*

Throw Away invited the clan of his friend to a feast of salmon berries and carelessly served the grease and berries in canoes that had not been cleaned sufficiently to do them honor. Fast Runner chose to take this as a gross insult. He refused the food, lying down with his black bear blanket drawn over his face, and all his relatives, seeing he was displeased, followed his example. The host urged them to eat, but Fast Runner had his speaker address him, complaining of the indignity: "Our Chief will not eat the dirty things you have offered, O dirty man." Throw Away scornfully replied: "Let it be as you say. You speak as if you were a person of very great wealth." Fast Runner replied, "Indeed I am a person of great wealth," and he sent his messengers to bring his copper Sea Monster. They gave it to him, and he pushed it under the fire, "to put out the fire of his rival." Throw Away sent also for his copper. His attendants brought him Looked at Askance and he pushed it also under the fire in the feasting-place, "to keep the fire burning." But Fast Runner had also another copper, Crane, and he sent for that and placed it upon the fire "to smother it." Throw Away had no other copper, so he could not add more fuel to keep his fire going and was defeated in the first round.

The following day Fast Runner returned the feast and sent his attendants to invite Throw Away. Throw Away, meanwhile, had pledged property enough to borrow another copper. Therefore when the crabapples and grease were set before him, he refused in the words which Fast Runner had used the day before, and sent his attendants to bring the copper Day Face. With this he extinguished his rival's fire. Fast Runner rose and addressed them: "Now is my fire extinguished. But wait. Sit down again, and see the deed that I shall do." He . . . destroyed four canoes of his father-in-law's. His attendants brought them to the feasting-house and heaped them on the fire to take away the shame of having had their fire extinguished by Throw Away's copper. His guests at all costs had to remain where they were or admit defeat. The black bear blanket of Throw Away was scorched, and below his blanket the skin of his legs was blistered, but he held his ground. Only when the blaze had begun to die down, he arose as if nothing had happened and ate of the feast in order to show his complete indifference to the extravagance of his rival. . . .

Such contests were the peak of ambition. The Kwakiutl's picture of the ideal man was drawn up in terms of these contests. An old chieftainess addressed her son: "My tribe, I speak particularly to my son. Friends, you all know my name. You knew my father, and you know what he did with his property. He was reckless and did not care what he did. He gave away or killed slaves. He gave away or burned his canoes in the fire of the feast-house. He gave away sea-otter skins to his rivals in his own tribe or to chiefs of other tribes, or he cut them to pieces. You know that what I say is true. This, my son, is the road your father laid out for you, and on which you must walk. Your father was no common man. He was a true chief among the Koskimo. Do as your father did. Either tear up the button blankets or give them to the tribe which is our rival. That is all." Her son answered: "I will not block the road my father laid out for me. I will not break the law my chief laid down for me. I give these blankets to my rivals. The war that we are having now is sweet and strong." He distributed the blankets.

3 The American's Values

Who can say what all the 200 million Americans think is good, and what they think is bad? A free society gives no one that authority. And anyone who claimed to state the values of all of us would be viewed as a crackpot at worst and a thought-provoker at best. Our values are highly personal, and we even applaud the fact that Americans have differing values—at least until others' values get in our way!

Nevertheless, it is probably true that there are certain typically American values. And it is probably equally true that if any one American deserves a special hearing when he tries to give voice to our national values, that one American is the President of the United States. If that President has just won re-election by a huge majority, his words may be especially revealing of what most Americans think.

Today's reading consists of excerpts from the *Economic Report* which President Lyndon B. Johnson presented to Congress in January 1965. You will not understand all the ideas in it at this point; for example, the phrase "international balance" confuses many college graduates. Read the excerpts not to learn economic facts or ideas, but to see what they tell about President Johnson's view of "the good life" for Americans.

Values make themselves felt on three different levels: *1. The nation's values:* As a skillful politician, President Johnson will try to identify with the values which most Americans hold. *2. The President's values:* President Johnson could not keep his own values out of his report even if he tried. He sees the world around him in his own particular ways because of his own personality and experiences. His own values shape what subjects he chooses to talk about in such a report, and what he says about those subjects. *3. Your values:* You, in turn, cannot keep your values out of your reaction to the reading. What you see or do not see in the reading may depend in part on whether you approve or disapprove of the goals the reading describes. Also, you may react differently depending upon whether you like or dislike President Johnson.

As you read, keep these questions in mind:

1. What are the values President Johnson seems most interested in? Are there implicit (unspoken) values as well as explicit (specifically stated) values in the report?
2. How might President Johnson's values influence his behavior as President?
3. Which of President Johnson's values appeal to you? Which do you dislike? Why?
4. How are President Johnson's values similar to the Kwakiutl's? How are they dissimilar?

The State of the Economy

LYNDON B. JOHNSON

From Economic Report of the President, *January 1965 (Washington, D.C., 1965).*

I am pleased to report
that the state of our economy is excellent;
that the rising tide of our prosperity, drawing new strength from the 1964 tax cut, is about to enter its fifth consecutive year;
that, with sound policy measures, we can look forward to uninterrupted and vigorous expansion in the year ahead. . . .

Thus, the record of our past four years has been one of simultaneous advance toward full employment, rapid growth, price stability, and international balance.

We have proved that with proper policies these goals are not mutually inconsistent. They can be mutually reinforcing. . . .

The unparalleled economic achievements of these past four years have been founded on the imagination, prudence, and skill of our businessmen, workers, investors, farmers, and consumers. In our basically private economy, gains can come in no other way.

But since 1960 a new factor has emerged to invigorate private efforts. The vital margin of difference has come from government policies which have sustained a steady, but noninflationary, growth of markets. . . .

Our prosperity is widespread, but it is not complete. Our growth has been steady, but its permanence is not assured. Our achievements are great, but our tasks are unfinished.

Four years of steadily expanding job opportunities have not brought us to full employment. Some 3.7 million of our citizens want work but are unable to find it. Up to 1 million more—"the hidden unemployed"—would enter the labor force if the unemployment rate could be brought down just one percentage point. . . .

The promise in the Employment Act of job opportunities for all those able and wanting to work has not yet been fulfilled. We cannot rest until it is. . . .

The American economy is the most efficient and flexible in the world. But the task of improving its efficiency and flexibility is never done. . . .

American prosperity is widely shared. But too many are still precluded from its benefits by discrimination; by handicaps of illness, disability, old-age, or family circumstance; by unemployment or low productivity; by lack of mobility or bargaining power; by failure to receive the education and training from which they could benefit.

The war against poverty has begun; its prosecution is one of our most urgent tasks in the years ahead.

Our goals for individuals and our nation extend far beyond mere affluence. The quality of American life remains a constant concern.

The task of economic policy is to create a prosperous America. The unfinished task of prosperous Americans is to build a Great Society.

Our accomplishments have been many; these tasks remain unfinished:

to achieve full employment without inflation;

to restore external equilibrium and defend the dollar;

to enhance the efficiency and flexibility of our private and public economies;

to widen the benefits of prosperity;

to improve the quality of American life. . . .

The [new] Budget Message outlines my fiscal philosophy. We have four priorities:

to strengthen our national defense;

to meet our pressing human needs;

to maximize the efficiency of government operations;

to sustain the advance of our nation's economy.

In these priorities lies the key to our whole strategy of attack on waste:

the waste of lives and property and progress which is the cost of war;

the waste of human potential and self-respect which is the cost of poverty and lack of opportunity;

the waste of excessive government personnel, obsolete installations, and outmoded public services which is the cost of inefficient government;

the waste of men and facilities and resources which is the cost of economic stagnation. . . .

In our economic affairs, as in every other aspect of our lives, ceaseless change is the one constant.

Revolutionary changes in technology, in forms of economic organization, in commercial relations with our neighbors, in the structure and education of our labor force converge in our markets. Free choices in free markets—as always—accommodate these tides of change.

But the adjustments are sometimes slow or imperfect. And our standards for the performance of our economy are continually on the rise. No longer will we tolerate widespread involuntary idleness, unnecessary human hardship and misery, the impoverishment of whole areas, the spoiling of our natural heritage, the human and physical ugliness of our cities, the ravages of the business cycle, or the arbitrary redistribution of purchasing power through inflation.

But as our standards for the performance of our economy have risen, so has our ability to cope with our economic problems.

Economic policy has begun to liberate itself from the preconceptions of an earlier day, and from the bitterness of class or partisan division that becloud rational discussion and hamper rational action.

Our tools of economic policy are much better than existed a generation ago. We are able to proceed with much greater confidence and flexibility in seeking effective answers to the changing problems of our changing economy.

The accomplishments of the past four years are a measure of the constructive response that can be expected from workers, consumers, investors, managers, farmers, and merchants to effective public policies that strive to define and achieve the national interest in

full employment with stable prices;

rapid economic growth;

balance in our external relationships;

maximum efficiency in our public and private economies.

These perennial challenges to economic policy are not fully mastered; but we are well on our way to their solution.

As increasingly we do master them, economic policy can more than ever become the servant of our quest to make American society not only prosperous but progressive, not only affluent but humane, offering not only higher incomes but wider opportunities, its people enjoying not only full employment but fuller lives.

4 The Russian's Values

In Reading 3, we noted how hard it is to identify any one man who could presume to speak for 200 million Americans. We face the same difficulty in thinking about a "typical" citizen of the Soviet Union. In today's reading, as in Reading 3, the government of a nation is called upon to speak for its people. Just because the Soviet government is more centralized and undemocratic than ours does not mean that the leaders are completely out of step with the people. Even in a dictatorship, the leaders must in some way represent the people's values if they are to survive for very long.

Today's reading consists of excerpts from a report on the Twenty-third Congress of the Communist Party of the Soviet Union held in 1966. It was written in English by a Russian and was published by the Soviet government.

As in Reading 3, values make themselves felt on three different levels: *1. The Russian nation's values:* To keep popular support, Communist Party leaders will try to identify their ideas with the values of most Russians. *2. The Communist Party's values:* The Communist Party has its own distinctive view of history and its own distinctive ideas about what is right and wrong. *3. Your values:* You may have strong views about Soviet Communism. Those views will influence your reaction to the excerpts. Your views may even influence which statements you believe and which you doubt to be true.

As you read, consider the following questions:

1. What are the main values expressed? Are other values implicit?
2. What value is placed on an individual's desire for more material goods?
3. Which of the values appeal to you? Which do you dislike? Why?
4. How might a Soviet Communist Party member regard the values of the Kwakiutls? How might he regard the values expressed by President Johnson?

Progress: A Communist View

A. LAVROV

From Twenty-third Congress of the Communist Party of the Soviet Union (*Moscow: Novosti Press Agency Publishing House, 1966*).

Prerevolutionary Russia was an economically backward country. It was . . . a land of the sledgehammer and the wheelbarrow, the wooden plow and the spinning wheel. Despite its rich mineral deposits, the country was acutely short of metal. Its numerous villages were illuminated at night by the miserable flame of a smoky splinter. The people lived in want and overwhelming ignorance. . . .

Just five decades have passed since the day the October Revolution of 1917 won in Russia and the people took power in the country into their own hands. Yet the face of the country has changed beyond recognition. To be precise, it is no longer the country it used to be, but a completely new, socialist land.

The Communist Party, which raised the banner of Revolution in Russia, sees the entire meaning of its activities in making the life of the working people affluent, joyful, and happy. . . .

Public consumption funds are presently playing a role of increasing importance in the welfare of the people. These funds are drawn upon to provide free medical services and free education, and to pay out Government pensions for factory and office workers and collective farmers. . . .

Take education, for example. In countries where education has to be paid for, only [wealthy] families can provide their children with good education. But in the Soviet Union parents do not count their savings when they want to send a daughter to school or a son to an institution of higher learning—all education in the Soviet Union is free.

The same applies to medical services too. In Soviet hospitals, clinics, and sanatoriums . . . an individual is [treated not according to] the contents of his purse but solely [according to] the state of his health. If you are ill and need treatment, you will always be assisted, and all that is necessary will be done to make you healthy and cheerful again. And it will not cost you a penny. . . .

Soviet people take pride in the successes of their labor. But Soviet men and women have never glossed over still-existing shortcomings, or reconciled themselves to them. The country's achievements in recent years would have been even greater if all the possibilities inherent in the socialist system had been used better and fuller. The fact is that during the execution of the seven-year plan—and this was bluntly emphasized at the Congress—shortcomings were revealed in the development of some branches of the economy, and miscalculations . . . were evident in planning.

The targets in the field of agriculture were not met. The volume of agricultural production rose by only 14 per cent during the seven-year period.

The basic reasons for the slow advance of agriculture lay in violations of the requirements of the economic laws of production, neglect of the principles of material [reward] and of the correct combination of public and personal interests. Collective and state farms were sometimes given economically unsound tasks, and some headstrong executives believed that their one desire would be sufficient to secure the rising output of butter, milk, meat and grain. The weather, too, did not treat the farmers too kindly. First, the winter would be severe and without snow, then the summer would be hot and dry . . .

The slow growth rates of agricultural production had a bad influence on other branches of the economy, primarily on the light and food industry. As a result, it was not possible fully to achieve the planned improvement of the living standards of the working people. . . .

Imperialist propaganda is holding forth everywhere about a "crisis" in the Soviet economy and even about a "retreat from socialism." The propaganda-mongers are writing about the "borrowing of capitalist economic management methods," about "rehabilitation of the profit motive," and about "renunciation of state planning in favor of a market economy."

What can be said of all this?

These assertions are ridiculous from beginning to end. It is obvious to anybody that the unshakable foundation of the Soviet Union has always been and remains public ownership of the means of production. There can, naturally, be no question of any "backsliding of the Soviet Union into capitalism." There have long since been no capitalists in the Soviet Union, nor any exploitation of man by man or any social basis for the restoration of capitalism. In this case the bourgeois ideologists are indulging in wishful thinking. . . .

The advocates of capitalism [present] yet another [false theory]. They allege that only an economy based on private property can generate material [rewards]. These allegations have nothing in common with the truth. Socialism is a socio-economic [system] whose principle is [reward] according to the quantity and quality of labor, and, therefore, it implies . . . material incentive. . . .

In the next five years the real per capita income will increase by some 30 per cent as compared with the 20 per cent rise in the preceding five years.

Such a high growth of real incomes will result from the following measures.

Firstly, the [wages] of factory and office workers and collective farms will go up. The average wages of factory and office workers will rise by not less than 20 per cent in 1966–70. . . .

Secondly, the real incomes of the population will rise through the reduction of state retail prices for various foodstuffs and manufactured goods, primarily for children's goods.

And finally, there will be a considerable expansion of the public consumption funds. . . . The state will earmark these funds for the development of free education and free medical treatment, payments for holidays, the provision of free or cheap accommodation in sanatoriums and holiday homes, the upbringing of the rising generation, the maintenance of old people and disabled members of society and for various other payments and benefits to the population. Many other measures are also envisaged to create additional comforts for the people.

Chapter 2

The Economic Problem

STATING THE ISSUE Values alone tell us little about the life of a society. To become meaningful, those values must be translated into actions. In translating its values into actions, every society comes up against the problem of scarcity: Because both time and resources are limited, a society must choose between different ways of using them. As Reading 1 pointed out, the problem of scarcity is no more avoidable than death or taxes.

Because each society has a unique set of values, each society has its own way of attacking the problem of scarcity. Thus, each society also has a unique economic system. To compare economic systems, however, it is necessary to make rough classifications.

There are many possible systems of classifications. In Chapter 1, we often classified economic systems according to the value different societies placed upon progress.

In Chapter 2, we move on to classifying economic systems according to how the chief economic decisions are made. This system of classification will be the basis of the remainder of the course.

The last two readings in this chapter describe how the Eskimo society goes about answering the problem of scarcity. We begin with the Eskimos because their economic system is the least complicated. But the questions raised about the economic system of the Eskimos will apply also to the more complicated economic systems of the United States and the Soviet Union.

Dog-sleds and jet airplanes, igloos and apartment buildings, seal hunting and meat packing may look very different. But to the economist, they all have one thing in common: All of them are the products of economic decisions that are based on values. Eskimos, businessmen, and Communist Party officials all must confront the economic problem. All must decide what is to be produced, how it is to be produced, and for whom it is to be produced. These are the basic questions discussed in Chapter 2.

5 What, How, and For Whom

In Reading 1, you first met the central problem with which economics is concerned: scarcity. The dictionary defines *scarcity* as "the quality or condition of being scarce; especially: want of provisions for the support of life." Most of us think of scarcity in these terms; "scarce" means "not enough of something." But economists have a special definition for scarcity, around which the entire study of economics revolves.

Today's reading, an imaginary interview, develops in detail the economist's special meaning for scarcity. It also poses three problems, resulting from scarcity, with which all societies must deal. As you read, keep the following questions in mind:

1. What does an economist mean when he uses the term "scarcity"?
2. What evidence can you offer from your own experience that scarcity, as the economist defines the term, is a universal problem? Is there any evidence that it is not?
3. What applications can you think of for the principle that the cost of doing any one thing has to be measured in comparison to the alternatives that are given up by doing that one thing?

Interview: An Economist Confronts Scarcity

INTERVIEWER: Good evening. Our guest on *House of Wisdom* this week is Professor Adam Mills, economist at Smith State University. Dr. Mills, you know that our purpose on *House of Wisdom* is to talk about the core of each of the many scholarly disciplines. We want to know, within the space of just a few minutes, what economics is all about. A tall order, we admit—so let's jump right into the subject. I've noticed that a number of economics textbooks start by talking about Robinson Crusoe. Why is that? Is he a patron saint of the economists?

MILLS: Not a patron saint, but a folk hero perhaps. What economists like about him is that he presents the scarcity problem so sharply and simply. There he is—one man with his helper, few tools, little in the way of natural resources, and a desire to survive in comfort. His choices are harsh: He can spend the day looking for better food if he wants to—but only at the cost of giving up the time and the labor that could go into fixing a better shelter against the weather. Thus, the real cost of getting the food must be measured by what he has to give up in housing or whatever else he wants in order to get that food. And so——

INTERVIEWER: Just a minute. I understood you until you used the word *cost*. I've always thought of cost as measured in money terms. Where does money come into Crusoe's world?

MILLS: It doesn't—and that's what makes it so nice. Too often we get mixed up in our thinking by bringing money into the discussion. You see,

Crusoe's costs are real: so much labor, so much time, so much of the raw materials on the island. If his world were more complicated and he had to deal with many people, he'd probably use money to measure the worth of that labor and raw material. But money is only a convenient way to add units of labor, land, and so on. In itself, money is worth only the metal it is minted on or the paper it is printed on. Its practical worth depends upon how much of others' labor and produce one can buy with it.

INTERVIEWER: Let me see if I've got the point. Are you saying that, if I spend two dollars on a movie, the real cost has to be measured by thinking about the other things I could have bought with the same two dollars, such as a necktie or a bet at the racetrack?

MILLS: Exactly. The money unit—the dollar, in your case—simply helps you compare the cost of one thing versus another. You don't really care about the two pictures of George Washington on the dollar bills. You care about what those dollar bills will buy.

INTERVIEWER: Fine. I see that now—but how are you going to get me back from that island to the real world?

MILLS: Well, the choice problem is just as clear if you jump from two men on an island to the world's largest nation, China. The bitter facts of life in China make the scarcity problem desperate: too many people and too little rice, too little fertilizer to help grow more rice, too few goods to sell abroad to get money to buy fertilizer from other countries, too little machinery to produce more to sell abroad to get money to buy——Well, you get the picture.

INTERVIEWER: Yes, but it doesn't bring me home yet. What does scarcity have to do with us?

MILLS: A great deal. It's true that we're the wealthiest nation the world has ever seen. But we've got scarcity too. Every day in this country, we too are making choices. And, every time we choose to do one thing, we pay the cost of not doing something else we'd like to do—presumably something else we don't want to do quite as much.

INTERVIEWER: Give me an example. I know what you mean about choices for me as an individual; that's clear to me each time I spend my pay check. But how does this apply to the United States as a whole?

MILLS: A dramatic example right now is the race to the moon. If we want badly enough to be the first to land a man on the moon, we may be able to make it; at least, we've still got a fighting chance. But we must pay the cost of not using resources, such as scientific talent, for some of the other things we'd like to do: clearing our air and rivers of pollution, or licking the traffic mess, or even lowering taxes. We can of course do a little of all of those things. But we can never do as much on any one of them as some people might like, without giving up a little extra progress somewhere else.

INTERVIEWER: Then if I hear you rightly, you're politely pooh-poohing those writers who say that today the United States has conquered scarcity and that the problem from now on is how to get rid of all we produce.

MILLS: Yes, but I don't mean to be polite about it. I mean to insist, rudely if need be, that scarcity is here to stay. Granted, it's all relative: In India and China the problem of scarcity is much more a matter of life and death. But we still suffer from scarcity, for we cannot have all we want. Until I can find even a handful of Americans so wealthy that they say they don't want a single thing more, I'll go on believing in scarcity—and in the economic problem.

INTERVIEWER: You're saying too, aren't you, that the problem is not restricted by time, or place, or anything else?

MILLS: Right. No individual licks it. No family licks it. And no economic system licks it. But they all try—and that's what makes economics so central in our lives.

INTERVIEWER: Another thing I've noticed about economics texts is that they often refer to "What, how, and for whom." What's that all about?

MILLS: Actually those words are simply ways of examining the scarcity problem more specifically. Look at it this way: Because no society can escape scarcity, every society has to have a way of deciding what goods and services to produce, how to produce those goods and services, and for whom to produce them. The *what* question simply says, "Which among the limitless number of things that you'd like to have will you put at the top of your list of priorities?" The *how* question asks, "Out of all of the possible ways of manufacturing or delivering those goods and services, which methods will you choose? How will you choose to combine labor with your other resources to give you the most of what you want?" And the *for whom* question asks, "After you've produced as much of what you can with your existing resources, how are you going to divide the product among all those who'd like to have some of it? Will it be divided perfectly evenly? If not, who gets how much?"

INTERVIEWER: Now that I understand the questions, I wish I knew the answers to them.

MILLS: Well, that's what the rest of economics is all about—it's the study of the ways that men go about answering those questions and of the varieties of their answers.

INTERVIEWER: Why varieties? Economists, after all, claim to be scientists. Aren't they therefore moving towards the one best way of answering *what, how,* and *for whom?*

MILLS: Best for whom?

INTERVIEWER: Well, I suppose I mean best for the most people, or at least for——

MILLS: But don't you see? That's just the point: Men don't agree on what's best for the majority, because their values differ. That means that they'll continue to come up with different answers to the *what, how,* and *for whom* questions for just as long as differences in values persist. Economists can go a long way towards telling a society the least expensive and most satisfying way to achieve its goals. But the same answer won't work for a society with different values. We'll always have——

INTERVIEWER: Dr. Mills, I'm sorry but——

MILLS:——a variety of "best" or, at least, acceptable answers as to how to organize men's economic affairs.

INTERVIEWER: At this point I must interrupt, for you have illustrated one of your own points—the one about scarcity. We've run out of time. Let me see if I can sum up our discussion as you would put it: We had only so much time for this broadcast; we chose to do a certain few things with that time; and the cost of doing those few things has to be measured in comparison to all the other economic issues we might have talked about. Right?

MILLS: Right.

6 An Overview of Economic Systems

Reading 5 made the point that every society, confronted with the problem of scarcity, must decide what goods and services to produce, how to produce them, and for whom to produce them. Reading 6 presents a rough guide for comparing the ways different economic systems go about answering the *what, how,* and *for whom* questions.

To compare economic systems, we will classify them. But our classifications will raise as many questions as they will answer. The biologist can confidently classify animals as birds, mammals, fish, etc.—until he is confronted with a species like the duck-billed platypus, which seems to be a cross between bird and mammal. The economist, however, finds that every economic system is a little like the platypus—part one kind of system, and part another. Because of this, you should be wary of classifications of economic systems at the same time that you use the classifications for what they are worth.

As you read, keep these questions in mind:

1. Why is it useful to think of economic systems as falling into place along a spectrum?
2. What might a spectrum of American political parties show? What kinds of spectrums might be used to compare American political parties?
3. Think of several ways in which the American economic system is traditional. What elements of traditional, command, and market systems are evident in Kwakiutl society, as depicted in Reading 2? Which is strongest?

Economies Along Spectrums

There are nearly as many ways of organizing an economy to decide what, how, and for whom goods are to be produced as there are societies of men. The economy of every society is shaped by the history, values, and geography of that society. Still, for our purpose of comparing economic systems, we can divide the economies of the world into three broad classes.

First and oldest are the *traditional economies.* We have already met one example in the Kwakiutls. Traditional economies answer the *what, how,* and *for whom* questions mainly by following the ways of their forefathers. They emphasize continuity, not change. Their people would be puzzled by the abiding faith in continual progress held by most Americans.

Second, and nearly as ancient as the traditional economies, are the *command economies.* These economies are run from above by rulers. They answer the *what, how,* and *for whom* questions by following the commands of the rulers or ruling group. Most of these societies have also preferred continuity to change; the rulers have simply enforced the ways of their forefathers. Thus, command economies often have blended together with traditional economies. But recently, command economies have arisen that place great emphasis on change and progress. An outstanding example is the Soviet Union.

Third, and only a few centuries old, are the *market economies.* They are still few in number, but they include the wealthiest economies the world has ever seen—economies like those of the United States and Canada. Like the newer command economies, the market economies emphasize progress and change. But the *what, how,* and *for whom* questions are answered mainly in free marketplaces where men buy and sell according to their own tastes, making as much profit as they can.

Economic systems, however, cannot be placed in a single classification. The United States, for example, does not leave all economic decisions to the workings of the free marketplace. Local, state, and federal governments all affect the economy with nearly every law they pass and enforce. In no command economy, furthermore, is every minute detail of economic life dictated from the top. And finally, even primitive traditional economies, like the Kwakiutls, are not wholly governed by long-standing customs.

No economy, in fact, is totally a traditional, command, or market economy. Each has traces of all three systems. All of this suggests that it will not be very useful to think of neat, separate boxes labeled "traditional," "command," and "market." Instead, we might do better to think of the world's economies as we think of the colors along a rainbow, which is simply a spectrum of light. On a rainbow, one color looks very little different from the color right next to it. But colors widely separated along a rainbow are clearly quite different from each other.

One of our economic spectrums might arrange economic systems according to how much they rely on the decisions of free individuals to answer *what, how,* and *for whom.* At one extreme will be the pure market economies. At the other extreme will be the purely traditional and command economies. In practice, no economy will be at either end of the spectrum; each will be somewhere in between. So:

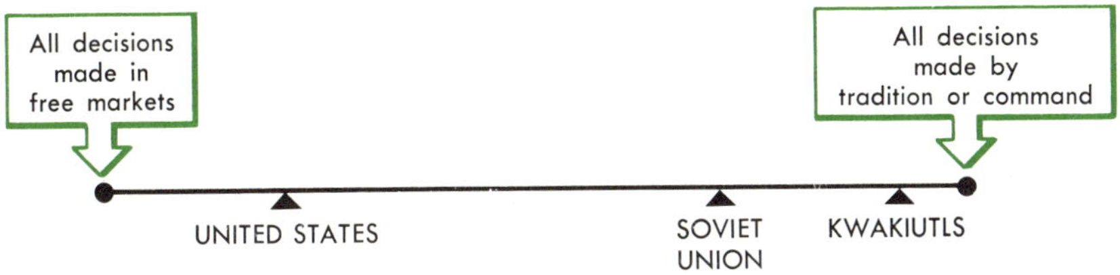

The spectrum, however, does not tell the whole story. Today, only a few of the traditional economies are stationary on the spectrum. And the United States, as governmental powers increase, seems to be shifting slowly toward the right end of the spectrum. Many observers believe that the Soviet Union is slowly shifting toward the left end. That does not mean, of course, that the United States and the Soviet Union will soon be alike. The two economies could move a long way toward each other on the spectrum and still remain far apart.

We might also use a second spectrum to compare the attitudes of different societies toward continuity and change. On this spectrum, the line-up would be quite different. Both the United States and the Soviet Union, for example, seem equally devoted to economic progress, no matter how much their methods of attaining that progress may differ. So:

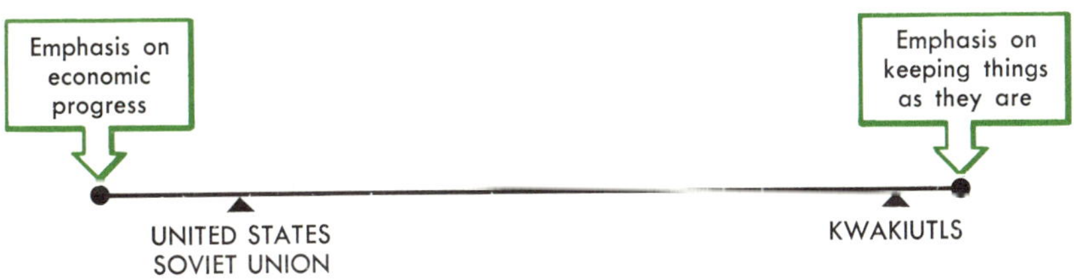

Comparing economies along a spectrum is more complicated than comparing them by means of those three tidy boxes labeled "traditional," "command," and "market." But it is also more accurate. The economies of human societies are almost as complicated as man himself. And man is a complicated and subtle animal.

In the weeks ahead we'll talk first about traditional economies, and then about command and market economies. But when we do, remember that no economy is purely one single type. Each economy may have unique features, but none is totally different from all others.

7 The Traditional Economy (I)

The next three readings will deal with the economic life of a traditional society—that of the Eskimos. Although there are hundreds of Eskimo tribes, nearly all of them have formed the same kind of economic system. We have learned about the economic system of the Eskimos mainly from the reports of explorers and anthropologists. Few economists have studied traditional economies in depth. That is particularly unfortunate because the Eskimos today are emerging from their traditional economy. In recent years the Canadian and American governments have embarked on programs to raise the Eskimos' standard of living by bringing them into the market systems of those two countries.

For the purposes of this lesson, however, we will look at the Eskimos as they were half a century ago, untouched by the benefits—and the drawbacks—of "modern" civilization. The excerpts that follow present glimpses of economic activity as reported by Vilhjalmur Stefansson (*stay*-fan-son), a Canadian-American explorer. As you will see, the values and customs of the Eskimos—such as their attachment to tradition and belief in superstitions—deeply affected their economy. As you read these first excerpts, keep the following questions in mind:

1. How might the attitudes portrayed in "The Hand of the Past" affect the Eskimos' readiness to change to newer ways of making a living?
2. How might superstitions affect the Eskimos' interest and skill in analyzing the economic forces that shape their lives?
3. How might the Eskimos' view of promises affect how successfully Eskimos could specialize in particular activities and then trade the product of their efforts with each other?
4. Think of some ways the attitudes expressed in these selections are found in an industrially advanced society like that of the United States. How strong are these attitudes in the United States?

1. The Hand of the Past: What Has Been Will Be

VILHJALMUR STEFANSSON

From My Life with the Eskimo, *copyright, 1913, by The Macmillan Company. Reprinted by permission of McIntosh and Otis, Inc.*

We returned home the same day and remained in camp, waiting for this band of Eskimo to call on us on their way to Point Barrow, for we wanted to buy from one of them a set of whale-bone sled-runners to use on our improvised sled. The next evening when they came, they camped beside us and immediately made preparations for setting fish nets. We had several excellent fish nets in our boat, and I had said to [the Eskimo] in the beginning that I thought we ought to put them out to see if we could catch any fish; but they said very definitely that there were no fish here.

At that time I had had no experience with Eskimo in a country new to them. I had dealt only with Eskimo near [their] home, and my experience with them was that they knew exactly where to put nets, and knew also what places were hopeless as fishing localities. I know now that the Eskimo . . . never expect to find anything in any place where no one has found it before, so far as they know, and never having heard of any one catching fish in Smith Bay they had felt sure there would not be any. . . . This was a valuable lesson to me, and has on many occasions encouraged me to go into districts that the Eskimo considered devoid of game and in which I have usually found plenty. . . .

It was the vanishing of the caribou from the interior coastal plain that drove down the Eskimo to the coast, and now it seems that the caribou are having a slight chance, for in large districts where formerly they had to face the hunter, their only enemy is now the wolf. . . . [T]he Eskimo expects to find everything next year as he found it last year; consequently the belief died hard that the foothills were inexhaustibly supplied with caribou. But when starvation had year after year taken off families by groups, the Eskimo finally realized that the caribou in large numbers were a thing of the past; and they were so firmly impressed with the fact, that now they are assured that no caribou are in the interior, as they once thought they would be there forever.

2. The Weight of Superstition: Miracles and Magicians

VILHJALMUR STEFANSSON

From My Life with the Eskimo, *copyright, 1913, by The Macmillan Company. Reprinted by permission of McIntosh and Otis, Inc.*

. . . [I]f you were to show an Eskimo a bow that would in the ordinary way shoot fifty yards farther than any bow he ever saw, the man would . . . understand exactly the principle on which it works, . . . and would find it to excel marvelously. But show him the work of the rifle, which he does not in the least understand, and he is face to face with a miracle; . . . he compares it with other miraculous things of which he has heard and which he may even think he has himself seen, and he finds it not at all beyond the average of miracles; for the wonders of our science and the wildest tales of our own mythologies pale beside the marvels which the Eskimo suppose to be happening all around them every day at the behest of their magicians. . . .

. . . When I showed them later my binoculars that made far-away things seem near and clear, they were of course interested; when I looked to the south or east and saw bands of caribou that were to them invisible, they applauded, and then followed the suggestion, "Now that you have looked for the caribou that are here today and found them, will you not also look for the caribou that are coming tomorrow, so that we can tell where to lie in ambush for them." When they heard that my glasses could not see into the future, they were disappointed and naturally the reverse of well impressed with our powers, for they knew that their own medicine-men had charms and magic paraphernalia that enabled them to see things the morrow was to bring forth.

3. The Impermanence of Promises: Each Man a Law unto Himself

VILHJALMUR STEFANSSON

From My Life with the Eskimo, *copyright, 1913, by The Macmillan Company. Reprinted by permission of McIntosh and Otis, Inc.*

. . . [W]e engaged to go with us to Banks Island a man whom we knew well and liked in a social way, but [for] whom we had no great [need]. Natkusiak and I were well able to provide food and raw material for clothing, but we needed an able woman to do sewing for us and especially for making waterproof sealskin boots, without which a summer in the swampy tundra and more especially a spring on the water-covered spring ice were very disagreeable things to face. I was a little surprised to find Kirkpuk and his wife willing to go with us, for they had a baby not more than six or eight weeks old, but they told me that they would leave the child with its grandmother, and that the arrangement was one that they had contemplated anyway; for had Kirkpuk not gone with us, he would, he said, have gone on a long hunt to Bear Lake, upon which journey the child would have been a burden. . . .

The next morning the weather had changed, but so, unfortunately, had Kirkpuk's mind. During the night he and his wife had had time to think of many things: how badly they would miss their baby if they did not see him for a year, and how they might never see him again for all they knew, going as they were with us into a dangerous and mysterious country; and anyway, Kirkpuk now recollected he had promised So-and-so that he would meet him that summer at Bear Lake. After breakfast he presented to me these and other reasons of the same sort . . . which made it imperative that he should break his agreement with us and return. I was a little unreasonably annoyed at this change of mind. There was nothing wrong about it from the Eskimo point of view. These people know nothing among themselves except absolute social equality. The relation of master and man is an unknown thing among them and therefore inconceivable.

A promise according to their way of thinking means merely that a man tells you what he feels like doing at that particular moment, and so long as his mind does not change he will be willing to carry out that intention; but whenever he does change his mind there is nothing to be done but to inform you that his mind has been changed, and the explanation is considered satisfactory and the agreement dissolved. Yesterday Kirkpuk had intended to go with me to Banks Island and he had told me so; this morning he intended to go to Bear Lake and accordingly informed me of that fact. The Eskimo individually behaves like a sovereign state. The laws of others do not bind him, and he makes new laws for himself whenever he likes.

8 The Traditional Economy (II)

Until very recently, the Eskimos made no new products. They produced food, clothing, and shelter just as their fathers had. They distributed goods according to time-honored patterns.

Eskimo society knew very little division of labor and little trade. Nearly every man was a hunter and nearly every woman a seamstress and cook. With families often widely separated, each father and mother had to know how to do every job essential to survival in the Arctic. Children learned their future occupations by watching their parents, and by playing with toy models of their parents' harpoons, bows, and needles. This educational system helped to pass on the traditional ways.

Today's reading concentrates on the ways Eskimos solved the questions of what, how, and for whom goods are to be produced.

As you read, consider the following questions:

1. How do the guiding principles introduced in the previous reading—"The Hand of the Past," "The Weight of Superstition," and "The Impermanence of Promises"—influence the Eskimos' answers to *what, how,* and *for whom?*
2. Compare the Eskimos' answers to *what, how* and *for whom* with a modern American's answers.

1. What To Produce: The Seal Versus the Caribou

VILHJALMUR STEFANSSON

From My Life with the Eskimo, *copyright, 1913, by The Macmillan Company. Reprinted by permission of McIntosh and Otis, Inc.*

The Noahanirgmiut [an Eskimo tribe] were still living on seal meat and were making no attempt to kill any of the numerous caribou that were continually migrating past.... They had never hunted caribou on the ice and had not considered it possible. It would in fact be a fairly hopeless thing for them to try it; and while no doubt some of them might occasionally secure an animal, they would waste so much time that the number of pounds of meat they obtained in a week's hunt in that way would be but a small fraction of the amount of seal meat they might have secured in the same time.

Besides that, this is the season which the Eskimo give up to the accumulation of blubber for the coming year.... By getting seals in the spring, . . . they secure an agreeable article of diet for the coming autumn and provide themselves as well with a sort of insurance against hard luck in the fall hunt. Each family will in the spring be able to lay away from three to seven bags of oil. Such a bag consists of the whole skin of the common seal. The animal has been skinned through the mouth in such a way that the few necessary openings in the skin can be easily sewed up or tied up with a thong. This makes a bag which will hold about three hundred pounds of blubber, so that a single family's store of oil for the fall will run from nine hundred to two thousand pounds.

2. How To Produce It: Catching a Seal

VILHJALMUR STEFANSSON

From My Life with the Eskimo, *copyright, 1913, by The Macmillan Company. Reprinted by permission of McIntosh and Otis, Inc.*

The whole principle of successfully stalking a seal is just in realizing from the first that he is bound to see you and that your only hope is in pretending that you are also a seal. If you act and look so as to convince him from the first that you are a brother seal, he will regard you with unconcern. [Imitating] a seal well enough to deceive a seal is not difficult, for, to begin with, we know from experience that his eyesight is poor. You can walk up without taking any special precautions until . . . you are within two hundred and fifty or three hundred yards. Then you have to begin to be more careful. You move ahead while he is asleep, and when he wakes up you stop motionless. You can safely proceed on all fours until within something less than two hundred yards, but after that you will have to play seal more faithfully. Your method of locomotion will then have to be that of the seal, which does not differ very materially from that of a snake, and which therefore has its disadvantages at a season of the year when the surface of the ice is covered with puddles of water anywhere from an inch to twenty inches in depth, as it is in spring and early summer. You must not only crawl ahead, seal-fashion, but you must be careful to always present a side view of your body to the seal, for a man coming head-on does not look particularly like a seal.

Until you are within a hundred yards or so the seal is not likely to notice you, but somewhere between the hundred yard and the seventy-five yard mark his attention will suddenly be attracted to you, and instead of going to sleep at the end of his ordinary short period of wakefulness, he will remain awake and stare at you steadily. The seal knows, exactly as well as the seal hunter knows, that no seal in this world will sleep continuously for as much as four minutes at a time. If you lie still that long, he will know you are no seal, and up will go his tail and down he will slide into the water in the twinkling of an eye.

When the seal . . . has been watching you carefully for twenty or thirty seconds, you must raise your head twelve or fifteen inches above the ice, look around seal-fashion, so that your eyes will sweep the whole circle of the horizon, and drop your head again upon the ice. By the time he has seen you repeat this process two or three times in the space of five or six minutes he will be convinced that you are a seal, and all his worries will be gone. From then on you can proceed more rapidly, crawling ahead while he sleeps and stopping while he remains awake, never doing anything unbecoming a seal. In this way you can crawl within five or ten yards of him if you like, and as a matter of fact I have known of expert seal hunters who under emergencies would go after a seal without any ordinary weapon and crawl so near him that they could seize him by a flipper, pull him away from his hole, and club or stab him.

3. For Whom To Produce It: Dividing the Seal

VILHJALMUR STEFANSSON

From My Life with the Eskimo, *copyright, 1913, by The Macmillan Company. Reprinted by permission of McIntosh and Otis, Inc.*

When we had entered the house the boiled pieces of seal meat had already been taken out of the pot and lay steaming on a sideboard. . . . My hostess picked out for me the lower joint of a seal's foreleg, squeezed it firmly between her hands to make sure nothing should later drip from it, and handed it to me, along with her own copper-bladed knife; the next most desirable piece was similarly squeezed and handed to her husband, and others in turn to the rest of the family. When this had been done, one extra piece was set aside in case I should want a second helping, and the rest of the boiled meat was divided into four portions, with the explanation to me that there were four families in the village who had no fresh seal meat.

The little adopted daughter of the house, a girl of seven or eight, had not begun to eat with the rest of us, for it was her task to take a small wooden platter and carry the four [small] pieces of boiled meat to the four families who had none of their own to cook. . . . Every house in the village in which any cooking was done had likewise sent four portions. . . . During our meal presents of food were also brought us from other houses; each housewife apparently knew exactly what the others had put in their pots, and whoever had anything to offer that was a little bit different would send some of that to the others, so that every minute or two a small girl messenger appeared in our door with a platter of something to contribute to our meal.

. . . [Many years ago, a certain Eskimo caught a huge bearded seal. Until he had killed it,] he had not thought of the other hunters, but now he looked around and saw that they were all far away. . . . [H]e felt sure that none of them had any idea what kind of a seal he had caught. (The hunters' law does not require that the hunters within sight be summoned to share at the cutting up of a common, small seal.) When a bearded seal is killed all the hunters within view must be called in to share the prize.

It had occurred to him that by keeping the thing secret (by pretending this was a common seal), he might keep the animal to himself, and especially the skin, for he knew that he could sell pieces of it to a neighboring tribe who seldom catch bearded seals, for numerous articles of value. Accordingly, he secretly cut the animal up, gave out the story that he had killed only a small seal, and pledged his wife to secrecy; but the story leaked out as such stories will. People came to him and took away from him both the skin and the meat and reproached him bitterly. He now repented his act and felt crushed by the disapproval of his people, but his punishment was to be made even heavier, for within a year he began to lose his eyesight and in another year he was stone blind. Since then he, poor miserable man, has been blind and a charge upon the community. Thus it was sure to go with those who did wicked things; and while he felt sure that I was a good man, nevertheless to know his story would do me no harm, and he wished I would pass it on to others, warning them to avoid selfish ways.

SUGGESTED READINGS

COMMITTEE FOR ECONOMIC DEVELOPMENT, *An Adaptive Program for Agriculture,* pp. 9–29.
 Question: What are the major values which lie behind each of these three approaches to the agriculture problem?

HEILBRONER, ROBERT, *The Worldly Philosophers,* Chapter 2.
 Question: What was the major value that had to be accepted before the market system could develop in Europe?

LISITZKY, GENE, *Four Ways of Being Human,* pp. 25–48.
 Question: How do the Semang answer the *what, how,* and *for whom* questions? How do their answers differ from the Eskimos'?

————, *Four Ways of Being Human,* pp. 167–203.
 Question: How do the Maoris answer the *what, how,* and *for whom* questions? How do their answers differ from the Eskimos'?

————, *Four Ways of Being Human,* pp. 240–98.
 Question: How do the Hopis answer the *what, how,* and *for whom* questions? How do their answers differ from the Eskimos'?

THEOBALD, ROBERT, *The Rich and the Poor,* pp. 18–29.
 Question: How may values retard economic growth in many poor countries?

WAGNER, LEWIS E., *What Are Economic Problems?* pp. 1–19.
 Question: To what degree do differing values alone explain differences among economic systems?

Unit Two

The Matter of Resources

THE GOODS AND SERVICES produced by a society are fashioned from the resources it has at hand. Most of us are used to thinking about resources only in terms of natural resources. But natural resources themselves do not automatically turn into useful goods and services. Human resources also are needed.

The human resources of a society are its people, together with their skills and values, who contribute to the society's economy. A population that is large, healthy, and open to new ideas will produce more than a population that is small, disease-ridden, and wedded to tradition.

The power of human resources, in turn, can be magnified by capital resources—goods used to produce other goods. A steel plow, for example, is a capital resource. With it, an American farmer today can raise far larger crops than could an American Indian farmer with his primitive tools. Thus, the natural resources of seeds and soil can yield more goods when better capital resources are introduced. By knowing what a society has in the way of resources, we can go on to evaluate how effectively it produces goods and services.

Chapter 3

Physical Resources

STATING THE ISSUE Despite the powers of modern science, it is doubtful that Lapland will ever become a major orange-growing region. The world's economic systems are limited by the geographical areas in which they exist. Some societies, like the United States and the Soviet Union, are fortunate enough to cover areas of great natural wealth. Given good human and capital resources, their chances of developing a wealthy and varied economy are great. Other societies, like that of the Eskimos, live in areas of more limited natural resources. It is doubtful that the Arctic region could ever have an economy like that of the United States.

No economic system, however, is totally dependent on its geography. Great Britain, despite its small supplies of most ores and fuels, has developed one of the world's most sophisticated industrial economies. The American Indians, on the other hand, had a primitive, pre-industrial economy despite the great natural wealth of the land on which they lived.

Chapter 3 asks two main questions: What natural resources does the society have available? And, How has it used those resources? First, it discusses the economic system of the Eskimos. We see how the values of a traditional society, combined with a severe climate, produced a primitive though hardy economic system. Next we examine the natural resources available to the United States. Then, Reading 11, a history of recent developments in the American coal industry, illustrates how imaginative use of capital resources can make a natural resource newly valuable. Reading 12 presents the natural resources of the Soviet Union and the progress its economic system has made in using those resources.

9 Resources in a Traditional Economy

Traditional economies, as we noted in Reading 2, often exist amidst bountiful natural resources. A society's level of technology and its values, however, determine how the available natural resources are used. Iron ore and the power of falling water, for example, are of little or no use to traditional societies. Similarly, an Eskimo can do things with the right kind of snow, a dead whale, and a dog team that would leave an American city dweller flabbergasted.

Resources are useful only if you know how to use them. This reading examines the resources of the Eskimo, as reported by Vilhjalmur Stefansson and Peter Freuchen who was a Danish explorer. Compared to modern America, Eskimo society seems frighteningly poor in resources. Yet, using their traditional skills, Eskimos have been able to employ those resources to fashion a distinctive economy which supports thousands of people.

As you read, consider the following questions:

1. What essential resources may be identified in these passages? Are any essential resources left out?
2. How does the Eskimo's know-how enable him to use the natural resources he finds? How might better technology make more use of those resources?
3. For much of the year, Eskimos wander about in search of game, sometimes building an igloo every day. Compare the Eskimos' use of the igloo to the use an American salesman makes of the motel.

1. Animal Life

PETER FREUCHEN

Reprinted by permission of The World Publishing Company from Peter Freuchen's Book of the Eskimos, *edited by Dagmar Freuchen. Copyright © 1961 by Peter Freuchen Estate. British rights controlled by Arthur Barker, Ltd.*

The animal life of the Arctic . . . is abundant, and it is characterized by sea mammals: seal, walrus, and whales that live on the fish, clams, and krill in the waters. Other special species are the polar bear, the arctic fox, the snow hare, the caribou, and the musk ox. It is upon these animals that the Eskimo has based his material culture; he feeds on their meat, he makes his clothes, his bed, his boats, and his summer tent from their skins, and most of his utensils from their bones and teeth. And let us not forget the millions of sea birds and waterfowl that in summer inhabit the cliffs and islands along the Arctic coasts.

2. Housing

VILHJALMUR STEFANSSON

From The Friendly Arctic: The Story of Five Years in Polar Regions, *copyright, 1921, by The Macmillan Company. Reprinted by permission of McIntosh and Otis, Inc.*

As a preliminary to the building of a house we find a snowbank that is of the right depth and consistency. With our soft deerskin boots we walk around on the drift, and if we see faint imprints of our feet but nowhere break through, we assume . . . that the drift is a suitable one, but examine it further by probing with a rod similar to a very slender cane. When the right bank has been found we get out our sixteen-inch butcher knives or twenty-inch machetes and cut the snow into domino-shaped blocks about four inches thick, fifteen to twenty inches wide and twenty to thirty-five inches long.

These blocks, according to their size and the density of the snow, will weigh from fifty to a hundred pounds, and must be strong enough to stand not only their own weight when propped up on edge or carried around, but if they are intended for the lower tiers of the house, must be capable of supporting the weight of three to five hundred pounds of other blocks resting upon them.

The house itself is built preferably on a level part of the drift where the snow is three or more feet deep. The first block is set on edge as a domino might be on a table, but with your knife you slightly undercut the inner edge so as to make the block lean inward at a very slight angle if the house is to be a big one, or at a considerable angle if it is to be a small one. . . .

The oval or circle that is to be the ground plan may be determined by eye as the builder sets up the blocks one after the other; but in practice I make an outline with a string with pegs at either end, one peg planted where the center of the house is to be and the other used to describe the circumference, somewhat as a schoolboy may use two pencils and a string to make a circle on a piece of paper. I find that even the best of snow-house builders . . . if they rely on the eye alone, will now and then err in the size of the house, making it uncomfortably small or unnecessarily large for the intended number of occupants. But with a string a simple mathematical calculation always tells how many feet of radius will accommodate the intended number of lodgers.

. . . [W]hen you once have your first block standing on edge, it is a simple matter to prop all the other blocks up by leaning one against the other. The nature of snow is such that when a block has been standing on a snowbank or leaning on another block for five or ten minutes in frosty weather, it is cemented to the other blocks and to the snow below at all points of contact and can be moved only by exerting force enough to break it.

When the first tier has been completed the second can be begun in any of several ways. The simplest is to select any point in the circle formed by your first tier, and from the top edge of one of the blocks make a diagonal cut downward to the bottom edge of the far corner of the same block, or of the second or third block. In the niche thus formed you place the first block of the second tier, its end abutting on the last block of the ground tier. After that you lean the second block of the second tier against the first block of the second tier, and so on, building up spirally.

The blocks of each tier must be inclined inward at a greater angle than those of the tier below and at less angle than those of the tier above. In other words, what you are trying to do is to build an approximately perfect dome.

3. Clothing

PETER FREUCHEN

Both men and women wear boots of sealskin, called *kamiks*. They are roomy, and inside there are stockings made of hare skins. For further protection of the feet, always the most exposed part of the body, they put a layer of dried grass in between the two pairs of soles, and this is changed every day. The men's kamiks reach the kneecap, where they meet a pair of shining white bearskin trousers. These are worn below the waist, somewhat loosely around the hips. A coat of fox fur covers the rest of the man—this has a hood which can be turned up to protect the head completely. The mittens are of seal or caribou skin.

The Eskimos have discovered that for maximum protection against the cold the hair of the fur must be outside. Under the coat they wear birdskin shirts with the feathers inside. These are the only tight-fitting garments. Otherwise, the skin clothes are loose and do not overlap too much, so as to allow for ventilation. For it is important that they be kept as dry as possible. If they should get too wet from perspiration and then be taken off, it could be difficult or even impossible to put them on again, as they would be frozen stiff.

In summer, the fox-fur coat is replaced by a seal-fur coat which is less warm. And in particularly [mild] weather, the birdskin shirt is often worn alone. When new it has a handsome dark-yellow color.

The coat has a snip both in front and behind, and the hood and the sleeves are brimmed with foxtails. Sometimes the men will wear two foxtails sewn together around each leg, just above the kamik, to take the bite off the cold air coming in.

The women's costume is essentially the same as the men's but their kamiks are much longer. They reach the crotch, and instead of trousers they wear short panties made of foxskin. The kamiks are brimmed on top with the mane hairs of the male bear, the longer the more elegant. The coat hoods are made of sealskin, pointed, and edged with foxtails.

10 Natural Resources in the American Economy

From the time of the first Indian settlers, the land that became the United States has attracted newcomers because of the natural wealth in its forests, streams, seas, mountains, and soil. For centuries, the generous and varied natural resources of this country have helped to make Americans an optimistic people, confident of continual progress.

Yet we should not exaggerate the role of natural resources. First, they are not unlimited. Careless exploitation can reduce their usefulness in the future. And even if our natural resources are used carefully, they may not be adequate to meet the needs of a constantly growing population. Second, natural resources alone do not make a nation wealthy. Capital and human resources are also needed to make use of the natural resources. In the 1960's, Americans use their natural resources in ways that the Indians never dreamed of.

Today's reading consists of charts, tables, and graphs, presenting statistics on some of our natural resources. Economists use statistics to measure and compare different aspects of the economy. Knowing how to use statistics can bring clarity to an otherwise hodge-podge of seemingly unconnected facts. Questions follow each set of statistics.

1. Population of the United States: 1870–1966

The source for these statistics is the United States Bureau of the Census, Statistical Abstract of the United States: 1966 (*Washington, D.C., 1966*).

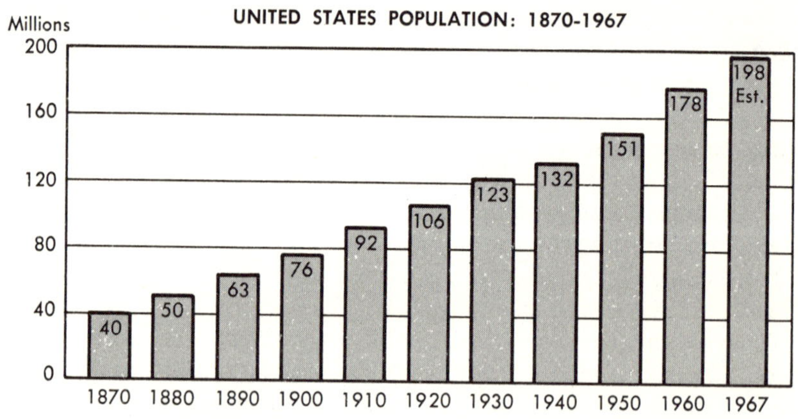

1. What has been the population trend in the United States? How has that trend affected the adequacy of our natural resources?
2. Relate some of the figures to other historical events. Why, for in-

stance, did the population rise sharply between 1890 and 1910? Why did it rise slowly during the 1930's?

2. Petroleum Products and Reserves in the United States

The source for these statistics is the United States Bureau of the Census, Statistical Abstract of the United States: 1966 *(Washington, D.C., 1966).*

Production		*Proved Reserves*	
1946–1950 (Average)	1,884	1950	25,268
1951–1955 (Average)	2,339	1955	30,012
1956–1960 (Average)	2,567	1960	31,613
1965	2,849	1965	31,352

(Figures given in millions of 42-gallon barrels. "Proved reserves" means petroleum that has been located but not yet extracted.)

1. Based on your knowledge of recent history and economic developments, give reasons for the steady rise in petroleum production since World War II.
2. How many times greater are the proved reserves than current production? What do you think the ratio of production to reserves would have been for the year 1492? What does this say about petroleum as a natural resource?
3. To estimate whether the United States will have enough petroleum in years to come, why must you have figures for population trends as well as figures for petroleum production and proved reserves? What other information would you need?

3. Natural Gas Products and Reserves in the United States

The source of these statistics is the United States Bureau of the Census, Statistical Abstract of the United States: 1966 *(Washington, D.C., 1966).*

Year	*Production*	*Proved Reserves*
1940	2,660	85,000
1950	6,282	184,585
1960	12,771	262,326
1964	15,547	281,251

(Figures given in billions of cubic feet. "Proved reserves" means natural gas that has been located but not yet extracted.)

1. Is natural gas being exploited more or less than petroleum? (Compare the ratios of production to proved reserves.)
2. Is natural gas production rising more slowly or more rapidly than petroleum production?
3. What information would you need to estimate whether the United States will have enough natural gas in the year 2000?

4. The Shifting Pattern of Energy Resources in the United States

The source of these statistics is the United States Bureau of the Census, Statistical Abstract of the United States: 1966 *(Washington, D.C., 1966).*

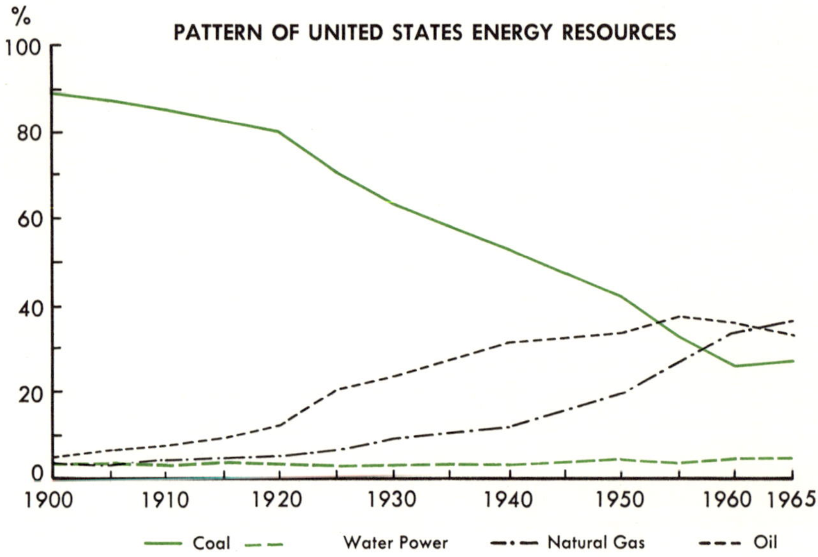

1. Which energy sources have been growing in importance? Which have been declining?
2. Does this graph tell you whether more or fewer tons of coal were consumed in 1964 than in 1900?
3. Give some possible reasons for the shifting pattern.

11 Capital Resources in the American Economy

Traditional economies like the Kwakiutl's differ most obviously from today's industrialized economies in their stocks of capital goods. *Capital goods* are goods used to produce other goods or services.

They may include tools, equipment, and transportation and communication systems. (A good is not a capital good, however, if it is totally consumed in the production of a good or service. A pound of flour used to make bread is not a capital good—once the bread is made, there is no more flour. The oven in which the bread is baked, on the other hand, is a capital good—it wears out only after repeated use.)

Because capital goods are used to produce other goods and services, they are essential to economic growth. Without them, even the brightest men would be reduced to using only their physical labor to wrest a living from the land and waters.

For capital goods to be produced, certain conditions must be met. First, a society must have the know-how—the technical skills—to produce those goods. That is simple enough: Even if you have all the necessary materials and labor at hand, you cannot build a factory unless you know how to do it.

Second, a society—or an individual or a company—must have an adequate source of consumption to keep alive while the capital goods are being produced. That source might be personal saving from preceding years. More often in the United States, a businessman will borrow from a bank. In other words, he will borrow from the savings of others, so that he and his employees can have an income during the construction period while no money is coming into the business. The businessman expects to be able to pay the interest for the bank loan from the increased profits he will make from his new factory.

That brings us to the third condition for the production of capital goods: an incentive. The businessman must feel hopeful that he will make enough added profit from his new factory to pay back the loan plus interest and to make a profit greater than he would if he were to use his loan in some other way. If a businessman does not expect to make a large enough profit —either because taxes are too high or anticipated sales too low—he will not build the new plant.

In the United States, a continual rise in population and rich natural resources have helped make businessmen more often hopeful than discouraged. In the last hundred years, the production of capital goods has gone on at a spectacular rate. By using new machinery, workers have been able to produce more and more. In other words, the production rate per worker has steadily risen.

In some instances, the introduction of new capital goods has saved entire industries. The coal industry is an example. By the late 1940's, the American coal industry was desperate. Fewer and fewer homes were being heated by coal, and most railroads had switched to diesel fuel. Using its traditional methods, the coal industry could not compete with newer sources of fuel. At the same time, the companies were faced with demands for better wages and working conditions from the vigorous United Mine Workers union, led by John L. Lewis. Today's reading tells how the coal industry met its crisis.

As you read, consider the following questions:

1. How did the coal industry meet the three conditions of know-how, adequate source of consumption goods, and incentive? What risks did the coal industry run in its new program?
2. What was the role of capital in reviving the coal industry? How have added capital goods affected the price of coal? the wages of miners? the profits of companies?
3. In exchange for higher wages, the United Mine Workers agreed to let the number of coal miners be reduced sharply. What might have happened if the union had refused to make that compromise?

Capital and the American Coal Industry

BUSINESS WEEK

Out of a miserable postwar past, bituminous coal is emerging into a future that is more competitive than ever—but also vastly more hopeful. Further, its prospects are well-grounded despite the amazing potential shown by two of the newer sources of power.

"I don't know how better to invest our funds than in coal," says George H. Love, chairman of Consolidation Coal Co., and probably the industry's outstanding executive. . . .

The most persuasive evidence of coal's fat future lies in the potential of its main customer—electric power. Short term and long, U.S. electric power and its demand for an energy source seem destined for tremendous growth. In energy transportation costs, coal seems to have better prospects than Canadian hydroelectric power; it also has several ways to compete with the "freight-free" atom. On the basis of this, coal should:

Double its sales to utilities in little more than a decade.

Triple those sales in little more than three decades—even if it then has a smaller share of the utility market. . . .

The very nature of the utility market—huge demands to be met daily at very tight costs—specifies with almost brutal selectivity just who is to share in its future.

Those who get the biggest slice will be the producers with the best located reserves, the most effectively mechanized mines, and the heaviest annual reinvestment in new reserves and higher capacity machinery and methods. These producers are the "career companies"—those that seek long-term contract business and continually reinvest the high cash flow that's characteristic of coal. . . . Topping the list of them is Love's Consol. . . .

The slump. In 1947, coal hit its all-time production record—630-million tons. But then its market changed. What had been its two best customers—rail and retail—slid from 40 per cent of total consumption in 1947 to 7 per cent in 1962. This drove out many producers, and threw coal reserves on the market for those who had the faith, and the credit, to expand. Out of these pressures, and from the growth of the utility market, the career company evolved. . . .

Expansion. By 1950, Consol . . . had picked up 225-million tons of strip coal reserves in southeastern Ohio, and 600-million tons of deep coal in northern West Virginia. In that time, too, the company plunged deep into research on liquid fuel from coal gasification, on low temperature carbonization, on the 100-cubic-yard stripping shovel, the tool that made possible today's highly efficient strip mining, and on the first commercial coal pipeline. Most such moves were previously unknown in the coal industry.

The transportation bind. Utility coal consumption has grown almost eight-fold in thirty years. Only fifteen years ago, it took several power plants to consume the production of a big new mine. Today, it frequently takes a new mine to supply one new power plant.

But coal's basic problem remained: it is solid, and expensive to transport compared with liquid, gaseous, electrical, or nuclear energy. So in taking advantage of its best market, the coal industry had to fight transportation costs.

Consol attacked that problem so vigorously that by 1957 it had a slurry pipeline* with a 1.2-million ton annual capacity operating between Cadiz, O., and Cleveland. The railroads brought that business back last spring with a 61¢-a-ton rate cut. Earlier, they had headed off a similar line to the Detroit area by cutting rates before the line was built. . . .

Cutting the cost. The pressures within the industry are matched by the pressures outside it. The dropping price of nuclear power and the advent of extra high voltage electrical transmission may force coal to reduce its delivered cost by 20 per cent, if it is to remain competitive. Some steps already have been taken toward this. . . .

One of a kind. Near Zanesville, O., Peabody operates the only machine of its kind—the push-button miner. This bizarre monster works in a strip mine, recovering coal too deep to strip but not recoverable by deep mining. A continuous boring head tunnels into an exposed seam, dragging behind it forty-three cars, each equipped with a conveyor. No miner accompanies the cutter underground. All controls are from the outside. Peabody won't discuss its costs, but experts believe they are low.

The push-button miner now is being adapted by its maker, Joy Mfg. Co., for use in deep mines. Joy developed the first continuous miner. It has been laboring ever since to perfect loading devices fast and flexible enough to keep up with a continuous miner and get loose coal away from

* Some coal is now shipped through pipelines in a soupy mixture called *slurry*.

the working face to the main haulage way. That's the biggest problem in continuous mining today.

Outlook. In 1947, coal production averaged 6.4 tons a man-day. Today in northern West Virginia, 26 tons a man-day is a good average. Joy's Pres. James M. Drain says confidently: "Within ten years, machinery will be available that will allow underground mines to produce as much as 70 tons of cleaned coal per shift per man on the payroll." . . .

Over the next decade, Drain believes, there may be more reduction in the cost of producing a ton of coal than has been made since the end of World War II. If this is done, it will be truly remarkable. Since 1947, coal doubled its average hourly wages, and added a 40¢-a-ton royalty payment for medical care, and still cut the average price by almost 50¢ a ton. . . .

12 Physical Resources in the Soviet Economy

Previous readings focused on the natural and capital resources of a traditional economy and an advanced market economy. Today we move to a command economy, that of the Soviet Union. The key question remains the same: What physical resources do people have to work with to produce the goods and services they want?

Few nations have changed as dramatically as the Soviet Union since the Communist Revolution in 1917. The Communists, besides leading a political revolution, were largely responsible for bringing the Industrial Revolution to Russia. Slowly, they have been transforming Russia from a land of farms to a land of factories. Their constant goal has been higher production through better use of resources. When the Communists came to power in 1917, Russia was the most backward major European country. Despite its large population and its huge territory, its industrial development was more than fifty years behind Great Britain's. The Communists, realizing this fact, eagerly set about building capital resources to make better use of their human and natural resources.

Since the Communist Revolution, the Soviet Union has made great strides in building their capital resources. But even today, the Communist leaders of the Soviet Union often talk as if their nation were still backward and primitive. While they congratulate themselves on the progress the Soviet Union has made, they continue to demand that the people concentrate their energies on building more capital resources.

As you read, keep these questions in mind:

1. What does it take to make a given natural resource, like iron ore, into something useful?
2. What accounts for the differences in the types of capital goods produced in the United States and the Soviet Union, as discussed on

page 42? What do those differences in capital goods show about the stages of development in the two countries? What do they show about how those two countries are answering the questions of what, how, and for whom to produce?

1. Natural Resources

The Soviet Union is the largest country in the world and probably the most self-sufficient in its natural resources. It is wealthy in nearly every important resource except natural rubber. But until the Communists came to power in 1917, most of Russia's resources lay unused in the forests and in the soil.

Most of Russia's mineral resources, for example, had not even been discovered by 1917. Some iron ore, copper, gold, and silver were mined in western Russia. But the vast lands of Siberia, that sprawl eastward from the Ural Mountains to the Pacific Ocean, were undeveloped. Today, the enormously expanded Soviet mining industry produces more iron ore than the United States, Communist China, and Canada combined. And an energetic prospecting program has discovered enough coal, manganese, lead, copper, zinc, bauxite, tungsten, mercury, potassium salts, and phosphates to make the Soviet Union the world's leader in proved reserves of every one of those minerals.

The table below shows the increase of energy produced in the Soviet Union. Because machinery needs energy, the table also gives us a rough idea of how much total production the Soviet Union is capable of.

PATTERNS IN RUSSIAN ENERGY SOURCES

Source of Energy	*1913*	*1921*	*1928*	*1940*	*1952*	*1963*
Electricity (billions of kilowatt hours)	2.0	0.5	5.0	48.3	119.1	412.0
Crude oil (millions of tons)	9.2	3.8	11.6	31.1	47.3	206.1
Coal (millions of tons)	29.1	9.5	35.5	165.9	300.9	532.0

Which energy sources have been gaining in relative importance? Which have been losing? How does this pattern compare to the pattern of energy sources in the United States shown on p. 36?

2. Capital Resources

As Russians have discovered and used long-hidden natural resources, they have created great amounts of machinery, buildings, railroads, and other equipment to produce and deliver goods and services. From the first, Communist leaders recognized that only by increasing productivity through giving the people capital resources could the country exploit its natural wealth. In 1919, Lenin, founder of the Russian Communist Party, told a Party congress:

> If we could tomorrow produce 100,000 first-class tractors, supply them with fuel, and with operators (you know perfectly well that this is a dream as yet), the average peasant would say, "I am for Communism."

Today there are more than a million tractors in the Soviet Union. With the help of that capital resource, the Russian farmer produces far more than he did fifty years ago, although his production still lags behind the American farmer's.

When the Communist Party came to power, it made a conscious decision to devote a large part of the nation's energy to producing capital goods. Thus, iron ore, nickel, and copper that might have gone into making pots or automobiles have gone, instead, largely into building steel mills and railroads. We shall see in later readings that this pattern has shifted somewhat in the 1960's. But even today, capital goods command the top priority in the Soviet Union's economic plans.

Only a few years ago, some of the Soviet leaders were boasting that their nation would out-produce the United States by 1970. Then the date for the "overtake" was shifted to 1975, and then to 1980. But whether or not the Soviet Union's total production matches that of the United States before the end of this century, two facts remain clear: The Soviet Union has the natural resources for great growth, and it has followed a policy of creating the capital resources needed for still greater growth.

Chapter 4

Human Resources

STATING THE ISSUE To an economist, we all represent human resources. It is human resources that create capital resources and put natural resources to work. Until that day when all computers learn to feed data to themselves, people will be vital for the success of an economy.

Economists have learned to identify characteristics of a society's population that affect its economy. Take the American Indians, for example. They lived in a land with plentiful natural resources, but developed only a primitive economy. Why? First, their population was kept small by crude medical practices and their failure to grow a large food supply. Second, their people were often sick—and sick people cannot do much labor. Third, their education was limited; they did not learn the technical skills and agricultural methods that would have produced economic growth. Fourth, and most important, they may not have been that interested in economic growth.

The belief in constant progress and ever-increasing wealth, which is so widespread in the United States today, would have made little sense to the Indians. They were content to live as their forefathers had lived before them. They did not regard themselves as poor and backward people. And that brings us back to the question of values. According to the values of modern Americans, the Indians were economic failures. But according to the Indians' own values, their economic system may have been adequate to meet the needs they felt were most important.

Chapter 4 first discusses human resources in an imaginary society. Then it considers the United States and the Soviet Union, societies which share a desire for economic growth. For each society, this chapter asks: What are its human resources? What kinds of human resources does it need to achieve its goals? How effectively is it using the human resources it has and training the human resources it wants in order to achieve its goals?

13 What Difference Do Human Resources Make?

Hiroshima, devastated by an atomic bomb in 1945, is today a bustling, prosperous city. The only trace of the devastation left on the city's buildings is one damaged structure left standing to remind the world of what had seemed once to be Hiroshima's doomsday. Hiroshima, as well as other heavily-bombed cities of World War II, was able to recover so completely because of its intelligent and hard-working people. With that human resource, the factories, railroads, schools, and homes could be rebuilt. Without that resource, a city, once bombed, would remain a wasteland. The people killed in World War II could not be brought back to life, but damaged capital resources could be repaired by the survivors.

The following reading examines the crucial role of human resources in developing an economy. As you read, keep these questions in mind:

1. What is the relationship between a society's population and its economic growth?
2. How educated, adequate, healthy, and willing was the manpower of the thirteen colonies in America in the mid-eighteenth century? How educated, adequate, healthy, and willing is the manpower of the United States today?
3. What is the relationship between human resources and capital resources?

Human Resources: Four Keys

Imagine great riches in metals, woods, soils, and waters—and even a stock of fine machinery and tools—set down in a remote village in the Andes Mountains. Some of the vital ingredients for economic progress would clearly be there. But, without people to want to use those material resources, to know how to use them, and to be free to use them, there would be little progress.

It is strange that man, who so often thinks of the whole physical world as existing for his personal satisfaction, should be so slow to recognize how essential human resources are to economic progress. For years, when economists and politicians talked about progress, they focused on the material resources needed for high standards of living.

So it was that when Americans and Russians first turned their attention to the underdeveloped two thirds of the world, they asked what natural wealth each poor country had and how it might get machinery to use its natural resources more fully. But the more that work was done on physical resources, the more it became clear that improved human resources were also needed to move the underdeveloped countries ahead.

Take that village in the Andes again. What human resources would it need in order to use effectively the material resources which we imagined it had suddenly been endowed with?

First, it would need educated manpower. Men would need to know how to get the most out of each separate resource, how to combine resources effectively (fertilizer with soil, for example), and how to use today's resources to produce still more resources for tomorrow (using tools, for example, to fashion still better tools). Such know-how might in part be learned through formal education. It can also be learned from on-the-job training and from experience. If the Andean village's best educated person is semi-literate, the process of educating manpower will be painfully slow. With help from outside, the villagers may learn quickly what men elsewhere, starting from scratch, had taken much longer to learn.

Second, it would need adequate manpower. Sheer numbers matter; a society cannot do much if it has too few adults available for productive effort. But numbers alone represent a poor asset at best. Many mouths to feed and few skills available to show how these mouths can best be fed will only perpetuate poverty.

Third, it would need healthy manpower. Those in their working years must be physically able to work. Disease and hunger can reduce today's productivity and slow the process of learning for tomorrow's productivity. This is why a poor country interested in growth may put high priority on an adequate system of sanitation and medical care. Such a system is viewed not as a luxury, but as a precondition for everything else the country wants.

Fourth, it would need willing manpower. Unless people want economic progress, their society will most likely fail to achieve it. The government of Burma, for example, has decided in recent years that it dislikes the types of economic progress achieved by both Communist and non-Communist nations. As a consequence, the Burmese government has refused most economic assistance from outside, saying in effect, "We'll stay as we are, thank you." Those countries strongly desiring growth have learned that the will to grow apparently must be accompanied by the willingness to sacrifice some present gains for future ones (a hard thing to ask where people are hungry today). And traditional societies must drop their opposition to change. Americans sometimes assume that the desire to work hard, to save, and to gain material rewards is built into all men. In fact, the belief that a society can make progress is relatively recent and far from universal. While the economist can say with some certainty that such an ambition is a necessary forerunner to a rising standard of living, he cannot say much at all about how to plant such ambition where it does not already exist.

These four requirements—educated, adequate, healthy, and willing manpower—are difficult ones to meet. Ambitious nations desiring to telescope the long process of building such manpower into a decade or two have learned that there are few shortcuts. To illustrate the point: Not only does it take time to produce the teachers who will teach the young, but it also takes time to produce the teachers who will teach the teachers of the young. Small wonder then that rich and poor countries alike are building human resources with a sense of urgency.

14 Human Resources in the American Economy (I)

Great natural resources alone would not have made the United States the richest nation in the history of the world. As earlier lessons pointed out, many underdeveloped countries have substantial natural resources, yet remain wretchedly poor. The United States has grown in wealth because it has had the human resources to develop its natural resources. Today's reading examines some of the strengths of the United States' human resources. As you read, keep the following questions in mind:

1. Why do you suppose the life expectancy for Americans is below that for some other peoples?
2. How is education an economic investment?
3. What ideas do the five excerpts at the end of this reading have in common? How do they differ?

The American as an Economic Resource

Ask an American the purpose of his country's economy, and he is likely to reply that its goal is the well-being of the individual or the family. Thus, he sees the individual chiefly as the consumer of the econ-

UNITED STATES POPULATION: 1870-1967

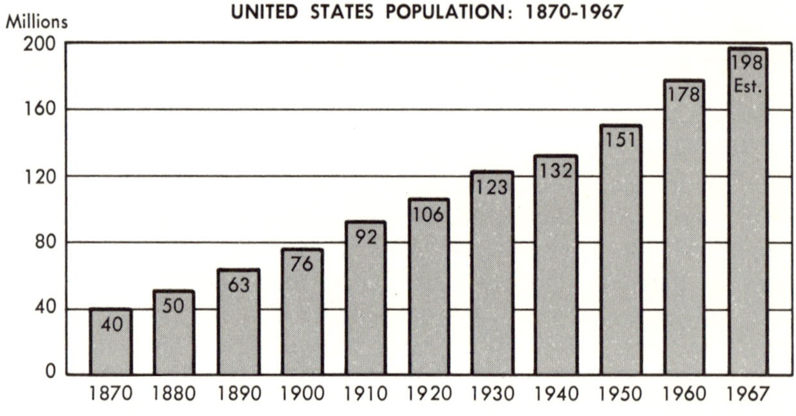

omy's bounty. But that same individual is also a producer of that bounty. He is a human resource.

American human resources have been so highly productive partly because they have been plentiful in relation to the available natural resources. As the graph on p. 46 indicates, the nation's population has risen rapidly.

Numbers alone do not make a country rich. India and China, for example, each has many more people than the United States, but they are about forty times as poor. The quality of the people also matters. That quality can be measured partly by health standards, for healthy people are more productive than people who are frequently sick. The health standards of the United States, as measured by life expectancy and infant mortality, are far better than the health standards of most countries. It is important to note, however, that the United States ranks slightly below some other advanced industrial nations. Following are statistics for a few selected countries.

SELECTED WORLD HEALTH STATISTICS

	Life Expectancy (in years)	*Number of deaths, per thousand, of infants under one year old*
United States	66.6 (Male) 73.4 (Female) (1963)	25.2 (1963)
Canada	68.4 (Male) 74.2 (Female) (1960–62)	26.3 (1963)
El Salvador	44.7 (Male) 47.4 (Female) (1951–61)	65.5 (1964)
India	41.9 (Male) 40.6 (Female) (1951–60)	81.0 (1962)
Japan	67.2 (Male) 72.3 (Female) (1963)	20.4 (1964)
Czechoslovakia	67.2 (Male) 72.8 (Female) (1962)	21.1 (1964)
Sweden	71.3 (Male) 75.4 (Female) (1962)	13.6 (1964)
United Kingdom	68.0 (Male) 73.9 (Female) (1961–63)	20.0 (1964)

Source: Demographic Yearbook, 1964, *pp. 550–57, 620–23. Copyright United Nations (New York, 1965). Reproduced by permission.*

Education in the United States is uneven. There are excellent schools, and poor ones. The number of college graduates is increasing rapidly, while there are still thousands of adults who cannot read or write. But the impact of American education on the economy seems clear: The educational system has helped to build a labor force of remarkable productivity. The percentage of seventeen-year-old Americans graduating from high school gives a rough guide to the nation's growing investment in education:

PERCENTAGE OF SEVENTEEN-YEAR OLDS GRADUATING FROM HIGH SCHOOL

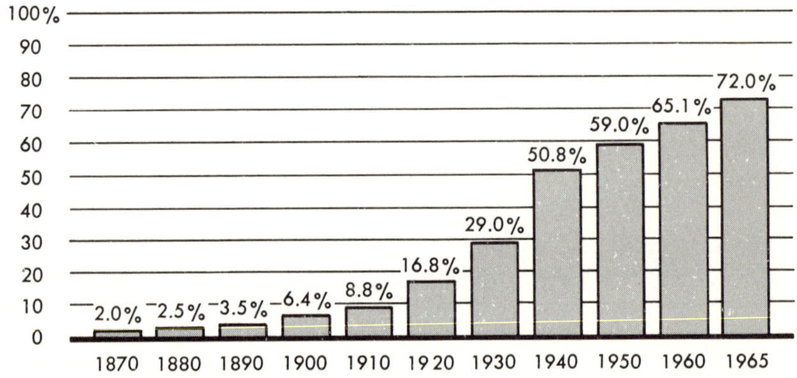

But statistics cannot tell the whole story. Historians and sociologists have long puzzled over whether or not any nation has a distinct national character. While they often disagree on what the national character of a particular nation is, most agree that there is something to the concept. Likewise, economists must consider a nation's economic spirit—its economic creed and behavior.

We have no certain way to measure or define just what the economic spirit of the United States has been. But we can conclude that it has permitted the human resources of the United States to become highly productive. Some of that spirit is captured in key documents that are part of the American heritage. Some brief excerpts follow:

From the Declaration of Independence, 1776:
We hold these truths to be self-evident, that all men are created equal, that they are endowed by their Creator with certain unalienable Rights, that among these are Life, Liberty and the pursuit of Happiness. That to secure these rights, Governments are instituted among Men, deriving their just powers from the consent of the governed.

From the Thirteenth Amendment to the Constitution, 1865:
Neither slavery nor involuntary servitude, except as punishment for crime whereof the party shall have been duly convicted, shall exist within the United States, or any place subject to their jurisdiction.

From the Employment Act of 1946:
The Congress hereby declares that it is the continuing policy and responsibility of the Federal Government to use all practicable means... with the assistance and cooperation of industry, agriculture, labor, and State and local governments, ... to foster and promote free competitive enterprise and the general welfare, conditions under which there will be afforded useful employment, for those able, willing, and seeking to work.

From the Taft-Hartley Act, 1947:
Employees shall have the right to self-organization, to form, join, or assist labor organizations, to bargain collectively through representatives of their own choosing, ... and shall also have the right to refrain from any or all such activities...

From the Elementary and Secondary Education Act of 1965:
In recognition of the special educational needs of children of low-income families and the impact that concentrations of low-income families have on the ability of local educational agencies to support adequate educational programs, the Congress hereby declares it to be the policy of the United States to provide assistance... to local educational agencies serving areas with concentrations of children from low-income families to expand and improve their educational programs by various means (including preschool programs) which contribute particularly to meeting the special educational needs of educationally deprived children.

15 Human Resources in the American Economy (II)

In your own view, the education you are now receiving may be satisfying your intellectual curiosity, preparing you for a well-paying job, or perhaps simply boring you. In the eyes of an economist, your education is supposedly increasing your value as a human resource of the United States.

Because the United States has a developed market economy, there is an enormous variety of jobs available and of skills needed. One of the problems of a developed market economy is getting the right people into the right jobs. Only in that way can the full potential of human resources be realized. Every American must decide, consciously or unconsciously, how he would like to use the human resource represented by himself. And for two individuals with the same abilities, the "right" choice may differ. Today's reading is a fictional account of young Americans making decisions that will have a profound influence on both their own lives and their country's economy.

As you read, keep the following questions in mind:

1. How accurate are the remarks of the assembly speaker? What values does he represent? To what extent has the United States realized those values?
2. Is discrimination most likely to be found in a market, command, or traditional economy? How does discrimination reduce an economy's supply of human resources?
3. What effect would it have on the nation's supply of human resources if every American went to college?

The Right Man for the Right Job

It's Career Day for the senior class at Washington High. The guest speaker at assembly is from a local service club—and if he hasn't actually put the class to sleep, he hasn't exactly inspired it either. Phrases like "the doorway to opportunity" and "no substitute for sweat, tears, and textbooks" float past the students. At least eight of them are daydreaming about their own career choices——

GEORGE A. wonders whether it's worth finishing high school. His grades are low, and his family takes little interest in his schoolwork. He's heard the guidance counselor quote all the statistics showing that high school graduates, on the average, make more money during their working lives than dropouts. Still, he knows he can get a job right now at a gas station, and he'd rather take home some money than study all the things he's supposed to care about in math and social studies.

ALICE B. wonders how anyone can ever figure out what he'd like to study after school. One minute she thinks she'd like to go on in math—her grades have been tops there. And the next she thinks nursing would be the best career—there she could do something worthwhile for other people. It's so hard to decide, and the choice has to be made soon.

RITA C. wonders whether it's worth going on to any further education after high school. She plans to get married in two years, when her fiancé returns from the Army. So why spend months and dollars getting further training, if she's only going to be in the labor market for a short time? On the other hand, she notices that more and more of mother's friends have gotten jobs after their children have begun to grow up. Some have taken courses before they started to work again. So how much should she invest now in building a skill that might lead to interesting work that will pay well far in the future?

EDWARD D. wonders whether he can make it as a professional baseball player. He's been a star at high school and has had small bonus offers from big-league scouts. He knows he'd like to play baseball, but he isn't sure he can take the chance. Most ballplayers, he knows, never make it out of the minor leagues. What do you do when your interests tell you to do one thing and hard facts seem to tell you to do another? There is that one chance in a thousand that he's the one who would make it big. Is it better to take that chance or plan now for a safer but less exciting career?

DONALD E. wonders what point there is in further education for him. He's a Negro, and he's never felt that his schooling had much to do with his own life. He never saw a Negro in any of his textbooks; he doesn't see a single Negro in the top jobs around town; and he keeps hearing about discrimination, while the newspapers claim that things are improving fast for the Negro. He knows that his own friends who finished high school have menial jobs—dishwasher, stockboy—or are out of work entirely. But he'd like to know whether or not anyone would really give him a full and fair chance if he got some more education.

DIANA F. wonders about discrimination too—but her concern is whether women have a fair chance to compete in the job market. She's been told that she should go to a junior college and acquire secretarial skills if she expects a good job in business. Strange, she thinks, that men in her class who have similar abilities don't need such skills. Why does a woman have to start as a secretary? And if she does start as a secretary, what chance will she have of working up to the kind of executive position she wants?

FRED G. has been planning all along to enter an apprenticeship in the typographical union. He knows that most fellows cannot get into it, but his father's a member and he's pretty sure he can pass the tests. Still, he worries about technological changes in the field. How can he know how much his skills will be worth if most printing is done by automated machinery in twenty years? If this happens, he will have sacrificed a lot to learn his skill and may have nothing to show for it. It must have been easier to decide in the old days, he thinks, when industry stood still a little longer.

TOM H. knows he wants to become a lawyer, but wonders what college he should go to. He's been accepted at both Harvard and the state university, but Harvard turned down his application for a scholarship. He could go to Harvard by borrowing and by working at part-time jobs through the school year. But would these sacrifices be worth it? Is Harvard really that much better than the state university? Every good school, he's heard, has some outstanding professors as well as some dull ones who should have retired years ago. And he can always try to go to Harvard for law school.

The Career Day speaker is coming to a close. "And so I remind you that the world is yours if you apply yourself fully and faithfully. No one, other than yourself, can keep you from going to the very top. You have but to decide what you want to do with your life—and you can achieve your goal. I envy you the chances that lie ahead." The students file out, headed for their first morning class.

16 Human Resources in the Soviet Economy

When Sputnik, man's first artificial satellite, began its cruise in October 1957, many Americans suddenly wondered what was wrong with their educational system. The Russians, they had agreed, could build steel mills and weapons. But how had they outstripped the Americans in space?

In Reading 12, we noted the vast physical resources of the Soviet Union. To develop those physical resources, the Soviet Union needed developed human resources. The Soviet Union had adequate manpower, for it had a large population. It had fairly healthy manpower. And it had willing manpower, for the Soviet government strongly favored economic development. The main problem remaining was to develop educated manpower. Reading 16 describes Soviet education today and notes the connection between Soviet education and Soviet national goals. As you read, keep the following questions in mind:

1. To what extent is American education designed to advance "the economic, social, and political purposes of the nation"?
2. Why do you suppose that Soviet students are required to study so much science and mathematics? How might that requirement be changed if Soviet production continues to rise?
3. What difficulties might an underdeveloped country in Asia or Africa encounter in trying to adopt the Soviet educational system?

Education: An Economic Tool

The Soviet Union may have gone further than any other nation in demonstrating the importance of educated manpower to achieve economic goals. Americans may question the narrowness and the values built into Soviet education. But they are left to stare at one overwhelming fact: In a relatively short period of time, the Russians changed education from a luxury for the few to a commonplace of life for almost all citizens.

The Communist leaders saw that with the "right" kind of education—in quantity and in emphasis—the Soviet Union could become prosperous and powerful. With the "wrong" kind of education—either in quantity or in emphasis—the Soviet Union would remain undistinguished from the other underdeveloped economies of the world. Accordingly, the Communist leaders gave education a central role in all of their planning. The results are obvious today. Soviet education is at once advanced and retarded, wide-ranging and inhibited, flexible and firmly fixed.

Americans have long been troubled by the issue of what control the federal government should exercise over the content of education. We have sought federal government aid for education but have been somewhat wary of it. So far, the Russians have shown no such doubts. Education has been viewed as an instrument in the total economic and social plan. Consequently, it has been totally controlled by the central government.

Look, for example, at the study program for the second semester of the ninth grade throughout the Soviet Union. The student will be in class six days a week, and each week will contain the following class periods:

Russian language and literature	4 periods
A foreign language, most often English	3 periods
Algebra and geometry	6 periods
Biology, physics, and chemistry	7 periods
History and geography	7 periods
Physical education	2 periods
Mechanical drawing	1 period
Shop course or work experience	2 periods

And in tenth grade, he or she will add astronomy, psychology and trigonometry to the list!

Thus, the Russian student will be ahead of his American counterpart in the study of a foreign language, in math and science, and in practical work experience. He may be behind the American in the arts and humanities and in learning a broad, free-ranging approach in the social studies. But, in the Soviet government's view, the Russian student will be better prepared to push the nation ahead in scientific endeavors and in economic growth. Exposing students to work experience is an attempt to make the Soviet Union's future intellectual leaders aware of the values and problems of manual workers. We do not know whether that effort pays off; we only know that the leaders of the Soviet Union feel that the attempt must be made.

The seriousness with which the Soviet Union seeks to develop its full potential in human resources is also shown by its great efforts to educate all children. The bitterly cold winters and vast distances make it a major problem simply to get all children to schools. But, from all available evidence, it seems clear that nearly every youngster goes to school from his seventh birthday through at least the eighth grade.

The Soviet government has also tried to make higher education available for everyone with ability, regardless of his wealth or geographical location. In practice, the Russians face some of the same practical difficulties that Americans do in trying to provide equal educational opportunity for all. Typically, city and suburban schools prepare students for higher education better than country schools. Furthermore, the children of the Soviet Union's leaders seem to face a better than even chance of getting into the best universities.

Although Soviet universities have expanded, there is still not nearly enough space for all who would like to attend. In part, the gap is bridged by an elaborate system of specialized institutes in practically every technical field that one can name. In those institutes, students receive heavy technical training as well as a generous amount of Marxist-Leninist philosophy.

Russian universities and specialized institutes seem to face a perpetual challenge: Minds that are trained to soar and dream in the pursuit of new knowledge may reach conclusions that the Soviet leaders do not like. Command societies must decide how much they can afford to let people think creatively for themselves. Command societies profit from the creativity of their people, as long as that creativity does not threaten the system itself. Since the death of Stalin in 1953, the Soviet Union has decided that it can afford to allow greater freedom of thought. But compared to the American student, the Russian student still has less exposure to the variety of human thought.

Supplementing the universities and the specialized institutes is a vast network of vocational-technical institutes. In these institutes the emphasis is heavily on job-training. They train men and women for the current needs of a developed economy; they have little to do with the production of new knowledge.

There are more than fifty million students registered in all of the Soviet Union's formal education programs. Their school days are guided by a carefully considered strategy for using human resources: The emphasis is upon teaching knowledge and skills that will contribute to the economic, social, and political purposes of the nation. The frills are few, and the days are demanding.

SUGGESTED READINGS

Committee for Economic Development, *Raising Low Incomes Through Improved Education,* pp. 15–40.

Question: How is education related to productivity and employment in present American society? Which of the committee's recommendations would be the most effective? Why?

Industrial Relations Center, University of Chicago, *Capital: Key to Progress,* pp. 5–31.

Question: Where do the capital resources for the American and Soviet economies come from?

Rieber, Alfred J. and Robert C. Nelson, editors, *The USSR and Communism,* pp. 10–33.

Question: What are the outstanding human and physical resources of the Soviet Union?

Senesh, Lawrence and Barbara Warne Newell, *Our Labor Force,* pp. 8–18.

Question: How have the human resources of the United States changed?

Unit Three

What and How in a Market Economy

IN EARLIER UNITS, we saw how the traditional society of the Eskimos answered the *what, how,* and *for whom* questions and thereby tried to solve the economic problem of scarcity. Now we move on to the second major type of economic system: the market economy. This unit examines the market economy's answers to the *what* and *how* questions. The *for whom* question is treated in Unit Five.

In a market society, the main economic decisions are made by consumers and producers, rather than by tradition or by the government. As the spectrums in Reading 6 suggested, no society has a purely traditional, market, or command system. The United States is no exception. Its economy is basically a market economy, but the workings of the free market have often been modified because of the value Americans place on security and fairness.

Chapter 5

Model of the Market

STATING THE ISSUE Every time you make a purchase, sell a good or service, take a job, or quit a job, you are making an economic decision in a market economy. Take the act of buying a shirt. When you buy the shirt, you—together with the store—are deciding that the shirt should be distributed to you (answering the *for whom* question). Your preferences, in turn, influence shirt manufacturers to produce the kinds of shirts that will sell (answering the *what* question). And the manufacturers, perhaps pressured by labor unions and regulated by government, must also decide what machinery to buy, whom to hire, and how to market the shirts to retail stores (answering the *how* question).

In a large market economy, millions of such decisions are made every day. Your decision to buy a shocking pink shirt instead of a white one will not in itself put the sellers of white shirts out of business. But the decisions of all of the millions of shirt buyers in the United States do control the fortunes of the shirt industry.

Although this process may sound simple, it is in fact highly complex. The problem is one of communication: Producers of goods and services must somehow correctly hear the messages of consumers of goods and services. Millions of economic decisions must be meshed together. If they do not, trouble will result. Manufacturers will make goods that consumers do not want to buy, and consumers will want to buy goods that manufacturers are not making.

Chapter 5 does not specifically describe the market economy of the United States, or that of any other society. Instead, it presents a model of a market economy—a simplified version. By using a model, we can concentrate simply on how a market economy is supposed to work. For the time being, we can leave out the complications that affect real market economies.

Our main questions will have a familiar ring: How does a market society decide what to produce? How does it decide how to produce it? And finally, how are the desires of consumers and the plans of producers coordinated?

17 The Market Economy as an Organizing Device

One of the interesting things about a market economy such as ours is that it is so terribly hard to describe to anyone how it works. How, for example, does it happen that just about the right number of units of any product are delivered to the right market for sale on the right day without there being someone sitting up on top giving all the orders? Because most of us have always lived in a market economy, we take its workings for granted. But if we had to describe it to someone who had never experienced such a system, we would probably be in hopeless trouble. And, in getting ourselves out of the trouble, we might develop a new appreciation for what an ingenious—and puzzling—system it is. Robert Heilbroner has imagined such a situation in today's reading.

As you read, keep the following questions in mind:

1. What is "the market"?
2. How are the *what, how,* and *for whom* questions answered in the bread and cheese economy?
3. If people want more cheese and less bread, what will happen to the price of good dairy acreage? Why?

1. "What You Suggest Is Madness"

ROBERT L. HEILBRONER

From The Making of Economic Society, *© 1962. Reprinted by permission of Prentice-Hall, Inc., Englewood Cliffs, New Jersey.*

. . . [A]ssume for a moment that we could act as economic advisers to a society which had not yet decided on its mode of economic organization. Suppose, for instance, that we were called on to act as consultants to one of the new nations emerging [on] the continent of Africa.

We could imagine the leaders of such a nation saying, "We have always experienced a highly tradition-bound way of life. Our men hunt and cultivate the fields and perform their tasks as they are brought up to do by the force of example and the instruction of their elders. We know, too, something of what can be done by economic command. We are prepared, if necessary, to sign an edict making it compulsory for many of our men to work on community projects for our national development. Tell us, is there any other way we can organize our society so that it will function successfully—or better yet, more successfully?"

Suppose we answered, "Yes, there is another way. Organize your society along the lines of a market economy."

"Very well," say the leaders. "What do we then tell people to do? How do we assign them to their various tasks?"

"That's the very point," we would answer. "In a market economy no one is assigned to any task. The very idea of a market society is that each person is allowed to decide for himself what to do."

There is consternation among the leaders. "You mean there is *no* assignment of some men to mining and others to cattle raising? No manner of selecting some for transportation and others for cloth weaving? You leave this to people to decide for themselves? But what happens if they do not decide correctly? What happens if no one volunteers to go into the mines, or if no one offers himself as a railway engineer?"

"You may rest assured," we tell the leaders, "none of that will happen. In a market society, all the jobs will be filled because it will be to people's advantage to fill them."

Our respondents accept this with uncertain expressions. "Now look," one of them finally says, "let us suppose that we take your advice and let our people do as they please. Now let's talk about something important, like cloth production. Just how do we fix the right level of cloth output in this 'market society' of yours?"

"But you don't," we reply.

"We don't! Then how do we know there will be enough cloth produced?"

"There will be," we tell him. "The market will see to that."

"Then how do we know there won't be *too much* cloth produced?" he asks triumphantly.

"Ah, but the market will see to that too!"

"But what *is* this market that will do all these wonderful things? Who runs it?"

"Oh, nobody runs the market," we answer. "It runs itself. In fact there really isn't any such *thing* as 'the market.' It's just a word we use to describe the way people behave."

"But I thought people behaved the way they wanted to!"

"And so they do," we say. "But never fear. They will want to behave the way you want them to behave."

"I am afraid," says the chief of the delegation, "that we are wasting our time. We thought you had in mind a serious proposal. But what you suggest is madness. It is inconceivable. Good day, sir." And with great dignity the delegation takes its leave.

2. A Model: By Bread and Cheese Alone

Perhaps the points made by Robert Heilbroner will become clearer if we look not at the complex, real world, but at a very simplified model or imaginary version of it.

Imagine a market economy somewhere in the world where only two products are produced and consumed. Men and women in that economy live entirely on bread and cheese. How does such an economy decide what to produce, how to produce it, and for whom to produce it?

To begin with, much of the *what* question is answered by the fact that these people just happen to like bread and cheese, and only bread and cheese. But how much of each? Because these people have a free market economy, we know that they will divide their spending between bread and cheese in whatever way appeals to their tastes. Let us assume that they have been spending half of their income on bread and half on cheese. Now suppose these people decide, of their own free will, that they want more cheese and less bread. What happens?

In the first place, the bakers and cheese-makers learn of the change in taste not from a king or commissar, but from simple observation. The bakers find themselves with bread unsold at the end of the day. That is a signal to them to cut back production. The cheese-makers, on the other hand, find that they have sold all their cheese before the end of the day. That is their signal to try to expand production.

But the chain of events has just begun. The cheese-makers cannot simply expand production at once. First, they will have to get more milk, more labor, and more equipment. If any of these ingredients is in short supply, the cheese-makers may change the way in which they make cheese as well as the quantity they make. If skilled labor, for example, is hard to come by, the cheese-makers may train more people, work their present staff overtime, cut corners in the cheese-making process, or try to devise new machinery to do part of the work that has been done by labor. From any of these changes, a new *how* answer would result.

At the same time, bakers will find that they must lay off some of their skilled workers as production is cut back. Those workers may be lucky enough to find jobs in the expanding cheese industry, but their new jobs will probably neither pay as well nor be at as high a skill level as their old jobs in the bread industry. Farmers with land that is fine for raising wheat but not so good for raising dairy cattle will also feel the squeeze. But their friends with good dairy lands will prosper. Thus, there will be a redistribution of income as a result of the shift in tastes from bread to cheese. The *for whom* question is answered not by law but by impersonal market forces: Those who gain from the shift in taste get more income with which they can buy more of the economy's bread and cheese than before. And those who lost from the shift in taste end up with less money to buy bread and cheese.

The real world, to which we will soon turn, is more complicated than this imaginary economy of bread-eaters and cheese-eaters. In the real world, there are thousands of products. But the same basic process is still at work. In a market economy, free market forces, responding to the dictates of consumers alone, make the major decisions about what goods are to be produced, how they are to be produced, and for whom they are to be produced.

18 Supply and Demand in the Market (I)

Today's lesson begins our closer examination of how markets work. At the core of these lessons—and of the market society—is the law of supply and demand. It is this law that Robert Heilbroner's economic advisers had such difficulty explaining to the African leaders. As you read, keep the following questions in mind:

1. What are supply and demand? What do they have to do with a market?
2. Describe a competitive market. Give examples.
3. Give an example of a product for which demand rarely changes.

1. The Law of Supply and Demand

A popular college textbook defines the law of supply and demand in this way: "The law of supply and demand states that the market price and the quantity sold will be determined by demand and supply in competitive markets." That is a perfectly satisfactory definition—as long as one knows the meaning of "market price," "quantity sold," "demand," "supply," and "competitive markets." Some simple examples, all involving the sale of ice cream of a certain quality at a certain time in a certain small city called A-Ville, will help to explain those terms.

1. The *market price* of a quart of ice cream is the sum of money for which it is actually sold.
2. The *quantity sold* means the number of quarts of ice cream sold during a given time period.
3. The *demand* means the entire list of quantities of ice cream that consumers would buy at various prices at a particular time. For example:

If the price were	*Consumers would want to buy*
$.80 per quart	500 quarts a week
.75	550
.70	600
.65	675
.60	750
.55	900
.50	1,100

The demand for ice cream is not as simple as "600 quarts." Instead, it is

600 quarts at a certain price, \$.70; but it is also 750 quarts at \$.60, only 550 quarts at \$.75, and so on. In other words, how much of anything people demand or want depends upon its price.

The ice cream example illustrates another point, and one familiar to students long before they began to study economics. As prices go up, people usually want less of that item; as prices go down, they usually want more of it. Less obvious is the fact that there are two reasons for this. Take the case of a drop in price. First, people want more of the item simply because it is now more attractive as compared to substitute products. (Ice cream, for example, becomes relatively more attractive if its price has fallen while the prices of other desserts have not changed.) Second, people can afford more of the item when its price drops. When the price of ice cream is \$.80 per quart, one can buy only three quarts for \$2.40. If the price drops to \$.60, one can buy four quarts for \$2.40.

4. The *supply* means the entire list of quantities of ice cream that producers would offer for sale at various prices. For example:

If the price were	*Producers would be willing to bring to market*
\$.80 per quart	875 quarts a week
.75	825
.70	750
.65	675
.60	600
.55	500
.50	400

Like the demand, the supply is not any one number like "600." Again, the supply depends on the price offered. If the price rises sharply it will pay ice cream plants to work overtime to produce more, even if their costs go up in the process. And it will pay some people not now in the ice cream business to come into the business with the hope of making money over and above all of their costs.

5. A *competitive market* means that there are enough ice cream plants in the area so that no one producer can restrict the quantity sold or the price charged. If there were only one ice cream plant in the city, that plant would have the market to itself. Anyone who wanted ice cream would have to buy it from that single plant, at the price it asked. A "competitive market" means too that no one buyer looms large enough to have much effect on the price that is charged. If there were only one buyer of ice cream, ice cream plants would have to sell at the price he offered, if they wanted to sell any ice cream at all.

2. A Long, Hot Summer for Ice Cream

In the rest of this reading, we'll look more closely at the demand side of our picture. We'll stick with ice cream but move to a larger city to examine what might cause a change in the demand for ice cream. And since demand has now been defined as a list of amounts that would be bought at different prices, a change in demand will mean a change throughout the list.

B-Ville is an industrial city of about half a million people. Its economy is based upon heavy industry; and income varies widely from time to time, depending on the prosperity of the mills. Our story begins in the winter of 1966–67. The winter was long and bitter; the spring was cool and rainy. By the beginning of summer, the ice cream business was terrible. Here is the demand picture for May 1967:

If the price were	*Consumers would want to buy*
$.80 per quart	50,000 quarts a week
.75	55,000
.70	60,000
.65	70,000
.60	85,000
.55	100,000
.50	120,000

During the summer, three developments affected the demand for ice cream and changed the market price. First came a sudden heat wave. The stores were besieged with demands for ice cream, and the demand picture was as follows:

If the price were	*Consumers would want to buy*
$.80 per quart	60,000 quarts a week
.75	70,000
.70	85,000
.65	100,000
.60	120,000
.55	150,000
.50	180,000

A week later, the mill workers went on strike. Forty thousand mill workers and their families suddenly had drastically reduced incomes, for the strike funds paid by the union were not nearly as large as what the men had made in wages. As a result, many businesses which depended upon mill workers for sales reduced hours for their employees and laid some of them off entirely. They, too, had smaller incomes. Within a week, the demand for ice cream had changed sharply:

If the price were	*Consumers would want to buy*
$.80 per quart	40,000 quarts
.75	42,000
.70	44,000
.65	48,000
.60	50,000
.55	55,000
.50	60,000

As if the strike were not enough, a national company began heavy advertising for a new diet ice cream made from vegetable oils and "guaranteed to contain not more than one tenth of one calorie per scoop." It quickly became popular with B-Ville's bikini-wearers. The table below shows how this development changed the demand for local ice cream:

If the price were	*Consumers would want to buy*
$.80 per quart	38,000 quarts
.75	40,000
.70	42,000
.65	44,000
.60	46,000
.55	48,000
.50	50,000

These events illustrate three factors that influence the demand for any product. First, demand depends in part upon people's tastes. (When the weather became warmer, people wanted more ice cream.) Second, demand depends in part upon people's incomes. (When the strike came, people cut back on their spending and bought less ice cream.) And finally, demand depends in part on the availability of substitute products. (When a new product came on the market, some people switched to it, and bought less local ice cream.)

19 Supply and Demand in the Market (II)

In the last lesson, we saw that demand for ice cream, or for anything else, depends on people's tastes and incomes, and on the availability of other products. Usually, the higher the price for anything, the less of it people will want to buy or be able to buy. And the lower the price, the more of it they will want and be able to buy. (Why are items like salt and drugs something of an exception?) Now we turn our attention to the supply side. As you read, keep the following questions in mind:

1. Which cost items are likely to vary most widely?
2. How will higher interest rates affect the number of new businesses started each year? Why?
3. Why couldn't a failing business survive simply by charging a high enough price to cover its costs and provide a modest profit?

The Sources of Supply

Common sense tells us that the higher the price a producer can get for his product, the more of it he will produce. This is true both for those producers already in the market who hope profitably to produce more to sell at the higher prices, and also for new producers lured into the field by higher prices.

Even if the price of ice cream rose to $6.00 a quart, it would do a producer no good if it cost him $6.10 to produce that quart of ice cream. A producer cannot look only at prices. He must also consider his costs:

1. The biggest cost item in many businesses is wages and salaries. Labor must be paid for, and it must be paid well enough to attract competent workers. In addition to wages and salaries, most employers now also pay such fringe benefits as pensions, vacations, Social Security, and sometimes health insurance.

2. A producer must buy and maintain machinery, probably more than he needed ten years ago. He will also have to rent or maintain a factory and office, and pay utility bills for electricity, gas, water, and telephone.

3. He must buy raw materials or semi-finished goods from other manufacturers. An ice cream company, for example, would need to buy milk from dairies, chocolate from a chocolate factory, fruit from farmers or distributors, and so on.

4. He will have selling expenses. Ice cream companies, for example, usually try to package their product colorfully to attract the eyes of the supermarket shoppers. That packaging costs money. So do advertising, and trucks to carry ice cream to the stores.

5. He will have to pay taxes on his business income, probably to the state and local government as well as to the federal government.

6. If he has borrowed money to run the business while he is waiting for the proceeds from sales to come in, he will have to pay interest charges to a bank.

7. And finally, he will have to make a profit, or else it will not be worthwhile for him to remain in business. The money, time, and skill a business-

man expends in his business could earn him money elsewhere. The owner of a new business, of course, may decide to take the chance that the higher profits he hopes to earn when his business becomes well-established will more than make up for low profits in the first years.

Producers vary in the efficiency with which they combine resources—labor, raw or semi-finished materials, machinery, and know-how. The most efficient producers can still make a profit even when market prices drop a long way. Less skillful producers, or those who live in an area with particularly high taxes or expensive labor, will probably be forced out of business if prices drop.

Business, then, is a gamble. A businessman gambles that he will produce efficiently enough to cover all his costs and still make a profit. And Americans have been unusually willing to take such gambles. Recently, about 425,000 businesses have been started each year. More than half are small retail businesses, but about 25,000 are manufacturing enterprises. Of these 425,000, about half are discontinued within two years, and two thirds fail within four years. And there is probably not a single producer who goes out of business who does not say, "I could have made it if only I could have gotten a little higher price for my product." But the market coolly, and usually impartially, enforces its law: Make a profit, or get out!

Thus, the supply side of the market—like the demand side—is dynamic and changing. Often, though, supply lags behind demand. A new fad, for example, can sweep the country in weeks, creating a new demand for some product almost overnight. But it takes time for producers to adjust to these changes. They must re-tool their machinery, retrain their employees, and find new sources of raw materials. The signals may have been clear enough, but producers cannot always respond to those signals immediately.

One last point before we put demand and supply together in the next lesson: We saw that selling expenses were one cost of doing business. And a big part of those expenses in the United States goes into advertising. The purpose? To change people's tastes so that they want the advertiser's brand more than they want that perpetual loser in the market place, "Brand X." In more technical terms, a supplier uses advertising to try to change consumers' demands. So supply and demand begin to interact even before a sale or purchase takes place.

20 A Way of Looking at Markets

Economists have a special tool which they use to sum up the supply and demand forces described in the last two readings. It is a diagram which, once mastered, proves useful over and over again in understanding how prices are set in a market. As you read, keep the following questions in mind:

1. Why does the demand curve slope downwards?
2. Why does the supply curve slope upwards?
3. What is the equilibrium price? Why are other prices unstable, as long as demand and supply do not change?

Supply and Demand Curves

Go back to the demand for ice cream, as discussed in Reading 18. We assumed that the demand for ice cream in A-Ville during a certain week was the following:

If the price were	*Consumers would want to buy*
$.80 per quart	500 quarts a week
.75	550
.70	600
.65	675
.60	750
.55	900
.50	1,100

Exactly that same information can be conveyed by a diagram. Start with a vertical and a horizontal line. Let points on the vertical line represent the various prices at which ice cream might sell. Points on the horizontal line will represent the total number of quarts that consumers would want to buy at various prices. So to show that if the price of ice cream

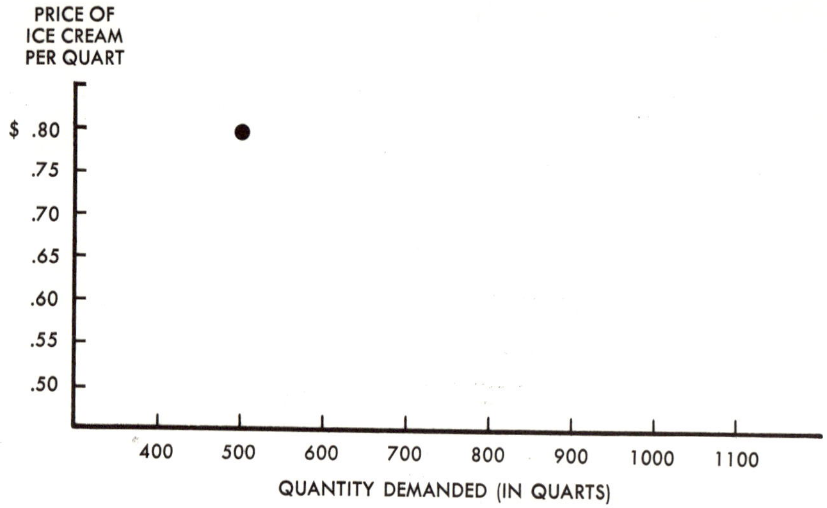

were $.80 per quart, consumers would want to buy 500 quarts, we put a ● directly opposite the $.80 mark, and directly above the 500 quart mark on the diagram on p. 66.

Next, we can fill in ●'s for the rest of the information from the table. There will be a ● opposite the $.75 mark and above the 550 mark, a ● opposite the $.70 mark and above the 600 mark, and so on. For convenience, we connect the ●'s with a line:

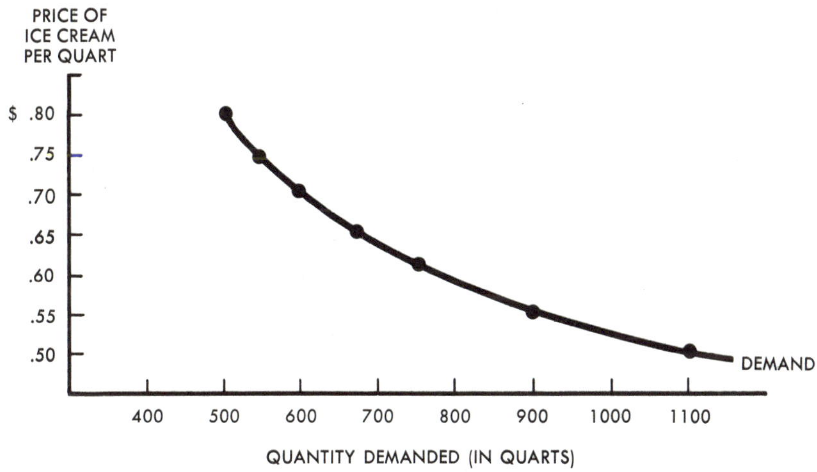

This curve now says all that we know about A-Ville's demand for ice cream. Its message is a familiar one: The higher the price, the less ice cream people will buy; the lower the price, the more they will buy. (Note that the downward slope of the demand curve represents falling prices, and not falling demand.)

We can make a similar diagram with the supply information for A-Ville given in Reading 18. There we assumed that A-Ville's supply of ice cream looked like this:

If the price were	*Producers would be willing to bring to market*
$.80 per quart	875 quarts a week
.75	825
.70	750
.65	675
.60	600
.55	500
.50	400

Transferred onto the diagram, that same information looks like this:

That upward sloping curve tells us again that the higher the price, the more that producers will be willing to bring to the market.

Now, putting the demand and supply curves together, we get:

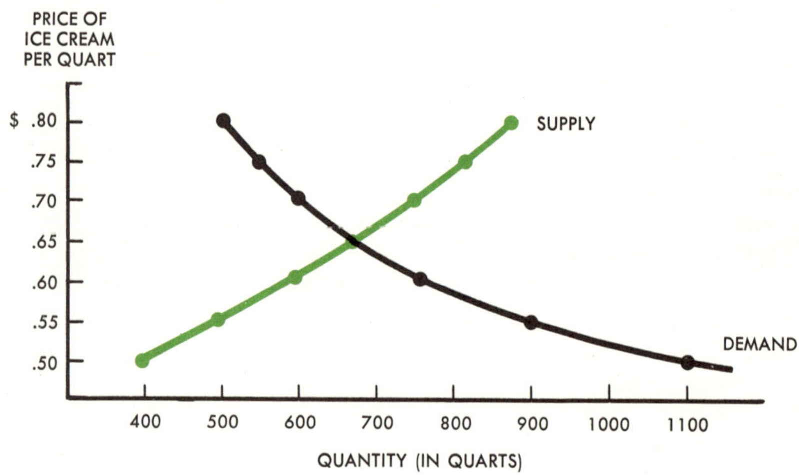

Those two intersecting curves portray the market for ice cream. To see what the diagram can tell us, we can examine what would happen in the market at three different prices:

1. Suppose the price for ice cream one morning were $.75. At that price, customers would be willing to buy only 550 quarts, but producers would be willing to bring 875 quarts to market. At $.75, supply would exceed demand:

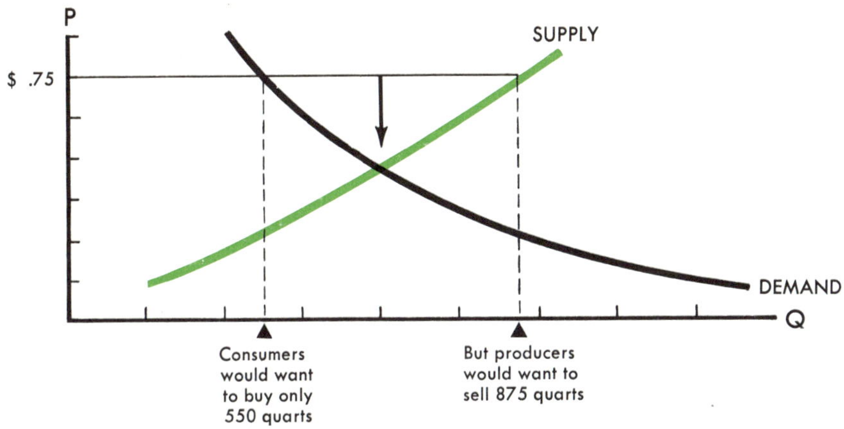

The situation would be unstable. Some producers, rather than have all their ice cream left, would be willing to cut prices. And customers, seeing that some producers are being stuck with larger quantities than they had counted on, will shop around for cut prices. Thus, the price of $.75 will be forced downward, as shown by the arrow on the diagram.

2. Suppose, on the other hand, that the price one morning were only $.50. At that bargain price, customers would be ready to buy 1,100 quarts. But producers would be willing to bring only 400 quarts to market. At $.50, demand would exceed supply:

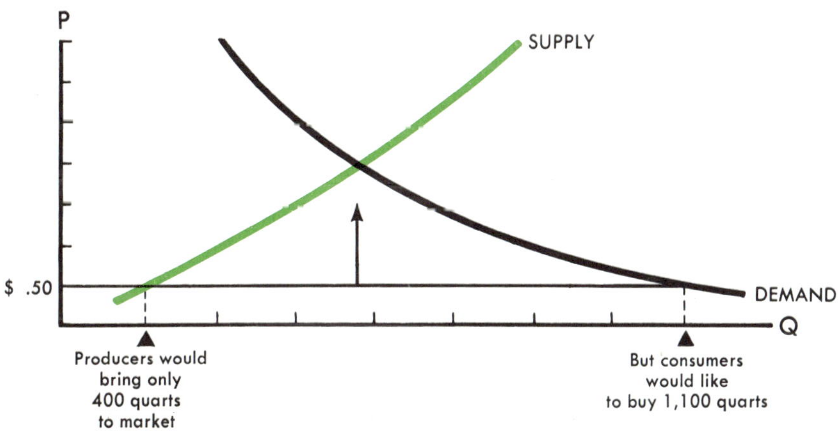

Again the situation is unstable. Rather than go without any ice cream, some consumers will be willing to pay more than $.50 a quart, and producers will see that they get more than $.50 a quart for their dwindling supply. So the price will be bid upward in the market, as shown by the arrow.

3. Now look at the price of $.65. At that price, consumers would be willing to buy 675 quarts. And producers would be willing to supply 675 quarts. At $.65, the demand would equal the supply:

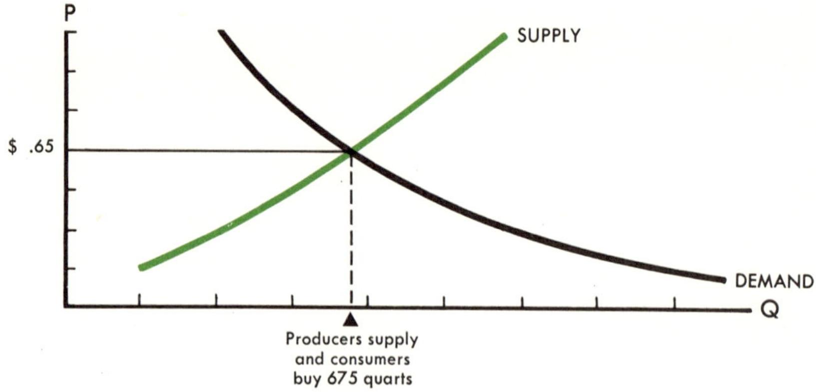

That is a stable situation. So long as consumers' incomes and desire for ice cream stay unchanged, and so long as producers' costs and desires to produce remain unchanged, ice cream will be sold for $.65. For that reason the price at which the demand and supply curves intersect is called an *equilibrium price.* That doesn't mean that everybody is happy with $.65 as the price for ice cream, because customers would still prefer a lower price, and producers would still prefer a higher one. But the equilibrium price, which matches the quantity demanded with the quantity supplied, will prevail until either the demand curve or the supply curve changes.

To repeat, these diagrams tell us nothing we did not know from the demand and supply tables. But they do help to put our available information into a more useful form. And they help to point out a key idea that Alfred Marshall, the British economist, first phrased so well: It is as useless to ask whether supply or demand determines price, as it is to ask whether the left or the right blade in a pair of scissors does the cutting. Both blades cut—and both supply and demand determine price.

21 How Markets Work: Some Further Examples

The purpose of this lesson is to test your understanding of supply and demand by looking at some concrete, factual situations. In the preceding lesson we assumed that supply and demand were unchanging. In fact, demand and supply continually fluctuate. It is in charting those fluctuations that the demand and supply diagrams prove most useful. As you read, keep the following questions in mind:

1. Why did the demand for hula hoops fluctuate? Why did the supply fluctuate?
2. What determines the demand for Utrillo paintings? What determines the supply?
3. How is a stock market different than a market for a product like pork? How is it similar?

1. The Case of the Hula Hoops

In July 1958, two men in San Gabriel, California, started the nation spinning into one of the most carefree fads of the decade. They invented the hula hoop.

The two men, owners of a small firm called the Wham-O Manufacturing Company, secured the aid of technicians from a major plastic company to design a simple plastic hoop about thirty inches in diameter. The hoop was meant to be placed around the body at waist height and then kept spinning there by rapid and rhythmical twisting of the hips. A simple enough idea, once somebody thought of it!

The fad spread at a dizzy pace. And its variations were endless. Some children and adults, too, specialized in seeing how many hoops they could keep going at one time using body, arms, and neck. Others entered contests to see how long they could keep the hoops spinning. There were classes in the finer points of hoopery, health clubs to promote the spinning habit, and "hoop-it-up" parties. Nor was the fad confined to the United States—France, Britain, and Japan soon joined in. And a Belgian expedition leaving for the Antarctic reportedly took a hoop along for the trip.

The Wham-O Manufacturing Company was not alone in the field for very long. By September 1958, at least twenty other companies were making hula hoops. Manufacturers of piping and hose quickly converted their equipment to turn out the simple plastic hoops. By mid-September, *Life* Magazine estimated that twenty million hoops had been sold for about $30 million. (Hoops sold from as low as $.79 to as high as $2.50 each.)

As quickly as it sprang up, the fad died away. The former manufacturers of piping and hose went back to making piping and hose. The retailers left with a large supply of hoops sold them at sacrifice prices; one of them cut his hoops in half and sold them as loops for decorative garden fence. So it was that a few years and twenty million hoops later, a child could ask his parents, "What's a hula hoop?"

Suppose we tell that same story with supply and demand diagrams. In these diagrams, "D_1"means the demand in Time Period 1; "D_2" means the demand in the next time period; and so on. And "S_1", "S_2", and so on refer to the supply of hula hoops in successive time periods.

ACT I:

A new product enters the market. There is only one producer, who turns out a limited number of hoops. But there is an almost instantaneous market for his product.

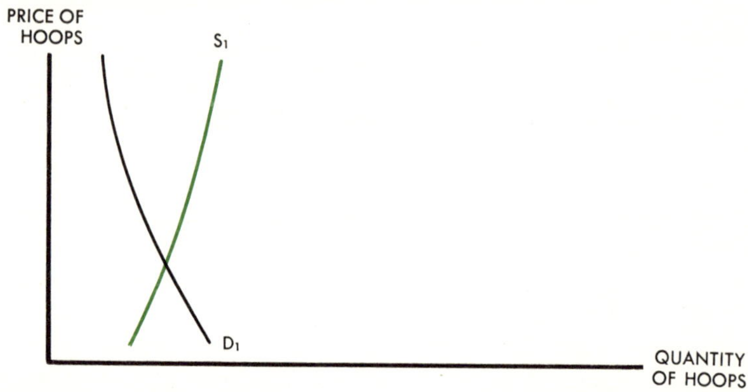

The price is high, and the quantity produced and sold rather small. (Why are the demand and supply curves so steep?)

ACT II:

The demand skyrockets as the fad sweeps the country:

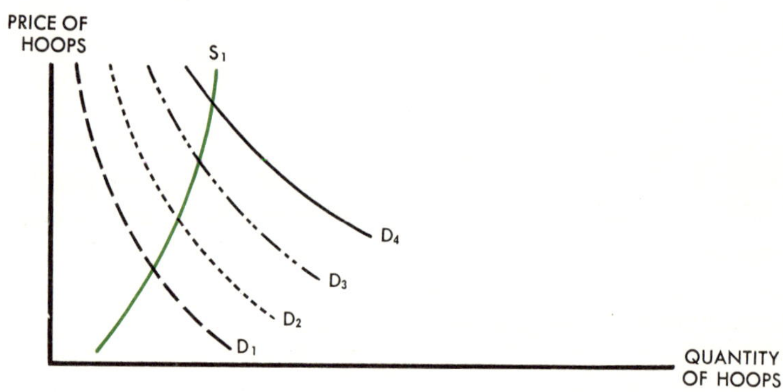

The equilibrium price rises sharply. We shift the demand curves to the right here to show the progress of the fad. The whole demand line moves in each instance because an increase in demand means customers will buy more hoops at each and every price.

ACT III:

It's an easy product to manufacture—and it isn't patented. More producers rush into the market, lured by the hope of matching the big sales and big profits of the first manufacturer.

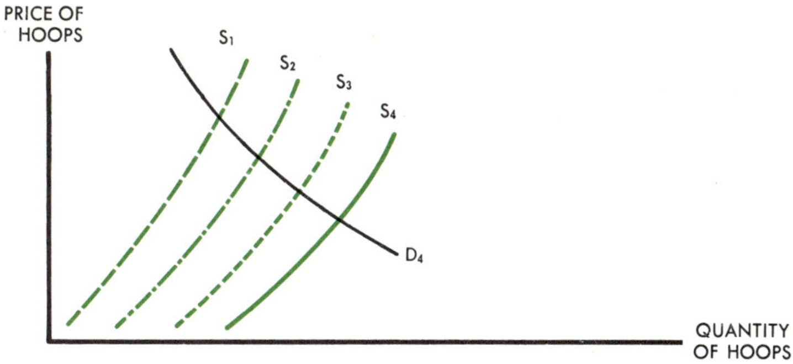

Prices drop somewhat as a larger supply comes onto the market and the demand stops rising. We shift the entire supply line to the right in each case to show that more hoops are supplied at every price.

ACT IV:

The fad is disappearing. A few slow-to-act producers are coming into the field, but the demand is falling off rapidly.

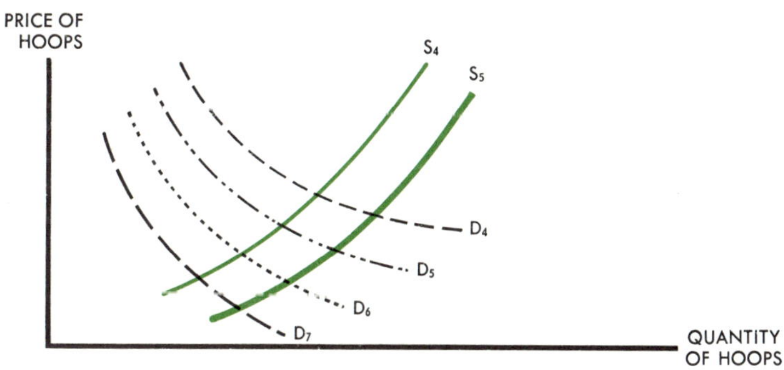

What happens to the price?

ACT V:

The fad is over. Customers stop buying. Producers stop producing.

2. The Case of the Utrillo Paintings

Maurice Utrillo was a French painter whose work so often featured the streets and buildings of the Montmartre section of Paris. Typically the colors in his paintings are light; in painting after painting there are white buildings bathed in sunlight. While a gallery filled with his work might be monotonous, each painting by itself has proved very popular. Prints of his works are to be found in many homes. When Utrillo died in 1955, it became known that a large collection of his work had still not come onto the market for sale. His widow, who owned the unsold paintings and who had managed his business affairs for many years, made it clear that she would be offering the paintings for sale only one at a time and at a slow rate over the years ahead.

What is Madame Utrillo trying to accomplish by selling the paintings slowly? How can her strategy be described in terms of supply and demand?

3. The Case of the New York Stock Exchange

The New York Stock Exchange is the world's largest trading market for the purchase and sale of shares of ownership (stock) in industry. Four or five million shares may exchange hands on a single day in that market, which is linked by telephone and teletype to stockbrokers' offices all over the country. (Stockbrokers act as go-betweens, or agents, for those who want to buy or sell stock.) Buyers and sellers have almost instant access to information on the prices at which stocks are changing hands. The price of any one stock may rise or fall sharply in any one day.

How does supply and demand analysis help to explain why the price of one stock might rise and the price of another drop in any one day? What might lie behind such a rise or fall?

Chapter 6

How America Modifies the Market

STATING THE ISSUE The guiding value in a market economy is free competition. From elementary school on, Americans are taught to accept and enjoy competition. We compete for grades in classes, for victories in sports, for profits in businesses, and for partners in marriage. "Let the best man win," we say. But at the same time, Americans learn another value—cooperation. We are taught to help one another in school, at play, in business, and in the home.

To some observers, the American society may seem two-faced—at least until they see that their own societies are seldom interested solely in competition or cooperation. But, as these observers look at us, they see us championing competition at one moment and cooperation at the next moment. In truth, there is a kind of tension between these two strands in our history. We have favored free competition in the marketplace. But, whenever competition has hurt too much or left some problem unsolved, we have not hesitated to use cooperation in its stead.

The chief instrument through which we have modified the market forces has been government. Where politically powerful groups have felt that free market forces hurt rather than helped them, they have used government's power to change the rules of the game. Every such change in the rules provokes strong controversy. Those who favor the changes say that they are either "making competition work still better" or "softening the harshest impacts of competition." Those in opposition have often claimed that those changes will "destroy the American way of life" or promote "creeping socialism."

In Chapter 6, we will see some of the ways in which the United States has modified its market economy. Two general questions will concern us: In what ways has the United States modified the pure market model presented in Chapter 5? And, to what extent does the United States have a free market economy?

22 Historical Backdrop for the American Economy

In the last chapter, we considered a model of the free market. Now we will look at the market as it actually exists in so-called market societies. As we shall soon see, not even the United States has a pure market economy. In fact, as today's reading points out, the United States has never had a free market economy—not even in the early, pioneering years of the nation.

Subsidies (direct grants of money to businesses by government), tariffs, and land grants to railroads were but a few of the ways in which government modified free competition by aiding businesses in the early 1800's. Later, the government took an active role in other areas of the economy. As you read, keep the following questions in mind:

1. How do tariffs and subsidies affect supply and demand in the market?
2. How could regulation of trusts be called an attempt to restore a free market economy?
3. Since 1800, has the economy of the United States become more free or less free? How?

American Economic Policy: "History, Not Logic"

WILLIAM L. LETWIN

From the Introduction to A Documentary History of American Economic Policy *(New York: Doubleday). Copyright © 1961 by William L. Letwin. Reprinted by permission.*

In reviewing the history of American economic policy, I shall . . . separate it into three eras, 1789 to 1862, 1862 to 1912, and 1912 to 1935. The first of these periods, from the foundation of the republic to the Civil War, offers the happiest ground for those who [look for] economic policy [in] the theoretical remarks of statesmen. Never since that time have so many American statesmen spoken so well, and never since have so many of them spoken the language of economic liberalism.

Nowhere is this language more clearly to be heard than in the voice of Thomas Jefferson. In his first inaugural address, delivered in 1801, after [listing] the rich opportunities available to Americans, he said:

> With all these blessings, what more is necessary to make us a happy and prosperous people? Still one thing more, fellow-citizens—a wise and frugal government, which shall restrain men from injuring one another, which shall leave them otherwise free to regulate their own pursuits of industry

> and improvement, and shall not take from the mouth of labor the bread it has earned. . . .

This statement of creed, much as it reflected the hopes of Jefferson and many other Americans then and since, is a poor guide to what government actually did during Jefferson's tenure of office, or at any other time.

The government, according to Jefferson, was to act seldom and tax little. . . . During his first administration, federal revenues were applied in large part to reducing the public debt incurred during the War of Independence. Once the public debt had been paid off, taxes were to be reduced still further—or so Jefferson must have planned. But nothing of the sort happened.

Four years later Jefferson made his second inaugural address. Revenues, largely obtained from tariff duties, had been rising; the debt was being reduced. Jefferson might have been expected to announce . . . that the tariff [soon] . . . would be reduced. He announced instead: "[The debt once paid,] the revenue . . . may . . . be applied, in time of peace, to rivers, canals, roads, arts, manufactures, education, and other great objects within each State."

Government would, in short, become an encourager and promoter of industry. No longer would it leave men "free to regulate their own pursuits of industry and improvement"; instead it would tax the citizens in order to benefit them, in order to . . . build the canals and stimulate the manufactures . . . which private enterprise could not be depended on to undertake. . . .

[But t]he chief authors of economic policy at this time were the state governments. . . . The activities of Massachusetts are a fair [example]. . . .

During the first half of the nineteenth century, the state of Massachusetts—or local bodies acting on its authority—regulated and inspected the production of lumber, flaxseed, potash, tobacco, and various foodstuffs. . . . Innkeepers . . . could do business only under license. Bridgekeepers, ferrymen, and millowners might charge only such fees as were prescribed by law. [Banks and corporations were also regulated.] . . .

At the other end of the scale was a widespread system of economic encouragement. Massachusetts subsidized fisheries, awarded bounties for the growing of hemp and the manufacture of sailcloth. . . . The state advanced loans to some entrepreneurs and exempted others from taxation—if, for example, they did such signal service as brewing more than a hundred barrels of beer annually. [Railroads were also aided.] . . .

Nor was Massachusetts indifferent to welfare. . . . The municipal authorities operated a system of poor relief. . . . A weak child-labor law was passed in 1836; a more effective one in 1858, setting standards of compulsory schooling for children who worked in factories. . . .

Other states did more and some did less than Massachusetts, but taken all together the states exercised a much greater influence on economic life during the first fifty years than did the federal government. Little by little, however, functions were transferred from the local to the central government. The case of internal improvements is characteristic of the transition. . . .

Besides absorbing gradually the major responsibility for internal improvement, the federal government itself had meanwhile [undertaken more economic activities] . . . than is often supposed. From the beginning it maintained a system of compulsory health insurance for seamen. It licensed fur traders, and established its own fur posts. . . . It subsidized codfishing and [shipbuilding,] . . . and regulated those industries in the interests of health and safety. Moreover, although there was no federal labor legislation before 1860, a ten-hour day was instituted for federal employees before 1840.

The most vital way, however, in which the federal government exercised its economic policy was through the tariff. In view of the fact that the United States [has usually] maintained . . . a deliberately protective tariff, one is bound to wonder how its economic policy could ever have been described as "negative." . . .

The characteristic feature of economic policy changed, during the second period, 1862–1912, from subsidy to regulation. . . .

With the completion of the transcontinental railroads, the period of fastest railroad building was over. . . . A vast block of public land had been handed over to the railroads, which were now selling that land at much increased prices. . . . Especially in the outlying rural sections of the country, railroads took advantage of their local monopoly powers to charge rates that seemed outrageously high. . . .

During the 1870's, accordingly, a powerful movement—misnamed the Granger movement, for farmers organized in the Grange supplied only part of its force—quickly grew up and brought about [governmental] regulation of railroad rates and service. . . .

During the period 1862 to 1912, . . . manufacturing [like the railroads] . . . now suddenly seemed no longer to need subsidy and encouragement. . . . An early proposal was that trusts [monopolistic corporations] be denied tariff protection. As a stronger attack was preferred, the Sherman Antitrust Law of 1890 was passed. That law made it a penal offense and civil wrong to form a combination in restraint of trade or to monopolize any industry . . .

[During the third period, from 1912 to 1935, economic policy was influenced by a desire to eliminate inequality or to promote fairness. When a certain group was believed to be at a disadvantage, the government sought to restore the balance. Labor unions, for instance, were given protection, as were farmers and small businessmen. Social Security was enacted to aid the elderly. Income taxes, made possible by the Sixteenth Amendment to the Constitution, were levied more heavily on the wealthy than on the poor. All of these measures were attempts to establish economic security, or to distribute the nation's income and wealth more equally.] . . .

The economic policy of the United States today is an amalgam of the chief tendencies . . . [of] each of the three periods. Economic development by hothouse methods still persists. American manufacturers are given preference over foreign suppliers in bidding for government contracts. Railroads, steamship lines and airlines continue to be aided. . . . The tariff is still frankly protective in certain of its branches. American bicycle manufacturers, for instance, are kept in business by a high wall that shuts out what are known as "cheap foreign goods." . . .

The regulatory mechanisms established during the second period and the security and redistribution measures of the third period are very much in evidence. In short, the development of economic policy in the United States has not consisted of a neat progression in which new policies have replaced outworn policies. What has happened, rather, is that the new policies have been added on to the old ones. . . . History, not logic, Justice Holmes said, is the life of the law; the same is true of the economic policy that has accumulated in the laws.

23 The Business Firm (I)

In the American economy, competition focuses on the business firm. Large or small, owned by one man or by thousands of stockholders, located in a single town or spread across the nation, the business firm is the institution in which most of the nation's economic decisions are made. Readings 23 and 24 trace the history of one business firm. They give you a chance to look at the role of competition in the economy through the eyes of men who had to meet a payroll and coordinate a complicated economic enterprise.

Founded in 1844, the Dennison Manufacturing Company developed with a growing economy. Today its seven divisions make and sell a large number of products. Competition from other firms frequently required company officials to reexamine what they were doing. Each new direction the company has taken has forced its leaders to make basic economic decisions. As you read the first part of the story of the Dennison Manufacturing Company, keep the following questions in mind:

1. What influenced the managers of the company to make the products they did at each stage of the company's development? What role did competition play in these decisions?
2. What influenced the company's decisions about how to produce its products? What role did competition play in these decisions?
3. Why did Eliphalet Dennison decide to invite partners into his

business? What were the advantages and disadvantages of a partnership compared to an individual proprietorship?

The Dennison Manufacturing Company (Part One)

R. W. HIDY and P. E. CAWEIN

Adapted from Case Studies in Business History and Economic Concepts *(Boston: D. C. Heath and Company, © 1967). Used by permission.*

By 1844, Andrew Dennison, a shoemaker of Brunswick, Maine, was experiencing the difficulty of competing successfully in a rapidly changing American economy. Like cobblers for centuries before him, he made shoes in his own shop. He would measure the foot size of a customer, then cut and stitch the leather by hand to fit each person's foot. . . .

Near Boston, shoemakers had long since begun to specialize. If several men worked together, each making a particular part of the shoe, shoes could be produced more quickly and cheaply. By adopting standard shoe sizes in a range of widths and lengths, people could make shoes in one place to be shipped to others. A customer could buy ready-made shoes less expensively than he could have a cobbler make him a pair.

Andrew Dennison could not compete with these mass-produced shoes, and looked about for a better way of earning a living. Andrew's two sons had moved to Boston to engage in the jewelry business. One of them, Aaron, was a successful watchmaker who later helped establish the Waltham Watch Company. For his business, he bought from France small jewelry boxes similar to those used by jewelers today to display their merchandise. The trip across the ocean on a sailing ship, however, made their delivery uncertain and their price high. Aaron took some sample boxes home to his father and two sisters with the idea that copies, made in the United States, would sell more cheaply and be more dependably delivered than the French boxes.

Andrew was persuaded to set up manufacturing of jewelry boxes. Using what money he had, he bought cardboard, fabric, wood, glue, and tools and, with the help of his family, started making jewelry boxes in his own home. To establish a price for his boxes, he added up his total cost for materials, wages, and transportation. Then he added 20 per cent to this cost which he would keep for himself. His son, Aaron, sold the boxes to jewelers in Boston and New York.

Before long, Andrew Dennison was able to increase his profit to 40 per cent. He did this in two ways. First, he raised his prices, although he still made sure that his prices were less than those of the French box makers. Secondly, he decreased the costs of manufacturing the boxes. By searching out new sources and buying larger shipments, he learned to obtain his raw materials more cheaply. The fact that each store originally demanded boxes of different sizes and shape made producing them slow work at first. He had learned a lesson from the changes in shoemaking, however. By persuading the stores to settle for a limited variety of boxes, he cut his producing costs.

Soon Andrew's second son, Eliphalet, became involved in the business. In 1849, he began to purchase supplies for the box business as an agent of his father. More important, he began to use his talents as a salesman to market or find buyers for his father's boxes.

Eliphalet recognized markets for other products similar to boxes, and knew that the more products they could sell the more money they could make. He was anxious to expand the business by diversifying, or manufacturing other products he was sure would sell. Soon the Dennisons hired neighbors to help, and were selling cards, fine cotton, tissue paper, and tags. They purchased their supplies in even larger quantities. Many of the new growing businesses in the United States found it cheaper to buy boxes and tags from Dennison, who specialized in their production, than to make their own as a sideline activity, as they traditionally had done.

The location of the Dennison business in Brunswick, Maine, was far from major markets. Delays in transportation by wagon over the poor New England roads occasionally caused loss of orders. Eliphalet suggested moving the business to Boston where the new railroads would provide fast regular delivery to New York and other eastern markets. His father, however, did not wish to leave his home town.

In 1855, Andrew Dennison agreed to sell the business to his son so that he could move it to Boston. Eliphalet had little cash, so he bought the business on credit; that is, he agreed to pay his father part of his earnings every year until $9,000 was paid. Eliphalet now rented a building in Roxbury, later to become part of Boston, and hired people in the area to work for him.

In 1858, Eliphalet added merchandise tags to his list of products. These were large tags for addresses or prices, with strings to tie them to packages or other articles for shipping. After eyes for the string were cut by machines, the tags were sent out to families who tied the strings to the tags. To expand his market, Eliphalet bought the business of a New York tag importer. Now he could sell tags to those companies that had previously bought from the New York company as well as to his original customers. Tags quickly became one of the most important products of the company, more important by far than the original jewelry boxes.

The Dennison Manufacturing Company grew rapidly, and as the company expanded, its profits increased. During both 1863 and 1864, profits came to almost 125 per cent return, or earnings, on capital invested in the company.

These large profits in the early stages of the business were used for *dividends* (the profits a company pays to its stockholders) and for expansion. Each of the persons who had supplied some of the money invested either in the original company or in later expansions received a yearly dividend. Some of the profit, however, was used for expansion. Equipment for manufacturing larger boxes, gummed labels, and sealing wax was added. Branch offices to expand sales were established in Philadelphia, Chicago, Cincinnati, and St. Louis.

Originally, the Dennison Manufacturing Company was an *individual proprietorship.* That is, it was the property of one individual, Andrew Dennison. He had supplied all of the capital or money to start the business; and he was personally liable for its debts. On the other hand, he could run the business as he saw fit and keep all of the profits which he did not use for expansion.

In 1863, after Eliphalet had been the individual proprietor for a while, he wanted to expand the business. He needed a larger *inventory,* or supply of merchandise on hand, so that he could fill orders as fast as they arrived. He also wanted to move to larger quarters and increase production and sales. All of these things required money. Therefore, Eliphalet took on three partners who supplied the needed capital and became part owners of the firm. Among them they contributed $8,000 to Eliphalet's business, which had an estimated value of about $15,000. The *partnership* agreement stated that each partner would receive dividends and have a voice in the company's management proportionate to his investment. Since Eliphalet had still contributed over half of the capital for the expanded business, he continued to have most influence over it. But his direct control of the business was somewhat lessened by having co-owners. In effect, he traded off the advantage of being the sole owner for the presumed greater advantage of getting more money for the business.

The Dennison Company, like many others, started in the home. The family members worked under the direction of the father. Later a few neighbors were hired. Hours were informal. If an employee's husband were ill, it did not matter if she stayed home a few days or kept irregular hours. Perhaps she would work late another time.

When Eliphalet moved to a factory in Roxbury and started hiring strangers to work for him, the labor situation changed. Then it was necessary to set down specific rules and hours. Still, however, Eliphalet probably knew most of his employees by name, and if they were doing something wrong he could scold them personally.

As the business continued to grow, however, the roster of employees grew so long that one manager could not possibly know them all. Discipline became a matter of rules rather than of personal relationships.

As a part of the rapid expansion of American business during the nineteenth century, the Dennison Manufacturing Company grew from a small home industry to a moderately large manufacturer. The growth of other businesses, most of which needed tags and labels, created an expanding market. An ample supply of natural resources and adequate amounts of labor and capital, combined with new, efficient transportation, stimulated rapid growth in many parts of the American economy. Dennison owner-managers rode the wave of that growth, and sales and profits continued to rise.

24 The Business Firm (II)

Today's reading carries the story of the Dennison Manufacturing Company from 1878 to 1929—a period of industrialization for most of the American economy. As in its earlier years, the Dennison Company faced important decisions, most of which involved the *what, how,* and *for whom* questions. Its answers to these questions determined its success at competing and making profits. Refer back to the study questions for Reading 23 on pp. 79–80, which also apply to this reading. And, as you read, keep these additional questions in mind:

1. Why did the Dennison Company incorporate? What role did competition play in the decision to incorporate?
2. How would Dennison's managers have been better off if they could have driven their competitors out of business or agreed with them to establish a high price for similar products? Would their customers have benefitted from either of these practices?

The Dennison Manufacturing Company (Part Two)

R. W. HIDY and P. E. CAWEIN

Adapted from Case Studies in Business History and Economic Concepts *(Boston: D. C. Heath and Company, © 1967). Used by permission.*

In 1878 the growing company changed from a partnership to a far more complicated legal organization known as a *corporation.* A corporation enables a large number of people to act legally as one individual person. That has three main advantages. In the first place, the corporation itself, and not its individual owners, is *liable* or responsible for any debts or lawsuits against it. This means that the individual who owns part of a corporation can only lose as much money as he has invested in it. Unlike the individual proprietor or the partner, he cannot be forced to use his home, his savings, and his other personal belongings to pay the company's debts.

Secondly, a corporation is not ordinarily dependent on the life of any of its owners. In a partnership, the death of a partner means that the business must be completely reorganized. A corporation, on the other hand, can usually continue to exist as long as its policies are successful and its owners, the stockholders, are satisfied. Should the stockholders become dissatisfied, they may change the board of directors or even vote to dissolve the corporation. If this latter happens, all of its property will be sold and its debts paid; then any money left will be paid to the owners in proportion to their shares of ownership.

The third advantage of a corporation, that it can raise great sums of money, is a direct result of the way in which it is formed. Men may invest in the company by putting their money at the disposal of the business. In return, they receive shares of *stock*, which are simply statements of ownership claims on the business. The limited liability feature mentioned above means that men will be more willing to put their money into this business, knowing that creditors cannot come upon them personally to meet any obligations of the business. This one element of risk, so common in individual proprietorships and partnerships, is missing in the corporation.

In the case of the Dennison Manufacturing Company, the value of the original capital put into the business at the time of incorporating was $150,000. Eliphalet Dennison and his son owned two thirds of the company, and Metcalf, one of the original partners, held the remaining third. The ownership capital of $150,000 was represented by 1,500 shares each originally valued at $100. The Dennisons received 1,000 shares, and Metcalf 500. (This then was a closely held corporation at first.) Printed stock certificates were legal proof of a stockholder's part ownership.

Dividends and control of the company are generally divided proportionately among all of the stockholders in a corporation. During each year, the managers reinvest some profit, if any, and distribute the rest among their stockholders as dividends. Each share of stock gives an owner the right to a dividend if a dividend is paid. Usually each share also entitles its holder to one vote in electing a board of directors responsible for guiding the company. In this case, the Dennisons had two thirds of the votes in electing the board of directors. These directors need not themselves be major stockholders, but they must come before the stockholders each year to report on the business. If the stockholders are dissatisfied, they may elect a new board or make changes in the existing one.

Should a stockholder wish to sell one or more of his shares of stock, he must find a buyer. If the corporation is a private one, he must find the buyer himself. Most large corporations, however, are public; this means that their stock is sold on a public market like the New York Stock Exchange. This is a place where any person can buy or sell shares of stock through *brokers* (middlemen who buy and sell stock for others).

The price of a certain stock on the exchange corresponds not to the original value of the company but to the current demand and supply situation for that stock. If investors expect a company to be very successful, they might compete with one another to buy its stock, until the shares sell for as much as two or three times the price that the current owners paid for them. On the other hand, if the shareholders expected the company to fail, they might all try to sell their stock and be unable to find buyers for it until they sold it for a fraction of what they had paid for it. If a company either grows fast or pays consistently good dividends, buyers are likely to bid its stock up.

Between the Civil War and World War I, the Dennison Manufacturing Company met serious competition for the first time. The patent on Eliphalet's merchandising tag ran out in 1880, and competitors started copying it freely. Dennison was forced to cut its prices by 12 per cent. Competition also forced the company to cut gummed label prices from 75 cents to 50 cents per carton. During this period, salesmen were frequently given the right to adjust prices themselves to obtain orders. In its effort to control the market for its products, Dennison bought out some of its competitors, advertised its wares, invented new products to meet new demands, and developed new methods of marketing.

Buying out competitors is very expensive, and, when it was discovered that some men were starting competing businesses with the sole purpose of selling out to Dennison for more than they were worth, Dennison discontinued this method of limiting competition.

Advertising was also used to meet growing competition. When a consumer thought of tags, Dennison wanted him to think of Dennison tags. To this end the company bought advertisements in city and town directories. To appeal to home consumers, it advertised in popular magazines like *The Ladies' Home Journal* and *The Youth's Companion.* In 1893 it established a booth at the Chicago World's Fair to display Dennison products.

As the way of life in the country changed, the Dennison Company tried to invent new products that would appeal to consumers. New styles of jewelry boxes and cases were introduced. Merchandise was made available in a greater variety of colors. Glues and pastes were added to Dennison's list of products. Paper napkins proved very profitable. A pamphlet, "The Art of Sealing a Letter," was circulated to stimulate sale of sealing wax. Demonstrators were sent to retail stores to give instructions on how to make such things as paper flowers and window decorations out of crepe paper.

Meanwhile, Dennison attempted to cut its costs by increasing efficiency in marketing. By 1890, increased advertising had so associated the name of Dennison with paper products that now it was able to send its own salesmen out to deal directly with the businesses, manufacturers and retailers who used Dennison products. Regular sales districts were set up so that salesmen came to know both the area and their customers personally.

Eliphalet's son, H. S. Dennison, became president of the company in 1917. Since he had previously been works manager, he brought an interest in production to the board of directors. Under his leadership a continuous effort was made to increase production efficiency and speed. Production costs were carefully watched. The price set on merchandise had to reflect the pressures of competition. But the company had to look at its costs of production and its need for profits to see if it could afford to sell at competitive prices. If its costs were too high to permit competitive pricing, either those costs had to be lowered or they had to get out of that product line.

Heavy sales at the turn of the century put a strain on the whole management to continue at high volume of production. For the first time in many years, new equipment was developed or purchased to speed production of shipping tags and boxes. Although the substitution of machinery for hand processes was expensive at first, the company had to make the changeover in order to assure future productive efficiency and future profit.

In 1901 an outside expert suggested that production could be made more efficient by the establishment of new departments to control inventories of raw materials and of finished goods. The raw materials department tried to keep supplies steady. Excess stock of any one material tied up the company's money where it was not needed. On the other hand, to run out of a material could stop production altogether. The finished products department made sure that the merchandise inventory in the warehouse was sufficient to supply branches and salesmen. By determining what items were in demand at the prevailing prices, it could tell the factory what products and how much were currently needed.

Another way in which the Dennison Manufacturing Company met competition and cut production costs was by reorganizing the company so that all of the different departments worked smoothly together. In 1906 six merchandising committees were established, one for each of Dennison's six lines: tags, jewelers' items, adhesives, crepe, Christmas items, and consumer goods (items sold directly for home use). Each committee consisted of men from three categories: salesmen concerned with markets and competition; producers concerned with methods and costs of production; and directors concerned with long-term expansion and profit. By 1911 the committee chairmen, located in Framingham, were devoting full time to coordinating all facets of the business.

These merchandising committees set up lines of communication which made further expansion of the company possible. In the 1920's, a period of general prosperity in the country, Dennison increased production facilities by opening a box factory near Marlboro, Massachusetts. It established Dennison companies in Canada and England to sell products throughout the British Empire. The company also began to export merchandise, setting up sales offices in South America and Europe. In 1929 it formed a special research department to develop new products and methods. From a small family firm, Dennison had grown into an international corporation. The next episode in its growth was about to begin.

25 The Case for Competition

A persistent problem in all societies is that of putting checks on power. There seem to be no exceptions to the general rule that unchecked power, whether it is the power of a state, an army, a church, or a private business institution, quickly becomes abused power.

This lesson has not been lost on those who defend free market economies most vigorously. When asked what check on the power of individual businesses will be both effective and consistent with freedom, they have answered, "Competition." The core of their argument has been that, so long as competition exists in markets, no one producer or group of producers can afford to abuse power by charging too much or by selling shoddy goods, for fear that consumers might turn away from them to buy from other producers. In line with that argument, one of the government's tasks is to keep competition alive and functioning.

Reading 25, written by an economics professor, argues the case for competition in strong terms. The next two readings, however, show that attitudes towards competition in the United States are mixed, and that producers often engage in non-competitive behavior.

Before starting today's reading, it is important to note that the American economy today is a long way from being perfectly competitive. (Whether it is more or less competitive than it was in the past is a continuing subject of debate among economists.) To be perfectly competitive, each industry would have to be characterized by:

1. a very large number of producers, each so small in relation to the total size of the market that his production will make no significant difference in either the market price or the quantity produced;
2. an identical product marketed by these producers so that the consumer has no preference as to which source he buys from;
3. easy entrance into this field of production, and easy exit for those who fail in it;
4. an absence of any collusion (secret agreements) among producers on price, quantities, or quality of goods sold.

To list all of those conditions is to remind ourselves that they apply to only one or two industries at best. Yet it is equally true that very few American industries are marked by the extreme opposite of pure competition: pure monopoly. Under pure monopoly, there would have to be:

1. only one producer of a product;
2. no satisfactory substitute for that product;
3. no practical way in which a rival could enter that field of production.

So, most of American industry is neither as perfectly competitive as the "pure competition" model requires, nor as monopolistic as the "pure monopoly" model requires. Most of our industries lie somewhere between those two extremes. Again we can use a spectrum to define the situation:

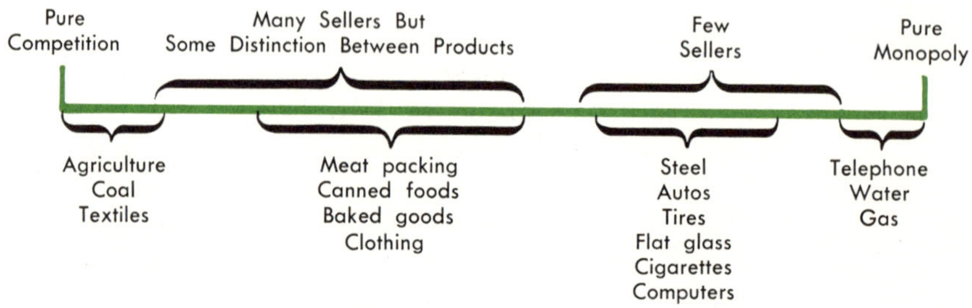

Agriculture falls at one end of the spectrum since there are thousands of producers of such products as wheat, and one farmer's wheat is just about the same as another's. Also, if wheat becomes too expensive, consumers can shift to other foods. The telephone company falls at the other end since technology and efficiency dictate that there be no more than one telephone company in any community. (Try to imagine the results of, say, a dozen telephone companies, each with its own system, competing for your family's business!) Also, for many purposes, there is no fully satisfactory substitute for the telephone. If telephone rates rose, it would be impractical for businesses to rip out their telephones and use a corps of special messengers to communicate with each other.

With this as background, let us turn to the arguments for keeping as much competition alive as is practical in a technologically advanced and free society. As you read, keep these questions in mind:

1. What is gained by maintaining competition?
2. Are there times when competition is not desirable in markets?

Competition in a Free Economy

JOHN MAURICE CLARK

From Alternative to Serfdom *(New York: Alfred A. Knopf, Inc., 1948), pp. 61–63. Copyright © 1960 by The Regents of the University of Michigan. Reprinted by permission.*

The chief agency on which defenders of the market economy have relied to keep self-interest within useful bounds and prevent it from becoming oppressive is the system of free competition. Without it, free exchange between unequals could still be tyranny and its freedom a sham.

Competition is an outstanding example of an institution that nearly everyone approves, yet almost no one carries his approval through consistently. This is partly a case of the familiar double standard—competition for the other fellow, protection for me—but it is only partly that. It is partly because competition has two opposites which we may call monopoly and security. . . . Nearly everyone favors competition as against monopoly, and nearly everyone wants [competition] limited in the interest of security. And hardly anyone pays much attention to the question [of] where one leaves off and the other begins. . . .

Competition is our main safeguard against exploitation. In our [complex] civilization we dare not trust the terms of exchange to tribal custom and sense of honor, as some primitive peoples can. Under self-interest, people of our advanced stage of culture would naturally incline to give as little and get as much as possible; they would increase their gains by reducing their services, by producing less to sell for more. But competition works the simple miracle whereby each one increases his individual gains by increasing his services rather than reducing them: He makes more by producing more to sell for less.

The question [of] how far this price-reducing pressure goes, and how far it is safe and desirable to have it go, is one of the key questions [about the] usefulness of competition. Put in other words, it is the question [of] whether competition threatens security [enough to require] some kind of protection. On this theme we might imagine [an argument] between prosecution and defense running somewhat in this fashion:

PROSECUTION: How can everybody get rich by selling for less? That is the way to make everybody poor.

DEFENSE: You get rich by having other people sell to you for less. And if you sell for less yourself, you haven't lost as much as you have gained. The essential thing is that, in trying to gain by selling for less, people produce more, and that extra product remains and is not canceled out. Some individuals may be ruined if they sell for too little—it's up to their common sense to stop short of that. But how can everybody get poor by all producing more?

PROSECUTION: When prices and wages all go down together in a slump, that seems to make the slump deeper, not lift us out of it. And in ordinary times millions of workers have injured their health and grown prematurely old, farmers have mined their soil and made dust-bowls, and irreplaceable treasures of coal and oil have been criminally wasted.

DEFENSE: I grant you these abuses are serious; the level of competition needs to be protected to prevent that sort of thing. And it ought to be possible to [soften] slumps, so that wages and prices would not be driven down to destructive levels. But if you let people peg their own wages and prices, then you are back in the condition in which they are all trying to get rich by selling for more—which can't make them all rich—and producing less, which ends by making everybody poorer. We may have to set limits on competition, but we can't afford to abolish it. It stimulates production; and if it is reasonably equal and fair, it safeguards distribution against the building up of privileged classes.

PROSECUTION: The little man hasn't a fair chance against the big one; and the majority of business enterprises end in failure.

DEFENSE: If the big man wins by efficiency, that is the customer's gain, meaning everybody's. If he wins in other ways, we should try to improve the rules so as to prevent it. If failures simply eliminate the inefficient, that is the price of progress.

26 Keeping Competition Alive (I)

As our political candidates continually remind us, free competition is one of the chief American economic values. Yet most Americans share another major value: the desire for security. Not only does the government, through such programs as Social Security, promote the security of individual citizens. But businesses, too, seek security through such measures as "fair trade" laws that permit manufacturers and retailers to make agreements setting minimum prices on certain goods. By setting minimum prices, competition is limited, for a retailer cannot try to attract customers by lowering his prices. But minimum prices also give retailers security from the fear of being driven out of business by price-cutting by discount stores. Labor unions, too, sometimes seek security at the expense of competition. Often, they hesitate to let younger men compete for better jobs, preferring to stick to the system of seniority. The desire for security, in fact, influences nearly every institution.

The following reading points out that many Americans talk as if they desire free competition, but at the same time try to restrict that competition. It is taken from a speech delivered to a group of businessmen by Charles F. Phillips, president of Bates College in Lewiston, Maine.

As you read, keep the following questions in mind:

1. Is security usually an explicit or an implicit value in the United States?
2. What harm do you think absolutely free competition could do? What good do you think it could do?
3. Judging from this article, to what extent do you think the United States has an economy based on free competition?

"Competition? Yes, But . . ."

CHARLES F. PHILLIPS

Published by the Foundation for Economic Education, Inc., Irvington-on-Hudson, New York. Reprinted by permission.

To ask an American businessman—whether he be grocer, baker, or candlestick maker—if he believes in competition is almost like asking for a sock on the nose. *Of course* he believes in competition—and he raises his voice to add emphasis to his answer.

But, after he has cooled off a bit from your question, you may find that he has his own definition of competition. For example, let's walk with him down the street toward [his] grocery store. . . . Across the way in a window of one of his competitors is a large sign, "Sugar, X cents per pound." You call it to his attention, and at once his brow knits. "That's unfair competition," he says. "That so-and-so has cut his price again to attract *my* customers." I remind him that he believes in competition. "Why, yes," he replies, "but not unfair and ruthless competition." And if you then ask him, "But why is it unfair for a competitor to cut his price?" he will explode, "Why, any darn fool knows that it is unfair to sell sugar for X cents. You can't make any money at that price. There ought to be a law in this state against such practices."

I wonder if the [grocer's] reaction does not illustrate a simple truth which can be expressed in the short but incomplete sentence: "We all like competition but . . ."

We all like competition since we know it is essential for our type of economy, and we like the freedoms which our economy gives to each of us—the freedom to enter or withdraw from any specific field or career; freedom to set our own prices; yes, even freedom to undersell somebody else and take business away from him.

But . . . all too often when a competitor really acts like a competitor and does something which hurts us—cuts a price, sells harder, improves quality—it becomes "unfair competition," and we run to our trade association . . . or the government for protection. . . .

We might begin [with a little history]. . . . If we go back to the [beginning of this] century, we find that small country merchants were going through the mail-order scare. Following the lead of Montgomery Ward Company and Sears, Roebuck & Company, mail-order firms were springing up in many parts of our country. To the small country retailer, this newer form of retailing was unfair. It did not employ salespeople. It did not involve the operation of a retail store. It could purchase in huge quantities. For these and other reasons, the local merchant was undersold and he objected to this result. Obviously, such competition was unfair! In a number of communities, "trade at home" clubs were organized, while some local retailers organized mail-order-catalogue burning parties. . . .

In the late 'twenties and early 'thirties, [small businessmen campaigned against the "unfair" competition of the growing chain stores. Chain stores, they claimed,] were monopolistic; were [harmful] to community life because of their absentee ownership, unfairness to local bankers, failure to pay their fair proportion of taxes; and were unfair to their employees through long hours, low wages, and offering little chance of advancement. . . . Customers were urged to curtail their purchases at chains. . . . The misnamed "fair trade" laws were encouraged, and in over twenty states special taxes discriminating against the chains were enacted.

We all like competition, but . . .

Pick up the trade paper of today, and you will discover that discount houses are a form of "unfair" competition. All over the country, they are . . . underselling the so-called established retailer. [According to] the executive secretary of the National Association of Retail Druggists, . . . they are trying to destroy "every established retailer in the United States . . . by unfair competition." . . .

Discount houses are even pointed to as being unfair to the consumer because, after all, they do not offer him all the services of the established retailer. Incidentally, whether the customer wants those services or not is rarely considered when this argument is advanced. . . .

We do not have to limit ourselves to illustrations from what we normally consider the retail field. Did you follow the ten-month strike of Local 15 of the United Hatters and Millinery Workers International Union against the Hat Corporation of America? The strike started in July of 1953, brought on basically by the union's demand that the company sign a contract [agreeing not to] open new plants outside of the Norwalk area [or to transfer] work now done in Norwalk to any outside plant.

What the union wanted was a limit on competition. It did not want its members to compete with workers in some other area where Hat Corporation might establish a factory. Fortunately, after ten months, the union lost its fight. It is worth contemplating, however, what would have happened had a similar strike been won when the United States was still located on the East Coast only. Obviously, it would still be located on the East Coast only; and equally obviously, its standard of living today would be far below what it now is.

Then, of course, there is the farmer—the so-called individualist, the man who stands on his own feet, and, as the politician puts it, "is the backbone of the nation." Here, of course, is someone who believes in competition. Yes, he does, but again there comes that "but"—and the "but" in his case is a big one, so big that through powerful lobbies he has forced through Congress price-support laws which give him protection far in excess of even that provided for the retailer through "fair trade." . . .

We all believe in competition, but . . .

I can even illustrate this attitude in the field of education—college education at that. Throughout the United States, colleges use scholarships to capture students- and I use the word "capture" deliberately. Sometimes we want them for their I.Q., sometimes for their A.P. (athletic prowess), and sometimes for both. At my college, of course, (or President Jones' college if he is the one doing the talking) we limit these scholarships to students who are in serious financial need; but, unfortunately (that is the word used by college presidents when several of them gather together in a room to discuss the situation), there are a few colleges which use scholarships as an unfair method of price-cutting. Don't you think, their conversation continues, our regional association can do something about this?

Even educators like competition, but . . .

Please do not think I am saying there is no such thing as unfair competition. When a competitor resorts to false and misleading advertising, engages in misbranding, and makes false and disparaging statements against competitors or their products, he is engaging in practices which all of us would denounce.

What I am saying is this: Much of what we daily refer to as unfair competition is really just keen competition. It is the kind of competition that is essential to our type of economic system. If we want to maintain the freedoms which our system gives us—to enter businesses of our choice, to produce the merchandise we please, to set our own prices—then we must accept the competition which is essential to that kind of an economy. We must not always look to our trade association or our government to protect us from the actions of our competitors.

27 Keeping Competition Alive (II): The Steel Industry

In some industries, only large firms can take advantage of the best technology and marketing methods. An industry dominated by only a few powerful producers is called an *oligopoly* (ol-i-*gop*-o-ly). (*Oligopoly* is Greek for "few sellers"; contrast *monopoly,* Greek for "one seller".)

General Motors, Ford, and Chrysler, which make nearly all American automobiles, constitute an oligopoly. So do the major steel companies, led by United States Steel. Competition in steel is somewhat limited because a buyer of steel has few sellers of steel with whom to bargain. But it should be noted that steel companies do compete among themselves for shares of the market. There is also some vigorous competition between steel and such products as aluminum, plastics, and concrete.

In early 1962, the Kennedy Administration was trying to prevent further inflation. Partly due to administration persuasion, the United Steel Workers union and the steel companies had agreed to a modest wage hike for the workers. President Kennedy was determined that a price rise would not soon follow. He believed that the companies were already making fair profits.

The following reading, taken from *The New York Times,* describes what happened when the steel companies decided to raise prices anyway. As you read, consider the following questions:

1. Why were other steel companies prepared to follow the lead of United States Steel? How much are the economic decisions of steel companies influenced by supply and demand?
2. What was the effect of the activities of the Kennedy Administration on free competition in steel?
3. What part did the government's role as a steel buyer play in the story?

The Steel Confrontation

WALLACE CARROLL

WASHINGTON, April 22—It was peaceful at the White House on the afternoon of Tuesday, April 10—so peaceful that the President of the United States thought he might have time for a nap or a little relaxed reading.

Just to be sure, he called his personal secretary, Mrs. Evelyn Lincoln, and asked what the rest of the day would bring.

"You have Mr. Blough at a quarter to six," said Mrs. Lincoln.

"Mr. Blough?" exclaimed the President.

"Yes," said Mrs. Lincoln.

There must be a mistake, thought the President. The steel negotiations had been wound up the previous week.

"Get me Kenny O'Donnell," he said.

But there had been no mistake—at least not on the part of Kenneth P. O'Donnell, the President's appointment secretary.

Whether Mr. Blough—Roger M. Blough, chairman of the board of United States Steel Corporation—had made a mistake was a different question.

For when he walked into the President's office two hours later with the news that his company had raised the price of steel, he set off seventy-two hours of activity such as he and his colleagues could not have expected. . . .

Early on that afternoon of April 10, Roger Blough had met with his colleagues of United States Steel's executive committee. . . .

For several months these men had been giving out hints, largely overlooked in Washington, that the company would have to raise prices to meet increasing costs.

The Kennedy Administration had striven last fall to prevent a steel price increase, and there had been no increase. It had pressed again for a modest wage contract this year, and a modest contract had been signed a few days earlier. The Administration expected no price increase now.

The company's executive committee reviewed the situation. The sales department had concurred in a recommendation to increase prices by 3½ per cent. . . .

Everyone realized that the move would not win any popularity prize, but the committee voted unanimously to go ahead.

With the decision made, Mr. Blough took a plane to Washington. . . .

A few minutes after 5:45 the President received him in his oval office. . . .

With little preliminary, Mr. Blough [informed the President that his company would raise prices immediately]. . . .

[After the meeting,] the President, who usually keeps his temper under rein, let go. He felt he had been double-crossed—deliberately. The office of the President had been affronted. The national interest had been flouted. . . .

It was clear that the Administration would fight. No one knew exactly what could be done, but from that moment the awesome power of the federal government began to move. . . .

By about 8 P.M. some decisions had been reached.

President Kennedy would deliver the first counter-attack at his news conference scheduled for 3:30 the following afternoon. . . .

At his home on Hillbrook Lane, Senator Estes Kefauver of Tennessee, chairman of the Senate Antitrust Subcommittee, was getting ready to go out for the evening. The phone rang. It was the President. Would Senator Kefauver publicly register "dismay" at the price increase and consider an investigation?

The Senator certainly would. He promised an investigation. So did the Justice Department.

The pressures on United States Steel were beginning to mount. But now some of the other titans of the industry began to fall in line behind Big Steel.

Shortly before noon [Wednesday, the President] was shown a news bulletin. Bethlehem Steel, second in size only to United States Steel, had announced a price increase.

Others followed in short order—Republic, Jones & Laughlin, Youngstown, and Wheeling . . .

When he faced the newsmen and television cameras at 3:30, President Kennedy spoke with cold fury. The price increase, he said, was a "wholly unjustifiable and irresponsible defiance of the public interest." The steel men had shown "utter contempt" for their fellow citizens.

He spoke approvingly of the proposed investigations. But what did he hope to accomplish that might still save the Administration's broad economic program? . . .

[Some of the President's economic advisers] argued that the principal thrust of the Administration's effort should be to convince one or two significant producers to hold out. In a market such as steel, they said, the high-priced sellers would have to come down if the others did not go up. . . .

As one member of the Big Twelve after another raised prices, only Armco, Inland, Kaiser, CF & I [Colorado Fuel & Iron] and McLouth were holding the line. These five hold-outs represented 14 per cent of total industry capacity . . .

Everything pointed to Inland as the key to the situation.

Inland Steel Corporation with headquarters in Chicago is a highly efficient producer. It could make a profit at lower prices than those of some of the bigger companies. And any company that sold in the Midwest, such as United States Steel, would feel Inland's price competition.

Moreover, there was a tradition of public service at Inland. . . .

At 7:45 that Wednesday morning, Philip D. Block, Jr., vice chairman of Inland, was called to the telephone in his apartment . . . in Chicago.

"Hello, P. D.," said Edward Gudeman, Under Secretary of Commerce, a former schoolmate and friend of Mr. Block's, calling from Washington. "What do you think of this price increase of United States Steel's?"

Mr. Block said he had been surprised. . . . [Other Administration officials also called people they knew at Inland.]

Though no concrete assurance was asked or volunteered in these conversations, the Administration gathered assurance that Inland would hold the line for at least another day or two.

Next came Armco, sixth largest in the nation. . . .

How many calls were made by President Kennedy himself cannot be told. But sometime during all the activity he talked to Edgar Kaiser, chairman of Kaiser Steel, in California. . . .

[At 3:30 P.M., Thursday, Roger Blough held a televised news conference.]

On several occasions, he said, he had made it clear that United States Steel was in a cost-price torque that could not be tolerated forever, that a company without profits is a company that cannot modernize, and that the price increase would add "almost negligibly" to the cost of other products—$10.64 for the steel in a standard automobile, $.03 for a toaster.

One question and answer in the fifty-eight-minute session caught the ears of people in Washington: Could United States Steel hold its new price if Armco and Inland stood pat?

"It would definitely affect us," conceded Mr. Blough. "I don't know how long we could maintain our position." . . .

Meanwhile, Justice Department agents appeared at the headquarters of United States Steel, Bethlehem, Jones & Laughlin and other companies and served subpoenas for documents bearing on the price increase and other matters.

And at 7 P.M. Attorney General Kennedy announced that the Justice Department had ordered a grand jury investigation of the increase. . . .

The first big news of [Friday] came [when] Joseph Block, Inland's chairman, told a reporter . . . :

"We do not feel that an advance in steel prices at this time would be in the national interest."

That news heartened the Administration but it did not stop planning or operations. . . .

At 11:45 Secretary McNamara said at his news conference that the Defense Department had ordered defense contractors to shift steel purchases to companies that had not raised prices. Later in the day the department awarded to the Lukens Steel Company, which had not raised prices, a contract for more than $5,000,000 worth of a special armor plate for Polaris-missile submarines.

At 12:15 President Kennedy and most of the Thursday group met again in the Cabinet Room. It was estimated at that time that the price line was being held on 16 per cent of the nation's steel capacity.

. . . This might be enough to force the bigger companies down again, but the sentiment of the meeting was that the retreat would not come soon.

Accordingly, preparations continued for a long struggle. . . .

[But suddenly the steel companies' united front crumbled. At 3:20 P.M. it was announced that Bethlehem Steel had withdrawn its price increase.]

The Administration had made no special effort with Bethlehem. To this day, officials here are uncertain what did it.

Among other things, Bethlehem's officials were struck by the Inland and Kaiser announcements that morning. Inland posed direct competition to Bethlehem's sales in the Midwest—the largest steel market—and Kaiser posed it on the West Coast.

Further, special questions were raised by the Pentagon's order to defense industries to shift their steel buying to mills that did not raise prices. What did this mean for Bethlehem's vast operations as a shipbuilder?

Whatever the compelling factors were, Bethlehem's decision brought the end of the battle clearly in sight. The competitive situation was such that United States Steel's executive committee was not called into session to reverse its action of the previous Tuesday. The company's officers acted on their own.

The big capitulation came at 5:28. . . .

United States Steel pulled back the price increase.

It was just seventy-two hours since Roger Blough had dropped in on Mr. Kennedy.

28 The American Executive

Although corporations play a central role in the American economy, their executives are little-known to the public. Most Americans cannot even name the chief officers of such gigantic companies as General Motors and American Telephone and Telegraph, though they can reel off the names of dozens of politicians and movie stars. But executives were not always so obscure. In the 1920's, one of the best-known Americans was Henry Ford, founder of the Ford Motor Company. The first part of today's reading is taken from *The Big Money,* a novel by John Dos Passos. The second excerpt describes the role of the American executive today. As you read, keep the following questions in mind:

1. How did Henry Ford's methods raise both supply and demand for automobiles?
2. What does Dos Passos seem to think of Henry Ford?
3. Why does a modern company need goodwill?
4. Why couldn't a company president simply give orders and disregard conflicting pressures?

1. Henry Ford and His Tin Lizzie

JOHN DOS PASSOS

"Mr. Ford, the automobileer," the featurewriter wrote in 1900, *"Mr. Ford the automobileer began by giving his steed three or four sharp jerks with the lever at the righthand side of the seat; that is, he pulled the lever up and down sharply in order, as he said, to mix air with gasoline and drive the charge into the exploding cylinder. . . . Mr. Ford slipped a small electric switch handle and there followed a puff, puff, puff. . . . The puffing of the machine assumed a higher key. She was flying along about eight miles an hour. The ruts in the road were deep, but the machine certainly went with a dreamlike smoothness. There was none of the bumping common even to a streetcar. . . . By this time the boulevard had been reached, and the automobileer, letting a lever fall a little, let her out. Whiz! She picked up speed with infinite rapidity. As she ran on there was a clattering behind, the new noise of the automobile. . . .*

He was the eldest son of an Irish immigrant who during the Civil War had married the daughter of a prosperous Pennsylvania Dutch farmer and settled down to farming near Dearborn in Wayne County, Michigan;

like plenty of other Americans, young Henry grew up hating the endless sogging through the mud about the chores, the hauling and pitching manure, the kerosene lamps to clean, the irk and sweat and solitude of the farm. . . .

He moved to Detroit, and in the brick barn behind his house tinkered for years in his spare time with a mechanical buggy that would be light enough to run over the clayey wagonroads of Wayne County, Michigan.

By 1900 he had a practicable car to promote.

He was forty years old before the Ford Motor Company was started and production began to move.

Speed was the first thing the early automobile manufacturers went after. Races advertised the makes of cars. . . .

But . . . [t]he speed he was busy with was speed in production, the records records in efficient output. . . .

Henry Ford had ideas about other things than the designing of motors, carburetors, magnetos, jigs and fixtures, punches and dies; he had ideas about sales,

that the big money was in economical quantity production, quick turnover, cheap interchangeable easilyreplaced standardized parts;

it wasn't until 1909, after years of arguing with his partners, that Ford put out the first Model T.

Henry Ford was right.

That season he sold more than ten thousand tin lizzies, ten years later he was selling almost a million a year.

In these years . . . [e]fficiency was the word. The same ingenuity that went into improving the performance of a machine could go into improving the performance of the workmen producing the machine.

In 1913 they established the assemblyline at Ford's. That season the profits were something like twentyfive million dollars, but they had trouble in keeping the men on the job, machinists didn't seem to like it at Ford's.

Henry Ford had ideas about other things than production.

He was the largest automobile manufacturer in the world; he paid high wages; maybe if the steady workers thought they were getting a cut (a very small cut) in the profits, it would give trained men an inducement to stick to their jobs,

wellpaid workers might save enough money to buy a tin lizzie; the first day Ford's announced that cleancut properlymarried American workers who wanted jobs had a chance to make five bucks a day (of course it turned out that there were strings to it; always there were strings to it)

such an enormous crowd waited outside the Highland Park plant

all through the zero January night

that there was a riot when the gates were opened. . . .

in 1922 Henry Ford sold one million three hundred and thirtytwo thousand two hundred and nine tin lizzies; he was the richest man in the world.

Good roads had followed the narrow ruts made in the mud by the Model T. The great automotive boom was on. At Ford's production was improving all the time; less waste, more spotters, strawbosses, . . . the . . . speedup everywhere, reach under, adjust washer, screw down bolt, shove in cotterpin, reachunder adjustwasher, screwdown bolt, reachunderadjustscrewdownreachunderadjust until every ounce of life was sucked off into production and at night the workmen went home grey shaking husks . . .

Ford owned every detail of the process from the ore in the hills until the car rolled off the end of the assemblyline under its own power, the plants were rationalized to the last tenthousandth of an inch . . .

in 1926 the production cycle was reduced to eightyone hours from the ore in the mine to the finished salable car proceeding under its own power,

but the Model T was obsolete.

New Era prosperity . . .
(there were strings to it, always there were strings to it)
had killed Tin Lizzie.
Ford's was just one of many automobile plants. . . .

2. The Modern Executive

Times have changed dramatically for the American business executive. In 1883, it was possible for William H. Vanderbilt, the railroad builder, to reply to a reporter's question, "The public be damned." Today, the executive works in an atmosphere of pulls and counterpulls, and of expectations that he will move the organization ahead yet not ruffle too many feathers in the process.

It is easy to give a general definition of the job of the executive, whether he is a corporate president or a plant manager: The executive aims to use whatever resources are available to produce the best product or service at the lowest cost. But there are many qualifications that must be added to that definition before any of today's executives will recognize it. The available resources are seldom fixed in quantity or quality; a little bargaining here and a little harassing there may change what he gets to work with in raw materials, in labor, in machinery, or in capital funds. Nor is the "best" product or service often firmly established; what is good enough today may be substandard tomorrow.

The story of Henry Ford is a classic example of how success produces its own blinders. When the Model T was enjoying its phenomenal success, Ford could say, "The public can have any color it wants as long as it's black." But new models came along from other manufacturers—and Ford fell behind, wondering why a model that once sold 1.3 million cars a year was no longer the favorite.

The outsider who looks at the formal organization chart of one of our large corporations would conclude that the president is supreme, responsible only to the board of directors who hired and can fire him. Thus:

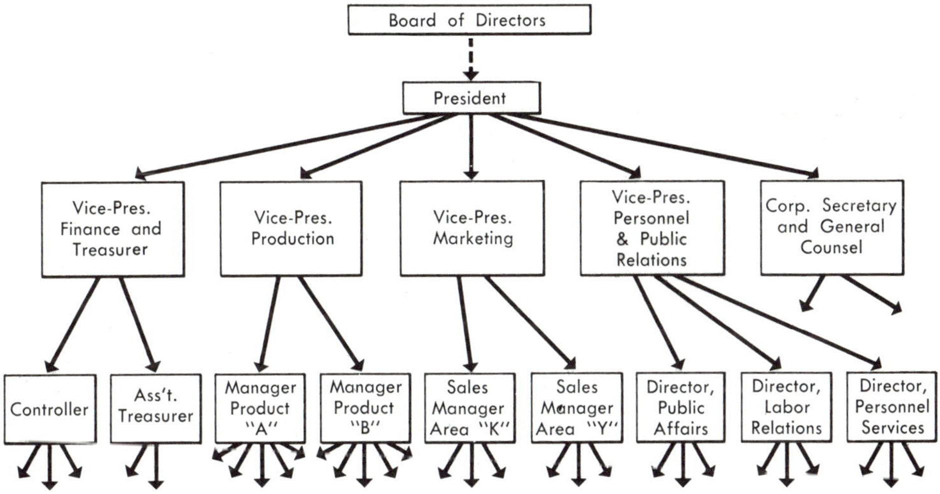

But the man who sits back of the president's desk probably sees the world in very different terms. He might wish that he could simply run the company by giving orders, but what he finds instead looks more like this:

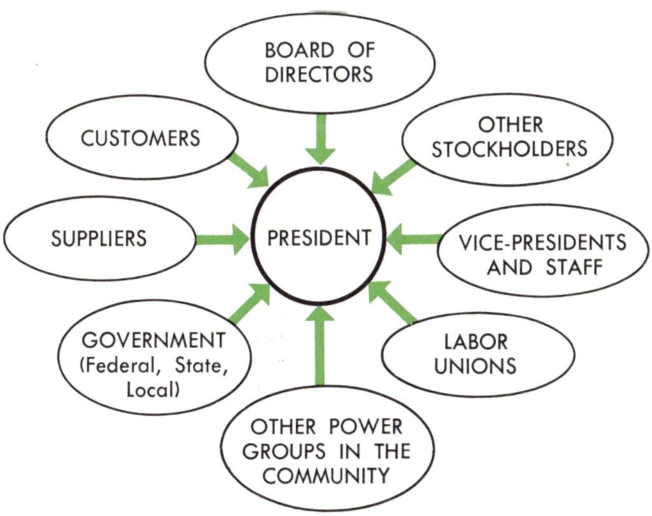

Instead of being at the top of a hierarchy, he is at the center of a whirlpool of pressures. And those pressures are often in conflict with one another:

The labor unions say: "Give us a wage increase, or we strike."

The board of directors and other stockholders say: "Resist the unions' demands, but don't interrupt production."

The government and such pressure groups as the NAACP say, "Break down all racial discrimination in your hiring."

Some of the vice-presidents and some other pressure groups, such as the White Citizens Council, say: "Don't upset the applecart."

Suppliers say: "Here's a better quality ingredient for your product. Of course, it costs a little more."

Customers say: "Keep your prices down."

The modern executive usually owns some stock in the business, but not nearly enough to control that business. Thus, the executive holds his job not because he owns the company, but because his professional managerial skills serve the company. And, if he is an able executive who can produce profits and goodwill alike, he is a much sought-after man in modern America.

29 Summary: The Changing Market Economy

In recent readings we have looked at how the United States modifies the pure market economy. Because America's economy is not a pure market economy, we have viewed it as a shifting point along the spectrum of economic systems. Although it depends mainly upon decentralized decision-making in the market, it also has elements of centralized planning and direction. Today's reading explores what has happened to the views of Adam Smith, the most famous advocate of a pure market economy.

As you read, think about these questions:

1. What are the major advantages and disadvantages that have been caused by the growing importance of government in the economy?
2. How well could the pure market system meet our problems of today?
3. In what ways does the United States have a "mixed" economy?

"Whatever Became of Adam Smith?"

"Well, they may have started off together, but they've sure drifted a long way apart ever since." The speaker was talking not about two individuals, but about two documents, both born in 1776. One was the Declaration of Independence; the other was Adam Smith's *The Wealth of Nations.*

Both of these documents have had enormous influence on the United States. The Declaration of Independence stated the philosophy of the revolution which gave the United States a chance to shape its own political destiny and to build a democratic society stressing individual freedom. *The Wealth of Nations,* written by an Englishman, stated the economic philosophy which became dominant in the United States.

In its time, *The Wealth of Nations* was as revolutionary as the Declaration of Independence. Before 1776, most European nations believed in mercantilism. Under this philosophy, governments sought to build industry in their countries by protecting new industries from foreign competition, and by regulating economic growth. This government direction, the mercantilists believed, would help an economy to grow.

Not so, said Adam Smith. Put man on his own and free him from the protection of a planning, prodding government, and he will achieve wonders that the world has never seen. Smith's main beliefs were these:

1. Men are moved most by their self-interest. They will work hardest and most imaginatively for personal profit.
2. In pursuit of personal profit, a producer may abuse his power. But the best way to regulate such abuse is the free marketplace. If a producer gets too greedy, a consumer can always buy from someone else—as long as the market is not controlled by monopolies.
3. By trying to protect new industries and regulate the economy, government would only disrupt the free market. The best role for government is simply to make sure that free competition prevails. Beyond that, government should follow the policy of *laissez-faire* (*less-say fair*)—it should allow the economy to operate on its own.

This was the philosophy behind the market economy. Smith believed that the greatest prosperity would result from free competition unfettered by government regulation or aid. And nowhere was Smith's philosophy more popular than in the United States.

But now we are told that the United States has abandoned Adam Smith. Recently, some say, the United States has been turning from free competition and laissez-faire toward government intervention and protection. No one denies that we have the richest society in the world. But our wealth was the product of the free past, according to this line of argument. Now we are on the road to ruin.

Is Smith dead?

On the surface, the coroner's report seems convincing enough. Play the alphabet game by listing the regulatory agencies and institutions that have recently been influencing our economy: the FTC (Federal Trade

Commission), FPC (Federal Power Commission), FCC (Federal Communications Commission), SEC (Securities and Exchange Commission), FDA (Food and Drug Administration), FHA (Federal Housing Administration), CAB (Civil Aeronautics Board), NLRB (National Labor Relations Board), and so on until one ends with JFK and LBJ. American government today regulates, produces, subsidizes, taxes, protects, educates, sells, and buys. And what would Smith have thought of that?

Before we decide that Smith would have deplored such agencies, let us pause to ask why the government's role in the economy has grown. Government is bigger today for at least four major reasons:

1. *National defense.* Smith saw the need for governmental action to protect the nation as clearly as we do. What he could not foresee was how large the job would become as technology advanced. About half of the federal government's $100 billion annual budget is spent on defense. And a large part of that is accounted for by the search for further technological improvement: developing nuclear weapons, developing protection against others' nuclear weapons, and seeking leadership in outer space.

2. *Large-scale industry.* Again, Smith saw the need for government to set certain rules to keep the forces of free competition working. What he could not foresee was how new technology and new markets would produce large-scale industry. As businesses grow, they threaten to lessen free competition by gaining control of markets. Today, we are engaged in a kind of balancing act: We want competition, but we also want the benefits of large-scale production and distribution. The alphabet agencies listed above are efforts to keep that balance.

3. *Emphasis on human rights alongside property rights.* Smith surely would have said that he believed in human rights as strongly as we do. But he would have added that the free market was the best protection for those rights. To a large extent, we still agree with him. The free market continues to protect such rights as the right to change jobs or the right to move to another state. But at certain fringe points we have modified the workings of the free market. We have, for example, passed laws setting minimum wages. But possibly Smith might see, amidst all the debate on the "welfare state," that most economic decisions are still made in the free market. We have been tinkering with markets, not destroying them.

4. *New social concerns.* Finally, Smith could scarcely have foreseen the social problems caused by a large population. Smith lived in a much smaller world and believed that economic decisions should be made as close to home as possible. Our metropolitan areas, with their many governments, might well have confused him as much as they do us. In this and in many other areas, we have come to favor far more government intervention than Smith recommended. We agree with him that govern-

ment should do only what individuals cannot do as well for themselves, but we find that this test produces different answers than it did in the past.

Where, then, do we come out? Is Adam Smith only a historical curiosity?

There has indeed been a shift toward new responsibilities for government. But this is a matter of degree. In fact, the United States never had a completely free market economy. Even our pioneers were aided by federal land grants (which may mean that Smith never would have approved of us anyway). And today we are not discarding the market economy. Bit by bit we are still experimenting in the search for an economy which takes the best elements of free markets and adds to them the benefits—and the costs—of some types of government regulation.

Smith would find much in our economy to applaud. He would also find much to dismay him. But perhaps he would have the tolerance to realize that not much is fixed yet. And maybe he would share some of our own mixed feelings about this mixed economy—the same feelings with which Robert McCloskey once described the cottagers' departure from Maine at the end of a summer: "A little bit sad about the place you're leaving; a little bit glad about the place you're going."

SUGGESTED READINGS

Dunbar, Robert G., *The Farmer and the American Way*, pp. 22–30.
Question: What was the connection between the Industrial Revolution and the Agricultural Revolution?

____________, *The Farmer and the American Way*, pp. 32–45.
Question: What have been the major changes in the American farmer's answers to the *what* and *how* questions?

Federal Reserve Bank of Philadelphia, *The Price System*, pp. 1–9.
Question: Why have Americans modified the free market described by Adam Smith?

____________, *Automation*, pp. 1–9.
Question: What are the advantages of automation? What are some of the problems which automation brings?

Heilbroner, Robert, *The Worldly Philosophers*, Chapter 3.
Question: What is the major argument of Adam Smith's book *The Wealth of Nations?* On what evidence did Smith base his conclusions?

Industrial Relations Center, University of Chicago, *Competitive Prices in Action*, pp. 5–28.
Question: What are some of the areas in which competition has been limited in the American economy? Why those areas?

Korey, Edward L., "Business in a Changing World," *Business and the American Way,* pp. 33–43.

Question: What impact may large corporations have on competition in the economy?

———, "Business in a Changing World," *Business and the American Way,* pp. 55–76.

Question: What major changes have taken place in American business since World War II?

Koster-Dana Corporation, *Inside the Modern Corporation,* pp. 2–15.

Question: Draw a chart which shows how a corporation is organized.

Unit Four

What and How in a Command Economy

HAVING STUDIED the traditional and market economies, we will now look at the command economy. This unit examines the command economy's answers to the *what* and *how* questions. The *for whom* question is left for Unit 5.

Command economies confront the same economic questions as traditional and market economies. But they go about answering the questions largely by centralized planning. The government, not the consumers and producers, makes the main economic decisions. As we have often noted before, no economy is run purely by tradition, market, or command. The Soviet Union, the most successful command economy in the world, is no exception. While the government makes the main economic decisions in the Soviet Union, consumers, producers, and tradition all have their influence.

Chapter 7

Model of the Command Economy

STATING THE ISSUE To a Communist, the American free market system looks like a jumble. Countless economic decisions are made by millions of people. "How can all of those decisions be coordinated?" the Communist might ask. "How can it possibly work?" Soviet Communist leaders approached those questions and concluded that the market system worked only for the benefit of the few—the owners of property. For Russia, they constructed a system in which the government, acting in the name of the people, would make the major economic decisions. They looked forward to the day when economics would be logical, rational, and orderly.

Their task was not an easy one. As we shall see in Chapter 7, the government of a command economy must make many of the millions of decisions that the consumers and producers make in a market economy. Even with computers, the job of coordinating those decisions is staggering.

Chapter 7 presents a model of a command economy, just as Chapter 5 presented a model of a market economy. As in Chapter 5, we will use a simplified, small-scale model to concentrate on how the economic system is supposed to work. The complications of real life are left for Chapter 8.

Our main questions are these: How does a command economy decide what to produce? How does it decide how to produce it? And how does it go about putting its decisions into action? As you study this chapter, compare your answers to those major questions with the answers you came up with for the traditional and market economies.

30 The Command Economy as an Organizing Device (I)

As a political system, communism must try to solve many of the same problems that democracies solve. A communist state, like a democracy, needs some method of choosing leaders, making decisions, and carrying out those decisions. The solutions to those problems may be markedly different, but because human behavior is basically the same everywhere, the problems themselves are similar in different countries. The same holds for economic systems. A command society, like a market society and a traditional society, must decide what to produce, how to produce it, and for whom to produce it. This reading begins our exploration of how a command society goes about answering those basic economic questions. As you read, keep the following questions in mind:

1. What is the connection between economic scarcity and economic interrelatedness?
2. Give an example of interrelatedness in the Eskimos' society.
3. How might the War Production Board have avoided the shortages of casein and corn?

Command Economy and Market Economy: Common Problems

At first blush, the command economies of the world seem easier to understand than the market economies. Their answers to the three economic questions have a surface simplicity:

What goods and services shall be produced? Whatever the planners decide.
How shall they be produced? However the planners choose.
For whom shall they be produced? For whomever the planners decide.

Those replies are shorter than any that the market economies can offer. And, if you happened to like the decisions made by the planners as to what would be produced, how you would fit into the production process, and how much of the final product came to you, it could be a pleasant enough system for you to live under.

But that early appearance of simplicity vanishes once we look beyond the surface answers to the economic questions. The planned economy turns out to be an enormously complex system, particularly when, as in the case of a wealthy society (the Soviet Union, for example) or a poor but ambitious one (China), there is a national determination to make the economy substantially more productive each year.

The command economy offers no way of ducking the problems of economic choices. All that it does is to transfer the place where the choices are made from individuals and decentralized institutions to a centralized planning agency. In a planned economy, as well as in a market economy, a bar of steel used for one purpose is not available for some other purpose.

But why should a planned economy be so difficult to manage? What is so hard about making centralized decisions? The answer to those questions turns upon the interrelatedness of all economic decisions. A decision made in any one sector of the economy has an impact upon many other sectors. The effects spread out like ripples in a pool and touch many places where you might least expect an impact.

Take a decision to produce more steel. To produce more steel, you'll need more coal and more iron ore and more manganese. But you can't have those things without using steel itself for more railroad cars and more miles of track to get the raw materials to the steel mill. And then you'll need still more steel to build the new steel mill. The result? You'll have to use a substantial part of the steel produced today for building the steel plants and transportation systems of tomorrow. In other words, a decision to raise steel production will mean that, for the time being, less steel will be available for consumption.

In market economies, we often lose sight of the interrelatedness of all economic decisions. In market economies, decisions are less obvious and the market mechanisms adjust smoothly through changes in prices to changes in demand and supply. But occasionally, when we interfere with the market mechanisms, we see the problem of interrelatedness in sharp focus.

Consider price controls, which the United States resorted to during World War II. Because of unusually high demand or unusually restricted supply of some items, the government stepped in and said that free markets would not be allowed to operate. Rather than letting prices rise to the point where the number of units that can be sold would just equal the

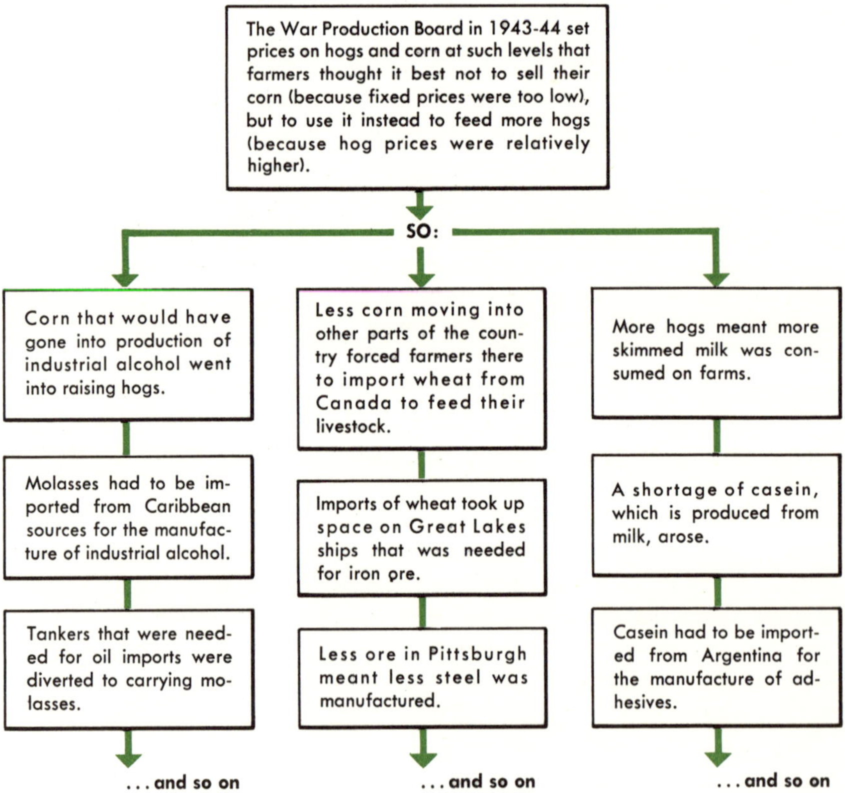

number that are available for sale, a ceiling was placed on prices by the War Production Board, which acted as the planner.

The War Production Board soon found that a price ceiling did more than prevent a spiraling price increase for a particular product. A price ceiling in one area quickly affected other areas. The diagram on p. 110 is a famous example from World War II of what happens when price decisions are made not by the market but by planners.

Of course, interrelatedness applies in a market economy as much as it does in a planned economy. The differences between planned and market economies, then, lie not in the presence or absence of interrelatedness, but in the ways the economies adjust to that interrelatedness.

What the planned or controlled economy does is to lift more decisions to the point of conscious, open, centralized decision-making. Those who run the controlled economies must face on a large scale the same kinds of decisions that individuals face in any society. Theirs is the task of deciding, for thousands or even millions of persons, how what people desire will be adapted to fit what people can have.

31 The Command Economy as an Organizing Device (II)

American Presidents have usually found that even they cannot simply give an order and expect it to be obeyed. Civil servants have power of their own, for a President needs their cooperation to carry out his programs. If a President's civil servants continually resisted the President's orders, the President would find his path difficult.

The same holds for those in charge of command economies. They, too, cannot simply give orders and then sit back comfortably. They, too, must win the cooperation of their subordinates. Those in charge of a command economy face yet another problem: giving the orders that will make their economy work smoothly. Their commands, as the last reading suggested, must somehow smoothly substitute for the invisible mechanism of a free market. Today's reading, which is about an imaginary command society, considers in more detail the problems planners face. As you read, think about the following questions:

1. What value does the Wisterian government place on economic growth?
2. What are the advantages of decentralizing decisions? What are the dangers?
3. What limits the power of the Planning Czar?

Planning Your Orsles and Your Wampsickles

Today you made it. After years of struggling and hoping and fighting, you're on top. You are the Planning Czar for all of the Island of Wisteria. No more do you have to fit your economic activities into somebody else's plans. From now on, the plans are yours—as long as the Ruling Czar has confidence in you.

The first day in office is enough to tell you that you'll never be able to make all the decisions yourself. There are just too many of them. True, Wisteria produces and consumes only five products: fliglets, iglons, marthrons, orsles, and wampsickles.* But there are different qualities, colors, and sizes of each. And iglons that work well in one part of the island are almost useless in other parts.

More than that, marthrons are used in the production of orsles; orsles are used in the production of iglons; and iglons are used in the production of marthrons. So, if you decide that you'll aim at a 10 per cent increase in the production of iglons next year, you'll have to allocate more orsles to the iglon production centers. To get those extra orsles, you must either increase the total production of orsles or cut down the supply of orsles used for other purposes.

Cutting down the orsle supply would not be a popular decision. First, nearly all the islanders like orsles. Second, and more important perhaps, you and the Ruling Czar love orsles. So you toy with the idea of increasing orsle production, too. But to produce more orsles so that there can be more iglons, you'll need to use up more marthrons in the production process. And to get more marthrons, you need to divert some of the extra iglons to the marthron industry. Circles began to swim around you.

There must be a way out of this. Too many decisions are being made in one office. You decide to decentralize decisions about each product, while still making the coordinating decisions yourself. It all looks so neat on paper:

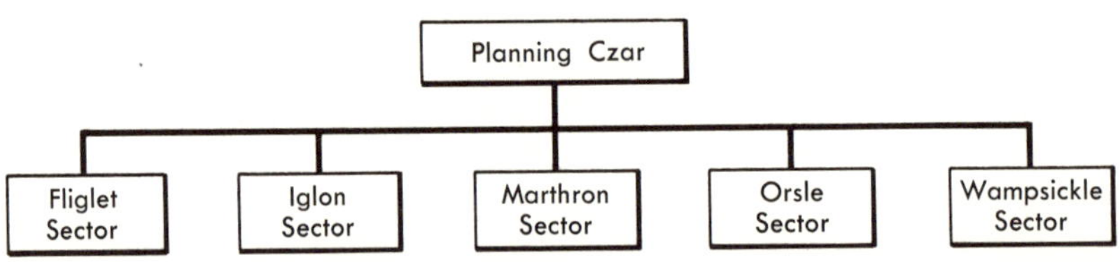

But it doesn't work quite so neatly. Each of your five Sub-Czars still has too many decisions to make. Each region of the island seems to have distinct enough problems that you decide to go another step towards decentralization. You set up separate planning offices within each production sector for each of the island's regions. The paper design still looks neat:

* Most Wisterians do not pronounce the *p* in wampsickle.

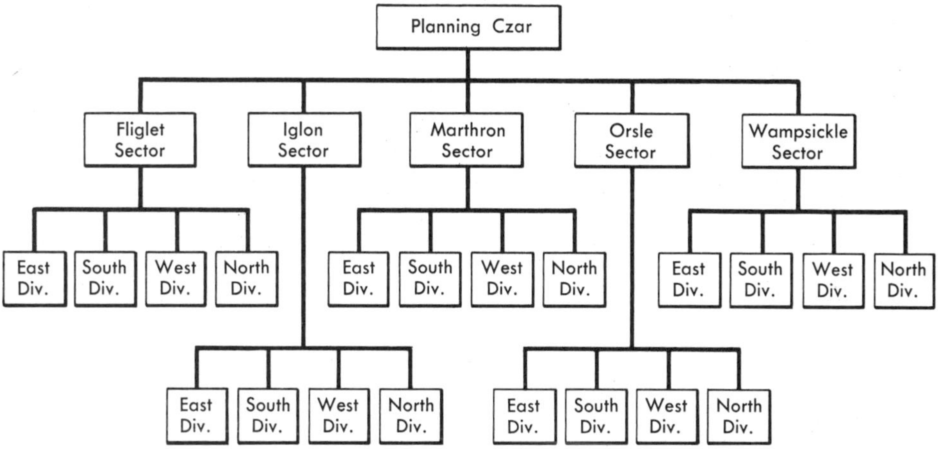

It then dawns on you that you can't have all the decisions coordinated at the top; there are too many of them. For example, the number, size, and quality of the wampsickles produced in the East Division affects the production of fliglets in the North Division, since the North has always relied upon the East for the particular type of wampsickle best suited to its fliglet production. So, some of your Sub-Sub-Czars must be in close contact with one another. You can leave the paper design just the way it is, but it won't tell you much about the actual flow of information and decisions within the island's economy.

Your hope is that you can concentrate on the broad targets at the top level, make them more specific at the second level, and still more specific at the third level. But problems at any one level have a way of getting back to the top very quickly. Two examples from your first days in office:

1. The orsle workers in the West Division are falling far behind in their scheduled production. It's not actually a strike, since no one would dare to strike openly. But somehow they are turning out less and less per day. The plant managers report that the orsle workers are angry because they are forced to pay more and more for fliglets in their part of the island, while their wages have not risen. You'd like to raise wages in the West Division, if only to make the workers happy and get the production of badly needed West Division orsles back on target. But you're worried: A wage increase in one region will make workers in other regions expect raises. What should you do?

2. The managers of the South Division's marthron plants complain that the quality of iglons they are getting to work with has fallen off badly. The iglons look as good as ever, but once they are fed into the marthron machines they often crack or crumble. Complaints to the iglon plant managers are either ignored or are answered with explanations that the iglon plant managers can no longer get the quality of orsles that they need. Everyone is blaming someone else. And the quality problem is spreading.

For a while, you toy with the idea of resigning. But the power and prestige are too attractive. You think about recommending to the Ruling Czar that you loosen up on the plans and controls and let people make more economic decisions for themselves. But you stop short on that thought when you recall that, in the old days when there was no plan, a few people were very rich but most Wisterians were very poor. And the island made little economic progress from year to year. Even today, you suspect that if the islanders were free to decide what should be produced, they would choose tons of wampsickles and very little iglons. Wampsickles give much short-range consumption happiness. But iglons, you realize, are essential for building the nation's capacity for producing more goods and services in the future. Iglons are also needed to build the military machinery with which to defend Wisteria against possible attack from neighboring islands.

Being the Planning Czar isn't turning out to be as much fun as you had hoped. But maybe it would help if you could sort out the various thought processes you are expected to go through. Where in your work are plain cold facts, the data on which statisticians could agree, useful? Where is it that you are expected to apply know-how, an awareness of technical possibilities and strategies? And where are you called upon to make value judgments, decisions about what is good for the people and the island and what is bad for them? You make a chart that evening at home. The chart has blanks under "Facts," "Know-how," and "Judgment" next to the following questions:

1. What productive resources will be available for use during the year?
2. What are the possible uses to which these resources may be put?
3. Which of those possible uses will be best to choose?
4. How will the choices of what is to be produced be made effective throughout the economy?

You decide to put *x*'s in the appropriate blanks, deciding which of the four questions can be answered by facts, which by know-how, and which by judgment.

It turns out to be a useful device. You're challenged by the value judgments you're forced to make, and convinced that you'll have to design a better fact-gathering system and better access to know-how for the areas where personal judgments count for less. But that must wait until tomorrow. Tomorrow you're planning to get organized.

Before going to sleep, you leaf idly through an old issue of a *New Yorker* Magazine from the United States. Your eye falls on a cartoon showing two Russians walking alongside the Kremlin walls. One is saying to the other, "In a democracy, it would be nothing but choice, choice, choice all the time." Your smile is a weak one. They should see my job, you think.

Chapter 8

How the Soviet Union Modifies the Command Economy

STATING THE ISSUE The guiding principle in a command economy is that overall planning from the top can produce better results than free competition. As Chapter 7 suggested, putting that principle into practice is no easy matter. And the Soviet Union's leaders were given little guidance in the writings of Karl Marx. Marx was an economist and historian, not a nation-builder. His central idea was that the societies of mankind go through a series of stages of development. The next-to-last stage, Marx believed, was capitalism. The final stage would be Communism. The facts of history, however, did not follow Marx's theory. Communism came to Russia while capitalism was still weak, and industries few. Russia thus skipped most of a full stage of development in Marx's scheme of things.

Marx believed that the transition from capitalism to Communism would be fairly easy—once the workers were in control. In the new Communist state, he thought, government itself would soon prove unnecessary, for the workers would happily cooperate. According to the modern leaders of the Soviet Union—who still consider themselves to be followers of Marx—the Soviet Union is not yet a Communist state. Rather, they claim, the Soviet Union is on the road to Communism. And it still has two tasks to accomplish: It must complete the industrialization that should have happened during the capitalist stage; and it must instill a full spirit of cooperation in the nation's citizens.

Chapter 8 examines the efforts the Soviet Union has made to put its theories into effect. Our main questions are similar to those for Chapter 6: In what ways has the Soviet Union modified the pure command economy model presented in Chapter 7? To what extent does the Soviet Union have a command economy?

32 Historical Backdrop for the Soviet Economy

Historians of the Soviet Union have long debated, but never finally decided, just how much the Soviet Union owes to prerevolutionary, czarist Russia. In other words, they have wondered how revolutionary the Communist Revolution has been. In the field of foreign policy, for example, the Communist seizure of Eastern Europe after World War II was strongly reminiscent of the czarist seizure of eastern Poland centuries before.

In economic policy, too, historians have found evidence both of change since the Communist Revolution and of continuity with what went on before the Revolution. Today's reading briefly analyzes the economic history of czarist Russia and the Soviet Union. As you read, keep the following questions in mind:

1. What elements of traditional, command, and free market economies were present in czarist Russia? Which are present in the Soviet Union?
2. How does the structure of the modern Soviet economy differ from the structure of the czarist economy?

Russia and the Soviet Union: Revolution or Evolution?

While the Industrial Revolution swept western Europe and the United States in the nineteenth century, Russia remained an agricultural land, steeped in tradition. Most peasants were tied to the land by the debts they owed their landlords.

Major agricultural reforms were finally begun in 1906—by the czarist government itself. The year before, the Russian navy had been disastrously defeated by the Japanese. The Russian government had also faced —and crushed—a workers' revolt at home. The workers' revolt had been touched off by the high cost of food. The government realized that the traditional system of farming, by which each village owned farm land communally, was wasteful. Peasants worked widely separated strips of land and had little incentive to improve their methods. Thus, the reforms of 1906 permitted peasants to own their land and to farm consolidated plots of land instead of isolated strips.

Like agricultural reforms, industrial development was inaugurated by the czarist government. In the 1890's, the major powers of Europe were locked in a tense and consuming cold war. Secret alliances were formed and broken. Nations competed for colonies in Africa and Asia. The general European peace that had lasted since the defeat of Napoleon in 1815 seemed frail.

Although Russia could field a huge army, its industrial system was backward. The government realized that the next war would be decided not by numbers alone, but by military technology and industrial strength. Mainly for these reasons, the czarist government started to encourage industrial development in the 1890's. The government made large loans to private companies for the construction of railroads. Smaller amounts were borrowed, through the government, from foreign investors. At the same time, mines and steel mills were expanded, again with government aid and foreign investments.

The spurt of the 1890's did not last, however. Agriculture still lagged behind, and when the peasants did not produce much grain, they could not pay large taxes. Without revenue, the government could not sponsor new industry. High farm prices, along with governmental corruption and the absence of democracy, kept the workers resentful. And increasingly, the government was devoting its energies to suppressing the new revolutionary movements.

There had been occasional peasant revolts in Russia for centuries. But in the late nineteenth century, a new class of reformers emerged. Many were students or workers in the factories and on the new railroads. A few were attracted to the ideas of Karl Marx. Because the Marxist group led by Lenin was the one that finally gained power, we will concentrate on it.

Lenin and his followers believed in a revolution which would make the workers themselves the owners of the means of production. All private enterprise would be abolished. All would work for the state and would share work and play.

During the first years of the twentieth century, Lenin's Communist Party remained insignificant. Its membership was tiny, and its leaders were hounded by the czarist secret police. But World War I, which began in 1914, severely weakened the czarist government. Russian armies, poorly led and poorly supplied, suffered enormous casualties at the hands of the Germans.

In March 1917, the czarist government collapsed. The new government was led by reformers who hoped to fight the war with renewed vigor. But Russia remained sick: Food prices were high; the soldiers were tired of fighting. The reformers failed to control the flood of discontent. In November 1917, Lenin's Communist Party overthrew the new government. Although the Communist Party was small, it was tightly organized when no other group was. Few Russians supported, or even understood, Lenin's program. But the Communists promised bread to the workers, land to the peasants, and peace to the nation. The new government quickly signed a peace treaty with Germany, surrendering large tracts of territory to the Germans.

Changing the nation's name from Russia to the Union of Soviet Socialist Republics did not change the economy overnight. The Communists inherited the prerevolutionary economy of Russia. A peasant agriculture supported a small industrial system designed mainly to serve the needs of the military. Now that the Communists were in control, they had to decide how to complete their revolution—how to turn Russia into a Communist state.

In its first years, the Communist government had to contend with civil war. A miscellaneous coalition of reformers and czarists, aided by foreign countries including the United States, fought the Communist government until 1921. During these years, Lenin improvised to save the economy from chaos. After unsuccessful experimentation with less sweeping measures, the Communist government nationalized all industry. That is, all factories were placed under government ownership and control.

The peasants were a more serious problem. To the peasants, the Revolution had meant no more landlords. They looked forward to growing their own crops and selling them for the highest prices they could get. Soviet industries, however, were largely turning out military weapons. The cities had little to give the peasants in exchange for food. Thus, the peasants had little incentive to raise production. The Communist armies tried to solve this problem by forcibly seizing crops. But this action earned the bitter hatred of the peasants.

To soften the peasants' anger, Lenin inaugurated the New Economic Policy (NEP) as soon as the civil war was over. Under NEP, crops were no longer seized. Instead, peasants paid their taxes with crops. But they could sell whatever crops were left over on the free market. To give the peasants an incentive, Lenin also encouraged the development of small factories which produced consumer goods for sale to the peasants. Soon a flourishing free market economy arose.

Lenin, however, viewed NEP as only a temporary measure to let the nation and the Communist Party recover from the civil war. Lenin believed that the Soviet Union's only hope was heavy industry—industry which produces goods like machines which can be used to build even more industry. Heavy industry would eventually raise the standard of living in the Soviet Union. It would also furnish the military power needed to fend off the invasion Lenin expected from the capitalist nations of western Europe. But heavy industry does not produce consumer goods of the sort that could be used to pay the peasants in exchange for crops. Thus, the old problem remained: How could enough crops be obtained from the peasants to feed the growing number of workers needed to build heavy industry?

Lenin himself died in 1924, too soon to try to answer that problem. After a bitter power struggle, he was succeeded by Joseph Stalin, who was a far more brutal man. Stalin set rapid industrialization as his goal. His main tactic was all-out war on the peasantry. He decided that the only way to get more food from the peasants was to force them to work in large state-owned, or collective, farms. On large, consolidated farms, tractors could be used profitably. Starting in 1929, collective farms were established. Approximately five million peasants resisted, clinging to their private plots of land. Ruthlessly, Stalin had them killed or deported to Siberia.

At the same time, Stalin embarked on the first of a series of Five Year Plans to develop heavy industry. The private enterprise that flourished under NEP was abolished. There was no semblance of democracy. Stalin's police even suppressed loyal Communists who disapproved of Stalin's methods. The human costs were staggeringly high, but the cold economic results were remarkable. Within two decades, backward Russia became a leading industrial state. When Germany invaded the Soviet Union in World War II, the Red Army proved able to push the Germans back.

Stalin's brutal regime came to an end with his death in 1953. After a struggle among Communist leaders, Nikita Khrushchev emerged as head of the Soviet Union. Under Khrushchev's leadership, the Soviet Union began producing more consumer goods—the workers and peasants were finally to receive some comfort for their years of sacrifice. Partly because of his failure to solve the continuing problem of low agricultural production, Khrushchev was ousted from power in 1964. He was succeeded by two men: Leonid Brezhnev and Aleksei Kosygin. Under Brezhnev and Kosygin, the Soviet economy has continued to produce large quantities of consumer goods, along with building heavy industry. And agriculture remains a problem.

33 Making Planning Work (I)

Against the historical backdrop presented in the previous lesson, we now turn to look at how the Soviet Union manages its economic affairs today. Two key points from that historical review have had a particularly profound impact on Soviet economic development.

First, the Russian people have not known political freedom in the same sense in which we have known it. The builders of Communism did not create tyranny; but they continued it in altered form from the long czarist past.

Second, Russia began industrializing later than most of the Western powers. Because of this, and because of the mediocrity of much of its cropland, the Soviet Union has continued to struggle with the problem of conquering agricultural inefficiency even though its industrial development has moved ahead rapidly.

The next four lessons examine some of the ways the leaders of the Soviet Union have adapted Marx's ideas and the ideal of the planned economy to meet the realities of economic management and of Soviet life. As you read, keep the following questions in mind:

1. Who makes which economic decisions in the Soviet Union?
2. Why is centralized distribution of key resources a necessary part of a command economy?
3. In the United States, who makes the economic decisions that are made by the Communist Party in the Soviet Union? Who in the United States makes the economic decisions that the Gosplan makes in the Soviet Union?

The Core of the Command Economy

Every Soviet leader, from Lenin and Stalin to Khrushchev and Kosygin, has used similar words to describe his economic goals for the Soviet Union: much higher production for domestic development and for protection against outside aggression; improved health, educational, and cultural standards; shorter hours and better working conditions; and improved social services. In themselves, those phrases could easily form the political platform for an American Presidential candidate. But the means an American President and a Soviet leader would use to achieve those goals—as well as the particular definitions they would give to those phrases—differ markedly.

The model for the Soviet economy has been adjusted over the years to meet new problems and new opportunities. But five elements have remained at the core of the model: 1) nationalization of most productive resources; 2) centralized distribution of key materials; 3) collectivization of agriculture; 4) comprehensive planning; 5) control through the Communist Party. Let's take these one at a time:

1. Nationalization of most productive resources

Marxist economics starts with the assumption that most struggles between men are struggles between the "haves" and the "have-nots." The Marxist sees history as a series of such stories: slaveowner against slave, patrician against plebian, lord of the manor against serf, capitalist against wage-earner, and so on. From this eternal struggle, the Marxist sees but one way out: Abolish private ownership of the means of production (capital) by giving the means of production to all of the people instead of to the few.

On this point, the real world of the Soviet Union comes close to the model proposed by Marx. The Soviet Union's mines, mills, railroads, machines, large stores, and many other firms belong to the "people" in the sense that they are all parts of the vast governmental structure. Technically, then, there can be no private profit out of the use of productive resources. (We'll see later that there are problems on this score.) A Soviet factory worker who believes in Communism must, by definition, believe that he is working for all his fellow countrymen since they, through the government, are the real owners of the factory.

2. Centralized distribution of key materials

In a market economy, productive resources such as steel and timber and skilled labor and computers would go to whoever bids highest for them. In the Soviet Union, the government planners decide where those resources are to go. They say, "Here are our most important goals—and here is the way we'll use our available resources to achieve those goals."

No aspect of this distribution of key resources is more important than the split between resources to be used for today's consumer satisfaction and those to be used for tomorrow's consumer satisfaction. If they chose to, the Soviet planners could immediately raise today's standard of living by allocating more of the available resources to the kinds of consumer goods desired by the people. But they know that steel used for automobiles and steam irons will not be available for building more railroad cars or even more steel mills—and if such productive facilities as steel mills are not improved, how can the nation make even more automobiles and steam irons tomorrow? Their problem: Find a workable balance between giving the people what they want in the short run while providing for the long-run expansion of the nation's productive facilities.

3. Collectivization of agriculture

During NEP, there were about 25 million farms in the Soviet Union. By now, most of those farms have been combined into about forty thousand collective farms and an additional ten thousand still larger state farms. Whereas the average American farm has less than two workers, the average Soviet collective farm has over four hundred workers, and the average state farm has more than seven hundred.

As the last reading noted, the collective and state farms were formed to reduce the stubborn independence of the small landowners and to increase agricultural efficiency. But as was also noted, the human costs of welding small farms into collective farms was enormous. Agricultural production also suffered. And still today, the collective and state farms have not figured out how to persuade the farm laborer to work hard when he cannot profit by the fruits of his individual labor.

But it would be a mistake to blame all the problems of Soviet agriculture on collectivization. The fact is that the soil and climate of the Soviet Union make it a far more difficult place to farm than is the United States. And the Soviet Union's leaders would also argue that without collectivization, there would have been no way to eliminate the small landowners who refused to make the sacrifices necessary for industrialization.

4. Comprehensive planning

All of the separate pieces in the Soviet Union's economic jigsaw puzzle somehow have to be fitted together. This is the task of the Gosplan (State Planning Commission). The Gosplan is given general commands by the Central Committee of the Communist Party, which frames Five-Year Plans for the economy. But those general commands must eventually be translated into a myriad of closely interwoven, specific targets and allocations of resources. The Gosplan, a central planning agency, has help from subordinate commissions that govern different industries and regions. More intelligent use of statistics and better computers are also helping the planners fit the jigsaw puzzle together.

Even so, the planners' task remains unbelievably complex. The planners must somehow make most of the economic decisions that the free market makes in the United States. Outsiders know many of the mistakes the Soviet planners have made—there have been too many shortages and too many failures in achieving goals to hide those mistakes. But outsiders also find themselves amazed from time to time that the thing can work at all. Just as the United States is the most striking example of what a modified free market economy can achieve in industrial might, so the Soviet Union is the most striking example of what a modified command economy can achieve in industrial might. (We'll see later some of the modifications made recently in Soviet planning.)

5. Control through the Communist Party

As mentioned above, the Gosplan takes its orders from the Communist Party—and especially from the Central Committee of the Communist Party. The Communist Party is an elite group; it is deliberately kept small. In fact, only about 5 per cent of the adults in the Soviet Union today are party members. But once they are in, they play a part, however minor, in setting the goals for the nation. The men and women at the Gosplan are the key technicians whose skills determine whether or not the nation's goals are achieved. But the goals themselves—and the final control of the economy—still stays firmly in the hands of the Communist Party.

34 Making Planning Work (II): The Zis Man

In Reading 28, we saw that American business managers sometimes feel caught between competing pressures. On the one hand, they are told to compete as keenly as possible, and to expect to be measured by the results they achieve. On the other hand, they are told, by government, that they must compete only in certain "fair" ways and must not compete so successfully that they end up as monopolies.

Soviet managers, too, face dilemmas. They are told to produce results, or else face the consequences. But they are also told to produce those results within certain clearly defined restrictions. Chief among those restrictions is the volume of resources—such as manpower, raw materials, semi-finished goods, and electric power—that they are given to work with by the planners.

A Soviet plant manager stands between the planning officers and the shop superintendent. His interests are quite different in dealing with those above him and those below him. From the planners, he wants the lowest production quota together with the biggest block of resources. From his plant superintendent, he wants the maximum production from the smallest possible block of resources. (Now stop to ask, How does this differ, if at all, from the way you would expect an American plant manager of a multi-plant firm such as General Motors to view his own interests?)

In the following reading, a West German describes his encounter with a Soviet plant manager's unofficial assistant—the Zis man. As you read, think about the following questions:

1. What economic function does the Zis man perform?
2. Why do Soviet economic officials conspire to permit the Zis man to break the law? What do their actions indicate about his usefulness to the economy?
3. Do we have a counterpart of the Zis man in American society?

The Zis Man

KLAUS MEHNERT

From Soviet Man and His World. *New York: Frederick A. Praeger, Inc., 1962, pp. 84–87. Reprinted with permission of the publisher. British rights controlled by George Weidenfeld and Nicolson Ltd.*

A chance encounter at an airport in Siberia was very informative. I had arrived in the evening, and my plane was not due to leave until the next morning. At the airport hotel the receptionist told me that no beds were vacant at the moment, but that one would become available during the night.

I settled myself in an armchair in the lounge. A little later a passenger carrying two suitcases arrived . . . [H]e sat down beside me. . . . Having ordered the vodka, he plied me with questions about the economy. "Let us take as an example," he said, "the Volkswagen plant in Germany. Let's say the program for the year is . . . 500,000 cars. If you include one spare, then five tires will be needed for each car, or a total of 2.5 million tires. Suppose the factory then finds it can produce 30,000 more cars in a year. It will then need 150,000 more tires. What does the management do to get them? . . ."

I answered, "Volkswagen . . . would have no difficulty in getting extra tires from the firm that supplies them, since that firm, anticipating such a situation, will always keep a surplus on hand."

"I see. But let's suppose they can't get them like that—suppose the supplying firm just hasn't got them."

"In that case Volkswagen goes to another tire manufacturer."

"Direct? Just like that?"

"Yes, just like that."

"But suppose the second firm doesn't have 150,000 tires either, and no other tire manufacturer in the country has them? This could happen, couldn't it?"

". . . If that happened then the firm would turn to a tire company abroad."

"Could they get the necessary foreign currency?"

"No difficulty about that. . . ."

"Then in your country," he said with a laugh, "I should be out of a job." . . .

"What do you do for a living, then?" I asked, although I already had a fairly good idea.

"Me? My specialty is eliminating bottlenecks and oiling the wheels of industry."

"Ah!" I said. "So you're a Zis man?"

He laughed. "You know the expression?" (It is a play on words.) There is a car called the Zis, a product of the Zavod Imeni Stalina, the Stalin Factory (since renamed). But "Zis" also stands for "Znakomstva i svyazi" (connections and contacts).

I asked him, "How do you go about it?"

"I'll tell you. Let's say a factory is short of tires and can't get them anywhere. The director phones me. 'Stepan Alexeyevich,' he says, 'get me forty tires, will you? Our trucks are being held up, and our suppliers have let us down. The Glavk (the appropriate administrative department) can't help us, and the Ministry has let us down too. . . .' "

"Well, I go to the chief accountant: 'Maxim Ivanovich,' I say, 'the director told me to come to you. He wants me to get forty tires. Give me the money!' The accountant moans and groans. . . . He always does—as though he already had one foot in prison!" (The accountant is not allowed to make money available for any purpose not provided for in the plan, and Zis men, with their fairly heavy expense accounts, are not, of course, included.) "But he has to fork out anyway, because if we fall short of the target due to lack of tires, it won't be any more amusing for him than for the rest of us."

"So he overcomes his scruples and does something illegal?"

"What else can he do? We've got to complete the program. But he'll try to cover himself by getting the director to sign and pretending he doesn't know what it's all about. So in the end he gives me my travelling expenses—first class, of course, because we're an important firm—with some extra money for gifts and entertainment. . . . Before I set out, others let me know of their needs. One wants so much copper wire, another asks me to find him a skilled mechanic. . . ."

"What does the Party secretary in your factory think . . . ?"

"Him? Oh, he looks the other way. He's just as eager as anyone to see the plan fulfilled. . . . It's much better for him, too, if the factory where he is Party secretary reaches its quota."

"But surely, as Party secretary, he can count on being commended if he discovers irregularities and reports them?"

"Perhaps. But I know of one case where a Party secretary who had reported irregularities was reprimanded for being a bureaucratically minded grumbler. Still—let's assume he gets a pat on the back. It's the last he'll get, because from then on he won't be let in on any of the factory secrets. We're all equally interested in seeing that we meet the state's production demands. Director, chief cashier, Party secretary, staff, and the Ministry—everybody's on the side of the man who sees that the plan is carried out."

"What about the Ministry of Inspection and Supervision?"

"That's different. They've got their own machinery. Fulfillment of their plan isn't a question of goods produced, but a wrongdoers handed over. That's what they get their decorations for. But there are limits even to that. Counter-intelligence measures—the police are first-rate at that. But bookkeeping, no."

"So they all come to you with requests, and eventually you set off?"

"Yes. I travel here and there, visit people, chat with them, give them all kinds of presents, dine them, wine them, and promise them this, that, and the other, until at last I've got what I want."

35 The Soviet Executive

In Reading 28, we looked at the American business executive, first through a novelist's eyes and then through a discussion of the pulls and counterpulls surrounding a modern executive. In today's reading, we look at a Russian executive through the eyes of David Granick, an American economist who has observed the Soviet economy at close range.

The worlds in which the American and the Soviet executives operate seem strikingly different. Yet for all of the deep ideological differences between American and Soviet executives, they have much in common. When Soviet Premier Nikita Khrushchev visited the United States in 1959, he and his top associates seemed to find it easier to talk with and understand American business executives than American labor leaders, reporters, or government officials. This was not because American business executives were any more pro-Communist than their countrymen. It was rather because the Soviet leaders and the American executives found a common ground on which to talk: They were all managers of resources.

As you read, consider the following questions:

1. What are some of the pulls and counterpulls surrounding a Soviet executive?
2. How is the Soviet executive an "organization man"? How do his power and independence compare with those of Henry Ford in the early days of the Ford Motor Company?
3. Compare the economic roles of the Soviet executive and the modern American executive.

An Organization Man, Communist Style

DAVID GRANICK

From The Red Executive *(New York: Doubleday). Copyright © 1960 by David Granick. Reprinted by permission.*

The Soviet Union is a country in which the manager has no possibility of starting his own business and gaining future financial independence in this way. He cannot share in his firm's profits through becoming a partner or by stock options. He has no path to wealth through capital gains and stock purchases of growth companies.

Even when he has plenty of money, there are things he would badly like to have but which are simply not for sale. He cannot rent a larger or better-built apartment by looking in higher-rent areas; there are no free-enterprise builders ready to put up luxury apartments to meet the rental market. He can build his own house, and then own it outright. But he cannot build on the scale he wishes and can afford; building materials are scarce, and allocation orders are required for them. Thus, money cannot be transformed into better housing—for the profit incentive of builders is missing....

But, of course, the Soviet manager has financial incentives of his own. These are far from negligible.

Take salary and bonuses. In one Leningrad plant of the food industry which I visited, earnings of average workers were 700–800 rubles monthly. At the same time, the monthly salary of the plant director was 3,000 rubles, and he averaged monthly bonuses averaging 1,500–1,600 rubles. ... It seems reasonable to think of directors of plants with a labor force of five hundred to fifteen thousand employees as receiving something in the order of five to six times the earnings of the average worker.

The Red Executive has come far since the days of the Revolution. Today he is a college-educated engineer with a sound technical and administrative background, and he bears little resemblance to the flamboyant [fiery] Party director of the early days whose credentials were years in czarist prisons, escapes from exile, and oratory exercised in stirring the masses.... Today's executive combines sound training with the political assurance and power which permit him the freedom to make creative use of his training.

The Soviet manager may not live well when judged by the standards of his American counterpart, but he does quite satisfactorily compared to the ordinary Soviet citizen. He is given powerful monetary incentives to turn in a first-rate job. Yet never in his life will he have any certainty of [holding his job]. No civil service rules or old-school tie protect him; his superiors show a marked impatience with failure. This impatience, it is true, is now tempered more with common sense than was the case in the past. No longer, as often occurred during the mid–1930's, do production lapses lead swiftly to charges of sabotage and to a forced-labor camp. Nevertheless, blunders can result in swift demotion. The executive ulcer rate is high.

The Russian manager is a man with power, but he is no independent decision-maker. He is an organization man, filling a slot in an industrial bureaucracy which has lines reaching to the very heights of Soviet power. His production goals, his costs, and even his industrial research objectives are set for him. Moreover, he must establish and maintain successful contact with the members of other powerful bureaucracies—and in particular with that of the Communist Party.

But if the manager's goals are established for him, their achievement is often his personal responsibility. No excuse exists for failure. Often, the drive to meet quotas will force him into illegal activities;* this cannot be helped. . . .

The Soviet manager is oriented to production. Volume of output is the acid test of his work. Marketing is no problem; finance is a [minor] concern. But the purchasing department is the rock on which the factory organization stands; for supply shortages lead to production shortages. . . .

Although the situation is now [1960] in the process of change, raw materials and machinery are still the items of greatest scarcity to the Russian manager. It is these which are his bottlenecks. Labor, of course, is also a problem—but a labor-saving device is not nearly as valuable to him as one which saves materials or which permits more production from a machine. Thus, the Soviet manager tends to emphasize in his daily work different shortages than does the American company president or even the plant superintendent.

Well trained, well disciplined, politically conscious and active, the Red Executive seems a figure permanently established in the seats of the mighty. There is no justification for picturing him as a man in conflict with the Communist Party official, the two uneasily sharing power for the moment. Rather, the industrial manager and the Party secretary are old classmates, neighbors, and colleagues, seeing the world from the same perspective.

* The author seems to be referring to under-the-table deals to get more raw materials or labor than authorized, to cut corners on quality standards, or to ignore certain government-imposed restrictions on his operations. Remember the Zis man.

Neither the Red Executive nor his Party-official colleague is any longer the revolutionary of the 1920's to whom ideology was everything. Both are men well established in the second most powerful country in the world, with enormous personal stakes in world stability and in peace. When Marx in the *Communist Manifesto* appealed for world revolution, he addressed himself to the worker who had "nothing to lose but his chains." The Red Executive and the Party administrator have a great deal more to lose—and they know it well. Their attitude toward world revolution and other threats to peace . . . bear[s] the imprint of this knowledge.

36 Summary: The Changing Command Economy

In examining the economy of the United States, we saw that many modifications have been made in the pure market model. Bit by bit, Americans have introduced changes; our system today no longer has the simplicity which Adam Smith so strongly favored. We've tempered market forces to meet new problems created by massive industrialism and urbanization. But despite the modifications, the economy of the United States still remains basically a market economy.

The Soviet economy has likewise been undergoing change. Adam Smith, as we have seen, would probably have a hard time recognizing the United States in the last third of the twentieth century. But Karl Marx would have just as hard a time recognizing today's Soviet Union. New needs, new ideas, and new experiences have led the Soviet Union's leaders to experiment with changes—but still within the framework of a planned economy. Today's reading describes some of the recent changes in the Soviet economy. As you read, keep the following questions in mind:

1. In what ways are Professor Liberman's ideas like the ideas behind a market economy? How are they different?
2. How might a pure command economy be clumsy in the Soviet Union?
3. In what ways does the Soviet Union have a "mixed" economy?

Norms, Storms, and Reforms

EDWIN A. ROBERTS, JR.

From Russia Today, A Newsbook of The National Observer. *Dow Jones and Co., Inc., Silver Spring, Maryland, 1967. Reprinted by permission.*

In the United States, politics and economics are closely related. In the Soviet Union, they are Siamese twins.

On October 17, 1964, two days after Khrushchev was ousted, a *Pravda* editorial indicated that Nikita's fall was caused in large part by dissatisfaction with his economic policies. The editorial, without mentioning the man *Pravda* had been idolizing only a few days before, lashed out at "harebrained scheming, immature conclusions and hasty decisions and actions divorced from reality, bragging and phrase-mongering, commandism, unwillingness to take into account the achievements of science and practical experience."

On October 21, of the same year, the Kremlin announced that the nation's economic performance for the first nine months of 1964 was only 7 per cent above the same period for the previous year. This represented the smallest increase in Gross National Product (total value of goods and services produced during the year) in the Soviet Union since 1946.

The news seemed to shock the economic planners in a way that [would be] almost [beyond] understanding in a capitalist country....

Although heavy industry, especially steel, did indeed dramatically increase its production, the economy as a whole fell far short of the Khrushchev goals. And as the gap between predictions and performance became clearer, new heed was given those progressive academic voices who urged a new approach to problems of industrial inefficiency.

Best known among these innovators was Professor Y. G. Liberman [*lee*-ber-mun] of the Kharkov Engineering and Economics Institute. His famous manifesto first appeared in *Pravda* on September 9, 1962, and it made six points:

1. Production planning should be the responsibility of the factory manager, not of some remote bureaucrat in Moscow.
2. Financial incentives should be used to encourage workers to boost individual output.
3. Incentive pay should also be based on the performance of all plants in a given industry having essentially the same natural and technical problems.
4. Make centralized planning workable by limiting it to overall decisions for an industry or region, with various checks on Moscow bureaucrats and lower-ranking economic councils.
5. Take incentive funds out of the profits of enterprises.
6. Establish a flexible pricing system that is related to production and distribution costs.

On this last item, it should be pointed out that the Soviet Union has long used the State's power to set prices as a [way of] rationing [the goods and services produced]. . . . When there is a shortage of some commodity [product], its price is often raised out of sight, thereby keeping the merchandise in the stores until production can catch up with the demand, which sometimes never happens. But the shortage is less obvious to the consumer who, although he can't afford to buy the item, at least can see it in the store. . . .

The manifesto was at first greeted with jeers. Declared the Soviet journal, *Voprosy Ekonomiki:* "Some economists have made proposals which take very little account of the specific character of the planned economy. Their proposals would lead in varying degrees to divorcing the enterprise from the whole system of national planning."

The economics journal was making an old point. It was saying that central planning should pronounce the broad objectives while permitting the workers to solve their little problems themselves. The trouble was—and this is what the economics journal was reluctant to admit—that once you set a bureaucracy planning, it doesn't know where to stop. . . .

Central planners traditionally have also tried to isolate their sector of the economy from the national whole. This kind of planning works as long as it can be well defined. But as the economy becomes more complex, as several bureaus must work together, the tangle becomes unbelievable. . . .

The sameness of the output of factories borders on the bizarre. A red carpet with orange and green stripes covers hallways in the Metropol Hotel in Moscow, the Armory Chamber Museum in Moscow, the Hotel Dnipro in Kiev, and the Hotel Oreanda in Yalta. Once a carpet factory gets the wheels turning, apparently, there is a distinct—and understandable—reluctance to turn it off and switch to another pattern.

A recent cartoon in *Izvestia,* captioned "Twins Against Their Will," [claims] to show men, women, and children in the Volga village of Sengilei all wearing identical checked hats with earmuffs because that model is the only one produced in a nearby factory and sold in local stores.

One government report noted angrily: "Men's suits [from a Moscow factory] range in color from dirty-gray to yellow-green. . . . Linings show from under coats; coat backs are too narrow; sleeves hang askew. Labels are not honest. Sometimes size 42 will be smaller than size 40."

The incentive-system experiment to try to change all this was originally tried out in eighty enterprises in the consumer goods field. . . . Before the new system was introduced, the Moscow factory was told by the central planners what to produce. Consumer tastes were not taken into account . . . The plant's quota was two thousand suits a day and nobody seemed to care what sizes the suits were or whether anybody would buy them. . . .

Today the Moscow suit factory bases its production rate on the orders it receives from twenty-two retail stores. If the merchandise is unsatisfactory, the stores can return it. Returned goods mean lower profits for the factory and smaller bonuses for the workers. . . .

The Liberman plan is chiefly designed to eliminate two of Soviet industry's worst snags. One is the penchant [habit] of factory managers to "bargain" with planners for [only] modest increases in their production quotas so they can easily collect a handsome bonus for fulfilling them. This, of course, tends to retard growth.

The other snag comes about when management seeks to fulfill quotas by lowering quality or by failing to produce a full assortment of sizes and models. The planners . . . tried to prevent these practices by imprisoning the managers in a strait-jacket of regulations, directives, and detailed production plans. . . . Under Liberman's plan, [the factory manager] need worry about only three [indicators]: total volume, a breakdown of product types, and a delivery schedule.

And most important of all, performance is now based solely on profits.

A capitalist might still find the arrangement strangling, but it represents the most freedom managers have had since full-scale planning began in 1928. . . .

To work effectively, Western experts believe, the scheme might require even more decontrol than Liberman has called for—more, in fact, than it is politically possible for Premier Alexei N. Kosygin to push for at this time. It is only logical, for instance, that price control and centrally planned distribution be abandoned; then managers seeking to boost profits would be free to shop around for raw materials and haggle with suppliers over prices.

Mr. Kosygin, an economist himself with a sophisticated view of socialist economics, has conceded that the decision to [use] what are essentially capitalist techniques stems from the growing complexity of Soviet society.

The move to Libermanism is only the latest step in the liberalization of the Soviet economy that has gradually taken place since the death of Stalin in 1953.

SUGGESTED READINGS

HEILBRONER, ROBERT, *The Worldly Philosophers,* Chapter 6.
Question: Why did Marx believe that capitalism and free market economies were doomed? On what evidence did Marx base his conclusions?

RIEBER, ALFRED J. and ROBERT C. NELSON, editors, *The USSR and Communism,* pp. 66–84.
Question: Who were the reformers in czarist Russia? What kinds of economic reform did they propose?

————, *The USSR and Communism,* pp. 84–97.
Question: How did late nineteenth century reforms affect the Russian peasant? Why do you think the peasants were slow to rebel against the czars?

____________, *The USSR and Communism*, pp. 114–133.

Question: How did the early Russian Communist leaders disagree with Marx's economic views?

____________, *The USSR and Communism*, pp. 133–143.

Question: What are some significant differences between the command economies of the Soviet Union, Yugoslavia, Communist China, and Cuba? What role has economics played in the lack of unity among those Communist countries?

____________, *The USSR and Communism*, pp. 318–320.

Question: What major economic changes did Marx and Engels advocate in *The Communist Manifesto*?

SCHWARTZ, HARRY, editor, *The Many Faces of Communism*, pp. 66–72.

Question: How did the 1962 program of the Communist Party propose to solve the *what* and *how* problems?

____________, *The Many Faces of Communism*, pp. 82–88.

Question: What values underlie the decisions made by Soviet planners about what to produce?

Unit Five

Distributing What Economies Produce

MARKET AND COMMAND economies alike face the *for whom* question—in popular speech, the question of "Who gets what?" For most people, this is the most important question economics has to answer. After all, an economic system is a means to an end, and the end is the use of the goods and services an economy produces. The *for whom* question is also a moral question. Every society wants to distribute the goods and services it produces in a just way. Yet each society has its own definition of *just*.

Unit Five examines the distribution systems of the United States and the Soviet Union. It describes the aims of the distribution systems of the United States and the Soviet Union. It suggests how pursuit of those aims has led to modifications in the pure market model and the pure command model. And finally, it seeks to give you a basis upon which to judge how well the United States and the Soviet Union are achieving their goals of a just distribution of goods and services.

Chapter 9

Distribution in the Modified Market Economy

STATING THE ISSUE In a pure market economy, the *for whom* question would be answered wholly in the free marketplace. But a society does not have to choose between adopting a pure market economy or an economy with no free markets at all. To achieve their goals, Americans have often modified the free market when it suited their purposes to do so.

In the past seventy years, as Reading 22 pointed out, Americans have been increasingly concerned with the *for whom* question. Often through governmental measures, Americans have tried to establish a fairer distribution of the goods and services their society produces. But on this issue, as on the issue of free competition among producers and sellers, the feelings of Americans are not altogether clear. On the one hand, Americans often favor letting the winner take home the prizes. Why should the millionaire be taxed more heavily than the poor man, Americans sometimes ask. After all, the millionaire earned that money, didn't he? On the other hand, the great majority of Americans have, through their elected representatives, indeed voted to tax the rich man more heavily than the poor man. They have also voted for the Social Security system, which ensures an income for the elderly who can no longer work. And they have voted for a public welfare system, designed to feed, clothe, and house those who fail in the real-life game of free competition. These measures, as we shall see, take the edge off the harshness of the free marketplace without destroying it.

Besides considering governmental measures which affect distribution, Chapter 9 discusses labor unions, in which workers join together to exert a greater force in the marketplace than they could if they competed as individuals. Chapter 9 also considers the importance of profits in maintaining a healthy market economy.

In sum, Chapter 9 examines the results of Americans' efforts to make their distribution system a just system. It raises two general questions for you to consider: How has the United States modified the distribution system of a pure market economy? What would you reply if someone asked you how the United States answers the *for whom* question?

37 Model of the Factor Markets

In a market economy, the question of for whom the goods and services will be produced is answered this way: Goods and services are produced for those who have the money to pay for them. And, in turn, the question of who has the money to pay for them is determined by the success that people have in selling their labor, the use of their land, or the loan of their capital in the marketplace. Someone whose services are in high demand—a brain surgeon or movie star, for example—will receive a high return for his services. This means he will have more dollars than others with which to bid for other goods and services in markets, and more of the society's goods will end up in his hands than in the hands of someone whose services are in less demand.

Today's reading develops this idea of distribution in greater depth. As you read, keep the following questions in mind:

1. What is "a factor of production"?
2. How will the factors of production in an industrially advanced market economy differ from those in a traditional economy?
3. What are the similarities between Robinson Crusoe's island economy and the world of an owner of a small firm in the United States?

1. The Three Factors of Production

The production of any good or service usually requires some combination of three different types of resources:

1. *Labor:* All aspects of human effort expended in producing a good or a service, from the simplest task up to the task of combining all the other goods and services into the final good or service.
2. *Land:* All of the natural resources used to produce something else. More specifically, the term refers to soil, minerals, forests, waters, and, especially in urban and industrialized societies, the surface of the earth on which productive activities may be carried forward.
3. *Capital:* Those buildings, pieces of machinery, and tools which man has fashioned to help him produce still more goods and services. (In common speech, "capital" is sometimes also used to refer to the money spent in producing capital goods.)

The terms are not precise ones, but their general purpose is clear: They help us to categorize all of the elements involved in any production process. Labor, land, and capital are therefore called the *factors* of production.

The *for whom* question is at root simply a question about what part of the total production of an economy shall go to each of the various factors of production. A man pays $2,875 for a new automobile. What part of that shall go to each of the workers (assembly-line worker, maintenance man, salesman, transport driver, president) who had a hand in producing the car? What part shall go to those who own the iron-ore mines, the steel mills, the land where the auto plant and the showroom are located, and the farm where the cotton fibers used in the upholstery were raised? And what part shall go to those who provided the machinery and buildings for production and sales? And to those who loaned the company money during the time when wages and other bills were being paid out and no sales dollars were yet coming in?

Each factor of production—or, more exactly, each owner of a factor of production—receives a share of the final product. To see how those shares work, it might be useful to return to the world of Robinson Crusoe, first introduced in Reading 5, and even to add a little to that world in order to make an extra point or two.

2. Factor Markets: Crusoe and Friends

ACT 1: Crusoe alone on a desert island

So long as Robinson Crusoe's world is a one-man world, he has no distribution problem to think about. No one, so far as he yet knows, owns the island and can claim rent for his living there. No one has loaned him any equipment to use and can claim interest on an investment in such equipment. And no one works with him and can claim wages for his effort.

ACT 2: Enter the man Friday

Friday comes along. Now there's a distribution problem. How much of the product of their joint efforts will go to reward Friday? Crusoe has a tough decision. If he gives Friday too much in relation to what Friday produces, there will be too little left for himself. If he gives Friday too little, Friday may either revolt or just not work very hard. By trial and error, Crusoe finds a settlement with which he and Friday can live.

ACT 3: Enter a new man, Saturday

Here we leave Daniel Defoe's original book and make life on the island a bit more interesting. A man named Saturday joins Crusoe and Friday. What will he get from the newly enlarged production of food and shelter? Crusoe will probably weigh Saturday's contribution against Friday's. If Saturday is more productive, he'll demand more of the food and shelter. If he doesn't get it, he'll sulk enough to lower production—and a sulking Saturday is more serious for Crusoe than is a sulking Friday because each hour of Saturday's labor is more productive than Friday's. So it isn't an abstract principle of justice that leads Crusoe to give Saturday more food and more shelter than Friday. It's the cold fact that Saturday is worth more to him. Men are beginning to be rewarded in relation to their contributions.

ACT 4: Enter the landlord

One day, a man named Jeremy Hopper sails over to the island, proves he is the rightful owner, and demands payment in food for use of his land. If Hopper asks too much for the rent, Crusoe and his companions will spend their time fashioning a raft, and paddle to another island where rents are lower. If the rent is too low, it won't be worth Hopper's while to come to collect it and to keep up the tax payments on the island. Crusoe and Hopper reach a compromise settlement.

ACT 5: Hopper's treasures

Hopper has a good thing going. He also has equipment—shovels, hatchets, quality seed, hammers and nails—that he will lease to Crusoe in exchange for interest payments in food. How much will Crusoe be willing to pay for the use of a shovel? Not too much, because it won't be worth it to pay more than he will gain in the way of extra production from using the shovel. And how little will Hopper settle for in leasing the shovel? Not too little, because at a certain low payment rate Hopper will gain more by selling the shovel on some other island where it is more appreciated. Then Hopper could use the proceeds from that sale to fashion some piece of equipment more to Crusoe's or other islanders' likings. So again, Hopper and Crusoe haggle, and a further bargain is reached. By now, there is a full-blown distribution system on the island.

Is the system fair? It all depends on your definition of fairness. In a market economy, it's hard to feel sorry for Crusoe because he has to pay out a percentage of the food and shelter to Friday and Saturday, and a percentage of the food to Hopper. He shares with Friday and Saturday as long as he thinks it is to *his* advantage to do so—as long as what he gets from them in production is at least equal to what he must pay them for their effort. And Friday and Saturday, in turn, work for Crusoe as long as it is to *their* advantage to do so—as long as what he pays them for their effort is more than they could make on their own or by working on another island. Crusoe pays Hopper for the land use so long as he can profit by using that land. And he leases Hopper's tools when the return he'll get from them through higher production is at least equal to what he must pay for their use. How much Crusoe pays in wages to his men, rent to his landlord, and interest to the equipment-lender will depend on how much benefit he derives from each factor and on what alternatives Friday, Saturday, and Hopper have for selling their labor, land, and capital elsewhere.

The net result? Crusoe has a model of the market economy's factor markets on his hands.

3. Supply and Demand

Now let's go back from the island world to the more complex one of a full-blown market economy. The principles remain the same: Factors of production will tend to be rewarded by the price they command in the marketplace—that is, by the supply and demand for those services. Let a service be in high demand and low supply, and the return on that service (wages, rent, or interest) will be high. Let the service be in low demand and in high supply, and the return for the service will drop.

Clearly the demand for any particular factor of production will depend upon the demand for the good or service to be produced with that factor. Take the case of construction workers. Plasterers, painters, and plumbers are in demand if new housing is in demand. So we would expect their earnings to rise during a year when new homes are selling at a brisk rate. Moreover, we would expect earnings to be highest for those men among the construction workers whose services are essential to the final product. Plumbers will probably get more than plasterers because there is no satisfactory substitute for the plumber's services, while the plasterer can be avoided by installing wallboard.

The supply of any factor may either be fixed or flexible. The amount of land available in Manhattan, for example, is fixed. But the supply of labor from women in the economy is flexible; different wage rates will attract different numbers of women into the labor market. Sometimes the supply will adjust slowly to changes in factor prices. For example, if there were a sudden and dramatic increase in the demand for marine biologists, it would take years for the universities to turn out new graduates qualified to fill the jobs.

There are, of course, some significant differences between product markets and factor markets. But, at root, the factor markets, like the product markets, are governed by those old friends: supply and demand.

38 How Labor Markets Work (I)

In the market for labor, buyers of labor (employers) bargain with sellers of labor (workers), and agree on a price for the exchange (wages). So long as the labor markets work freely and with both sides well informed, we would expect that the greater the supply or the smaller the demand for any one type of labor, the lower the wage rate will be.

Clearly, one factor that makes for differences in wage rates is that not all workers are perfect substitutes for one another. Thus, there are thousands of distinct labor markets. Everyone, for example, cannot compete in the market for professional baseball players or opera singers. Only those who have acquired long and costly training can compete in the market for lawyers or nuclear physicists. When entrance into a particular market is severely restricted, while demand in that market is high, wages will tend to be very high. On the other hand, where entry into a market requires only a minimum of physical strength and intelligence (for instance, the services of messengers), wages will tend to be low. These differences, then, grow out of inequalities in the abilities and training of the workers themselves.

But wide differences in wage rates may prevail even between workers with similar ability and training. All the jobs open to men of a particular skill level have certain advantages and disadvantages. In a freely competitive market, the wage rate operates so that all the jobs turn out to be about equally attractive when the earnings are taken into account. Such wage differences, then, grow out of differences in the job themselves, not in the workers.

These two sets of factors, explaining wage differences through (1) differences between workers and (2) differences between jobs, were well stated and combined into a single list in 1776 by Adam Smith. Don't expect to understand every phrase in the reading, for Smith's language is old-fashioned. But he stated his main ideas clearly, and you should be able to follow them. As you read, keep the following questions in mind:

1. Who decides whether occupations are unpleasant or honorable? In which cases might Smith have chosen different examples were he writing today, instead of in the 1770's?
2. Which of Smith's five points applies to the wages of a musician? a schoolteacher? a sailor? a private in the army? an electrician? a clergyman?
3. What role do values play in setting wage differences? Give examples.

1. Of Wages in Different Employments of Labour

ADAM SMITH

From The Wealth of Nations, *Book I, Chapter 10. First published London, 1776.*

The five following are the principal circumstances which, so far as I have been able to observe, make . . . for a small pecuniary [monetary] gain in some employments, and . . . a great one in others. . . .

First, The wages of labour vary with the ease or hardship, the cleanliness or dirtiness, the honourableness or dishonourableness of the employment. Thus in most places, take the year round, a journeyman taylor earns less than a journeyman weaver. His work is much easier. A journeyman weaver earns less than a journeyman smith. His work is not always easier, but it is much cleanlier. A journeyman blacksmith, though an artificer, seldom earns so much in twelve hours as a collier [coal miner], who is only a labourer, does in eight. His work is not quite so dirty, is less dangerous, and is carried on in daylight, and above ground. Honour makes a great part of the reward of all honourable professions. In point of pecuniary gain, all things considered, they are generally under-[paid].... Disgrace has the contrary effect.... The most detestable of all employments, that of public executioner, is, in proportion to the quantity of work done, better paid than any common trade whatever....

Secondly, The wages of labour vary with the easiness and cheapness, or the difficulty and expense of learning the business....

The difference between the wages of skilled labour and those of common labour, is founded upon this principle....

The laws and customs of Europe, ... in order to qualify any person for exercising [skilled] labour, impose the necessity of an apprenticeship.... They leave [common labour] open to everybody. During the ... apprenticeship, the whole labour of the apprentice belongs to his master. In the meantime he must, in many cases, be maintained by his parents or relations, and in almost all cases must be cloathed by them. Some money too is commonly given to the master for teaching him his trade.... It is reasonable, therefore, that in Europe the wages of mechanics, artificers, and manufacturers should be somewhat higher than those of common labourers....

Education in the ingenious arts and in the liberal professions, is still more tedious and expensive. The [wages], therefore, of painters and sculptors, of lawyers and physicians, ought to be much more liberal: and it is so accordingly....

Thirdly, The wages of labour in different occupations vary with the constancy or inconstancy of employment.

Employment is much more constant in some trades than in others. In the greater part of manufactures, a journeyman may be pretty sure of employment almost every day in the year that he is able to work. A mason or bricklayer, on the contrary, can work neither in hard frost nor in foul weather, and his employment at all other times depends upon the occasional calls of his customers. He is liable, in consequence, to be frequently without any [work]. What he earns, therefore, while he is employed, must not only maintain him while he is idle, but make him some compensation for those anxious and desponding moments which the thought of so precarious a situation must sometimes occasion....

Fourthly, The wages of labour vary according to the small or great trust which must be reposed in the workmen.

The wages of goldsmiths and jewelers are everywhere superior to those of many other workmen, not only of equal, but of much superior ingenuity; on account of the precious materials with which they are entrusted.

We trust our health to the physician; our fortune and sometimes our life and reputation to the lawyer and attorney. Such confidence could not safely be reposed in people of a very mean or low condition. Their reward must be such, therefore, as may give them that rank in the society which so important a trust requires. The long time and the great expense which must be laid out in their education, when combined with this circumstance, necessarily enhance still further the price of their labour. . . .

Fifthly, The wages of labour in different employments vary according to the probability or improbability of success in them.

The probability that any particular person shall ever be qualified for the employment to which he is educated is very different in different occupations. In the greater part of mechanic trades, success is almost certain; but very uncertain in the liberal professions. Put your son apprentice to a shoemaker, there is little doubt of his learning to make a pair of shoes. But send him to study the law, it is at least twenty to one if ever he makes such proficiency as will enable him to live by the business.

2. An Exercise in Explaining Wage Differences

One way to test Adam Smith's analysis is to apply it to some specific wage data. In the table which follows, all the wage rates were in effect on the same date, and were decided by bargaining between employers and the Teamsters union.

Come to class tomorrow prepared to explain the data in terms of Smith's analysis. Does Smith's analysis explain all the reasons for the wage differences?

UNION HOURLY WAGE RATES FOR DRIVERS
JULY 1, 1965

Type of truck	*Wage rate in Boston*
Armored car	$2.77
Bakery (cookie, cracker)	2.66
Beer	3.11
Concrete	2.63
Coal	2.78
Department store parcel	2.73
Meatpacking	2.90
Newspaper (afternoon)	3.38
Oil	2.86
Railway Express	2.91
Refuse disposal	2.83

Source: United States Department of Labor Bulletin No. 1488

39 How Labor Markets Work (II)

Year in and year out, about two thirds of the national income of the United States goes to labor in the form of wages and fringe benefits. ("Labor" here means the human contributions made to the economy by everyone from street-sweeper to President.)

The distribution of that two-thirds share, however, changes over time, as some workers fare well and others fare badly. The prices of different types of labor change for reasons similar to those that cause prices of goods in the market to change. A rise in the demand for bricklayers has the same effect as a rise in the demand for bread: In both cases, prices go up. A rise in the supply of unskilled laborers will, in the absence of new demand for their services or of market restrictions, send the price down just as surely as a new flow of potatoes into a market will make potatoes cheaper.

Sometimes workers have objected to such a cold-blooded description of the market for their services, protesting that "labor is not a commodity." That point may deserve a debate on moral or value grounds. But it does not change the facts that labor is now exchanged in markets (the worker sells his services, and the employer buys them), that there are prices attached to those transactions, and that those prices respond to changing conditions.

Today's reading is designed to help show how labor markets work. If labor markets are to respond sensitively to changes in supply and demand, the worker must know what jobs are available, what conditions apply to those jobs, and how he can go about getting one of those jobs.

Following is a transcription of a recorded interview with a young unemployed New Hampshire rolling-machine operator. It was part of a detailed survey of the effects of a plant shutdown in the town to see what workers knew about labor markets and how they used their knowledge in seeking a new job.

As you read, keep these questions in mind:

1. What is Raymond's picture of the labor market? Where does his information come from?
2. What factors other than demand for labor affect Raymond's quest for a new job? How might these factors change the market conditions?
3. If all of Raymond's fellow unemployed mill workers responded as he did, how would wages in the New Hampshire town be affected? How might wages in Boston be affected?

The Job Hunt: An Interview

CHARLES A. MYERS and GEORGE P. SHULTZ

INTERVIEWER: These questions are mostly about what you have been doing since leaving the mill. . . .
RAYMOND: You know I'm not working. . . . I was laid off from (name of company) after working there a week, so I had to find another job.
INTERVIEWER: That is where you worked after leaving the mill, I take it. . . .
WIFE: Yeah, he was working there and the man that owned the cement-laying business died and that left Raymond without a job. . . .
RAYMOND: That's the way it happened. You see, the last days that I was at the mill I began thinking. Here I was, a man with a family to support. I've three kids, my wife, and my mother. None of them can work, so it's up to me. . . . I knew I didn't have any chance of keeping my job in the mill as rolling-machine operator because there were people that had been with the company much longer than I had been. . . . I knew this man that owned this small place . . . so I asked him for a job and then quit my job at the mill when he said that I could go to work with him. You see, he knew that I knew how to do the work.
INTERVIEWER: How do you mean he knew that you knew how to do the work?
RAYMOND: Well once before I worked for a contractor and this here fellow knew that I was pretty good at making cement. . . . He knew I'd worked for this Boston contractor. . . . I imagine I could still be working with the Boston contractor now, only he wanted me to go out of the state and I couldn't do that.
INTERVIEWER: You felt that you couldn't go out of the state to work with his company.
RAYMOND: Of course, I wouldn't think of leaving my family and going out of this city to work with him or anyone else. . . . If some company would offer me a job with a place to live with my family then I might move, but I think that companies that are likely to do that are few and far between, for they could get single men that didn't have no families to work for them.
INTERVIEWER: So before you'd work outside of (name of city), you'd have to have a place for your family.
RAYMOND: Yes, that and some good wages, too.
INTERVIEWER: Good wages? . . .
RAYMOND: The job I had at the mill paid $1.01 an hour, and I thought that was pretty fair for what I was doing. The $.80 an hour that I got at (name of company) was O.K. too, but that's different. I wasn't as satisfied with that, for that's a big come-down from what I was making at the mill. But that was a job and it was paying something and more than what I would have gotten had I not worked at all, or have gotten from Unemployment Compensation.
INTERVIEWER: Then you didn't use any State Employment Service after leaving the mill.
RAYMOND: No, I didn't even go there to find out if I could use it or

could get benefits. Many of my friends went there some time or other and they never got anything out of them down there. And so I thought what's the use? They probably have lots of people looking to them for jobs... whereas if I go looking for a job myself, I've only myself to worry about.

INTERVIEWER: So you have never used the State Employment office.

RAYMOND: No, and you haven't either, have you, Honey?

WIFE: No, they don't have any good jobs there, and it's too hard to get any money out of those birds. You see, Mrs. Hunter, it's this way. Those people down there have jobs so they don't really worry too much about those without 'em. Now if they were out of work for a while and really knew how hard it was to find a job, they'd get busy and really work to help the rest of us that don't have too many drags around town.

RAYMOND: That's the reason we haven't been down there. They really don't know how hard it is for us to find a job and they're always pushing you aside or trying to give you a job that doesn't pay enough to feed yourself, much less a family. I know, for my friends that have been there tell me all this....

I don't care now how far or how dirty the job is, what I need is a job so I can keep the family fed. We can't live forever on potatoes and the few things Mom canned this summer. Then too, when I think it over now, I imagine that there are more like myself who are out of jobs because of the mill closing down....

INTERVIEWER: Raymond, you said that you had been to other places to get a job. Did you know anything about the job or the plants before you inquired?

RAYMOND: No, I still don't know too much about the company.... None of my friends that used to work in the mill ever worked at any other place and so I don't know nothing about these other places....

INTERVIEWER: Now about (name of city), you say you've been to several industries, but can you tell me the picture as you see it for the whole town? Are there many jobs available?

RAYMOND: I don't know of any that I could do. I suppose there must be some for somebody, but none that I know of.

40 The Impact of Labor Unions (I)

Until the 1940's, labor unions were not a thoroughly accepted part of American life. Well into the twentieth century, millions of Americans agreed with Adam Smith that individual workers should make their own contracts with their employers. Labor unions, on the other hand, claimed the right of collective bargaining. They said that workers should be permitted to band together and negotiate as a group. Only in that way could workers get a fair deal from large and powerful companies.

This reading, through documentary excerpts and commentary, traces the rise of labor unions as an economic force. It is far from a complete history of American unions. Rather, it touches on some of the shifting attitudes toward unions.

As you read, keep the following questions in mind:

1. What place do unions have in a free market society? Do they make the United States more or less of a free market society?
2. Why do you think it was difficult to organize automobile and steel factories into craft unions?
3. How do unions go about trying to influence distribution?

The Emergence of Labor as an Economic Force

As long as factories remained small, unions remained weak. Before the Industrial Revolution, most employees worked alongside their bosses at skilled crafts. But the Industrial Revolution, by expanding factories and increasing job specialization, made the skilled craftsman less important. Many felt lost in the bigness of the new factories. And workers came to feel that they were being paid only for their time, not their talent. In the following excerpt, a young machinist answered a United States senator's questions in 1883:

From the testimony of John Morrison, August 28, 1883. U.S. Congress, Senate, Report of the Committee of the Senate upon the Relations between Labor and Capital *(Washington, D.C., 1885).*

Question: Is there any difference between the conditions under which machinery is made now and those which existed ten years ago?

Answer: A great deal of difference. . . . [T]he trade has been subdivided and those subdivisions have been again subdivided, so that a man never learns the machinist's trade now. . . . [O]ne man may make just a particular part of a machine and may not know anything whatever about another part of the same machine. In that way machinery is produced a great deal cheaper. . . . [But t]he man thinks of nothing else but that particular branch: He knows that he cannot leave that particular branch and go to any other; he has got no chance whatever to learn anything else because he is kept steadily and constantly at that particular thing. . . .

Question: And does he not finally acquire so much skill in the manipulation of his particular part of the business that he does it without any mental effort?

Answer: Almost. In fact he becomes almost a part of the machinery.

★ ★ ★

From the discontent of men like the machinist came the desire for unions. The first unions to gain lasting success were the craft unions that formed the American Federation of Labor in 1886. The craft unions were made up of those who worked in a particular craft. All plumbers, for example, could join the plumber's union. The AF of L, led by Samuel Gompers, tied the craft unions together into a loose federation. The AF of L leadership had little desire to organize the great numbers of unskilled workers. And it bitterly opposed socialism and other schemes to change American society. Its goals had been clearly expressed before a congressional hearing in 1883 by Adolph Strasser, one of Gompers' chief lieutenants and president of the cigar-makers union.

From the testimony of Adolph Strasser, President of the Cigar Makers' International Union of America and a founder of the American Federation of Labor, August 21, 1883. U.S. Congress, Senate, Report of the Committee of the Senate upon the Relations between Labor and Capital (*Washington, D.C., 1885*).

Question by Mr. Pugh: You are seeking to improve home matters first?

Answer: Yes, sir. I look first to the trade I represent; I look first to cigars, to the interests of men who employ me to represent their interests.

Question: I was only asking you in regard to your ultimate ends.

Answer: We have no ultimate ends. We are going on from day to day. We are fighting only for immediate objects—objects that can be realized in a few years.

Question by Mr. Call: You want something better to eat and to wear, and better houses to live in?

Answer: Yes; we want to dress better and to live better, and become better off and better citizens generally.

Question: I see that you are a little sensitive lest it should be thought that you are a mere theorizer. I do not look upon you in that light at all.

Answer: Well, we say in our constitution that we are opposed to theorists. . . . We are all practical men.

★ ★ ★

Although the AF of L secured better wages for many skilled craftsmen, millions of unskilled workers were still without a union. Many worked sixty hours a week for miserable wages. Often, when a union was formed, the companies refused to recognize it. That is, they refused to accept the union as the workers' representative. To try to force the companies to recognize them, the United Mine Workers went on strike in 1902. Before the strike was settled by the threats and persuasion of President Theodore Roosevelt, the following article appeared in *The New York Times:*

From The New York Times, *August 21, 1902.*

WILKES-BARRE, PA., Aug. 20.—W. F. Clark, a photographer of this city, recently addressed a letter to President Baer of the Philadelphia and Reading Railroad Company [owner of many coal mines], appealing to him as a Christian to settle the miners' strike. The writer said if Christ was taken more into our business affairs there would be less trouble in the world, and that if Mr. Baer granted the strikers a slight concession they would gladly return to work and the President of the Philadelphia and Reading would have the blessing of God and the respect of the nation.

President Baer replied as follows:

"I see you are evidently biased in your religious views in favor of the right of the working man to control a business in which he has no other interest than to secure fair wages for the work he does. I beg of you not to be discouraged. The rights and interests of the laboring man will be protected and cared for, not by the labor agitators, but by the Christian men to whom God in His infinite wisdom has given the control of the property interests of the country. Pray earnestly that the right may triumph, always remembering that the Lord God Omnipotent still reigns and that His reign is one of law and order, and not of violence and crime."

★ ★ ★

With the men in command of industry sharing much of Baer's philosphy, strikes of unskilled workers were defeated time and again. Sometimes company tactics were rough or underhanded, as the following glossary compiled by a congressional committee in 1938, suggests:

U.S. Congress, Senate, Committee on Education and Labor, Violations of Free Speech and Rights of Labor, *Senate Report 46, Part 3, 75th Cong., 2nd Sess., 1938.*

Fink .... One who makes a career of taking employment in struck plants or of acting as a strikebreaker, strike guard, or slugger.

Hooking .... Entrapping an employee into spying on fellow employees. Usually accomplished by approaching the prospective hooked man under a pretext and engaging him to write reports.

Hooker .... Detective agency official who induces workers to become spies.

Missionary .... A spy whose work it is to spread anti-union or anti-strike propaganda in the general neighborhood of a plant and particularly among the wives of workers. One not employed in the plant.

Operative .... A spy employed by an agency. Usually has a secret designation. [M]ay be a hooked man or professional spy.

Rough shadowing .... To keep a man under surveillance in such a manner that he knows that he is being followed and is intimidated.

Slugger	A specialized type of fink used to attack, assault, and beat up strikers or union leaders. Generally armed.
Strikebreaker	One whose trade it is to take employment in struck plants. Distinguishable from "scab," who is a workman. May pretend to work in the plant or act as a guard. A fink.

★ ★ ★

To succeed against such determined opposition, unskilled workers needed strong organization. In an era of huge mass-production industries such as the steel and auto industries, craft unions had limited effectiveness. Younger members of the AFL therefore proposed that industrial unions be formed. These unions would include all workers in a single industry, instead of all workers who followed a particular craft. When the older leadership of the AFL balked at this plan, some of the AFL's younger members left to form the Congress of Industrial Organizations (CIO) in 1935.

The new CIO was greatly aided by the New Deal government of President Franklin D. Roosevelt. The government enforced the newly passed National Labor Relations Act of 1935, which outlawed the tactics described in the glossary. It also established a board to conduct elections among the workers themselves to decide whether or not they wished to bargain collectively through a union.

Led by the CIO and aided by the government, large numbers of workers in mass-production industries were organized in the 1930's. The following excerpt is from a speech to the AFL convention of 1935 by John L. Lewis, head of the United Mine Workers. It was soon after that convention that Lewis helped to found the CIO.

Report of Proceedings, American Federation of Labor, *Vol. 55, pp. 534–542. Copyright © 1935. Reprinted by permission.*

I served an apprenticeship of five and one-half years as a general organizer for the American Federation of Labor before I became an officer of the United Mine Workers of America. During that period of time I worked in the steel industry, the rubber industry, the glass industry, the lumber industry, the copper industry, and other industries in most of the states of this Union.

Then, as now, the American Federation of Labor offered to the workers in these industries a plan of organization into federal labor unions or local trade unions with the understanding that when organized they would be segregated into the various organizations of their respective crafts. . . .

What is the record? Delegate Howard expressed it when he said that we laid claim to a membership of approximately three and a half million, out of an organizable number of approximately thirty-nine million. . . .

. . . Great combinations of capital have assembled great industrial plants, and they are strung across the borders of our several states from the north to the south and from the east to the west in such a manner that they have assembled to themselves tremendous power and influence, and they are almost 100 per cent effective in opposing organization of the workers under the policies of the American Federation of Labor.

What are we going to do about it? . . .

. . . The strength of a strong man is a prideful thing, but the unfortunate thing in life is that strong men do not remain strong. And that is just as true of unions and labor organizations as it is true of men and individuals. . . .

. . . The enemies of labor in this country will be encouraged and high wassail [revelry] will prevail at the banquet tables of the mighty throughout the country if the American Federation of Labor refuses to grant the petition of these industries that are fighting for the objectives of labor and to defend the rights of mankind.

41 The Impact of Labor Unions (II)

By the end of World War II, labor unions were well established in the United States. The organizing drives tapered off. The unions consolidated their gains by pressing for better wages and fringe benefits. But many workers remained outside of unions. And unions failed to grow as rapidly as the nation's population. As the labor leaders who had led the drives of the 1930's grew older, critics of the labor movement charged unions with stagnation. They lamented the disappearance of the fiery spirit of the 1930's. Even many industrial unions, they charged, were as uninterested in progress as the AFL had been when the CIO was formed.

Today's reading presents some of the current controversies on labor unions in the form of a dialogue between two workers. As you read, think about the following questions:

1. How do you think unions should meet the problem of automation?
2. How much of a duty does a union have to protect its own members?

Solidarity Forever?

(*It's lunch hour at the widget factory, two weeks before the monthly meeting of Local 225 of the Amalgamated Widget Workers of America.* JOHN OLDE *is nearing retirement age.* TOM YOUNG *is twenty-four.*)

JOHN OLDE: Coming to the next meeting, Tom? You're not there very often.
TOM YOUNG: Ah, I come whenever there's anything important.

OLDE: Why, there's always something important in the union. It's our——

YOUNG: Maybe it's all important to you, but to me, most of it's for the birds. We pay our dues—let the officers run a good union, and leave the rest of us alone.

OLDE: That's no way to talk. If it weren't for all of us supporting the union, we wouldn't have any power at all. The company'd walk right over us—just like they did in the '30's.

YOUNG: The '30's! That's all you guys think about. Look, it's the '60's now. Almost the '70's. (*Pause*) I'm sorry, Pop, I didn't mean to hurt you. It's just that—well, I like the union and all that, but I don't think we'll live or die because of it. Times have changed.

OLDE: Yes, I suppose they have. But I'm never that sure. Maybe some of us do live in the past, but we know what it was like before the plant was organized. In those days we didn't go to union meetings because we were scared to, not because we were bored by the union.

YOUNG: I didn't say I was bored. But the union's not going to collapse just because I don't show up at the meeting every month. And besides, we've got laws to protect the union and to give us Social Security, and——

OLDE: But Tom, that's just the point. We have those laws because the union stood up and howled for them. And we've got living wages now because we all stuck together.

YOUNG: I think you're kidding yourself about the past, Pop. You guys used to bicker plenty among yourselves, even back in the golden '30's. That's the thing about unions. They never really stick together for very long. The only time we get together is when something threatens all of us. But the companies haven't exactly tried to break up our union lately.

OLDE: But there still is something that's threatening all of us, Tom. Those longhairs in the research department have come up with an automated widget machine that can take the place of twenty workers. I'm retiring soon anyhow, but you guys will have to fight the machine to keep your jobs.

YOUNG: Yes, but what's the union doing about it? All the leaders can think of is "Don't bring the machines in, or we strike."

OLDE: Strikes worked in the old days. Without strikes, we wouldn't even have a union. So why not now?

YOUNG: Because the last time we went out on strike, we weren't out ten days before the President called our leaders and the company men to the White House and sweet-talked them. Only our leaders got sweet-talked more. And what did we end up with? Fifteen cents an hour higher pay, but five hundred fewer jobs. The machines are here to stay. And if this union's ever going to do me any good, it had better think up a way out of this mess. Fifteen cents an hour doesn't mean a thing if I lose my job in two years.

OLDE: Then come to our meetings, and speak up.

YOUNG: I tried that once, Pop. And you know what happened? No one listened. You older men have your jobs. If anybody gets bounced it's going to be younger guys without seniority.

OLDE: I don't understand that thinking, Tom. I know I'm getting old, but I didn't used to hear people talking that way about the union. It was "we" and "our" and "solidarity." Now it's all "me." We used to stick together, but now you younger fellows just don't seem to care.

YOUNG: Look, that solidarity stuff may have helped you. You'll get your union pension soon and you can go off to Florida and sit in the sun with your old lady. But I've got to think about me. I've got two kids and a life ahead of me, and all the union has to give me is an extra fifteen cents an hour. And in a few years, when those machines get going, it will probably be "Good-bye, Charlie."

OLDE: Well, what can you expect? When the Model T came along, three carriage-makers in my home town went out of business. That's just progress.

YOUNG: I know it's progress, and I know you can't fight the machines. But how about a little progress in this union? If machines are going to be making widgets, I'm going to need some other skill. And the union should be out there training me instead of waiting for the government to come along.

OLDE: But what would happen to the union? If we don't make a stand against the machines, soon there will only be office workers left, and there won't be any union.

YOUNG: All you can think about is the union. If it comes to that, I'd rather be one of those office workers than sit around feather-bedding or living off relief.

OLDE: You youngsters sure have a selfish streak. Your father and I worked alongside each other for thirty years, Tom. And he fought for the union. And one of the reasons he fought for the union was to make sure you'd have a job. Do you really think you'd have been hired as an apprentice if your father hadn't recommended you?

YOUNG: O.K., so Dad's done a lot for me, and I'm grateful to him. But I remember a colored fellow back in high school. He was a top student and on the football team, and he couldn't get an apprenticeship in this union. And don't tell me you don't know why he couldn't.

OLDE: But Tom, we've got to protect our own. I agree that Negroes should get a better deal, but should we take in an outsider rather than the son of one of our own members?

YOUNG: You're talking like this is a ritzy country club, and the next minute you'll be saying this union is democratic. I've got pride in myself. And if I can only get a job because somebody else isn't getting a fair shake, then I don't want that job. And all our leaders do about discrimination is to make speeches. They've got to wake up. The Civil War is over.

OLDE: It's no use arguing with you, Tom. All I can say is that if you care that much about our union, come to the next meeting—and bring some of your pals. If you fellows want to change things, you'll have to stick up for what you believe.

YOUNG: Uh, the meeting's the twenty-seventh, isn't it?

OLDE: Yeah.

YOUNG: Gee, I've got tickets to the ball game that night. But I'll make it there the time after that, Pop. I really will.

42 The Role of Profits

No aspect of the American distribution process is subject to more emotion, error, and myth than the share going to profits. The myths begin with what part of the sales dollar goes to profits. In recent years, the nation's largest corporations have had average profits of about 5 per cent on their sales dollars. Yet, when thousands of high school students across the country were asked a few years ago what the average profit was in business, their estimates broke down in this way:

Estimates of profits	*% of students*
Less than 3%	4
3% to 6%	13
7% to 10%	17
11% to 15%	12
16% to 25%	18
Over 25%	12
No opinion	24

A poll of the students' parents might well have shown the same—or greater—exaggeration.

Perhaps myths and emotions alike may be traced to the fact that profits are often defined as the share of the sales dollar left over after all of the other factors of production have been paid—that is, after all labor costs, materials charges, utility bills, interest charges, and taxes (except profit taxes) have been paid. Because the profits share comes last in this process, one can slip into the habit of thinking of it as being both the least essential, and—if you think of the other payments as being small in total—the biggest in bulk.

But in fact, no share of the sales dollar is made more or less important by its place in the pay-out process. Returns to each of the productive factors—labor, land, and capital (including the funds loaned by investors to keep the business operating and growing)—are essential if all the factors are to work together. It is true that some firms occasionally do make very large unexpected profits; but that happens rarely. More often it is probably true that if all the profits of a firm were divided among all the workers in that firm or among all the customers of that firm, neither workers nor customers would gain much in the process. And those who had invested in the firm in the hope of earning dividends would have every incentive to pull their money out at once.

Profits fulfill a number of roles in a market society:

1. They attract the funds necessary for establishing and operating a business.
2. They act as signals to encourage investment where consumer demand is large, and to discourage it where demand is small.
3. They serve as a measure of how well individual firms and their managers are performing.
4. They encourage men to experiment with new products and with new approaches to producing old products.
5. They provide existing firms with funds for expansion and research.

That profits fulfill important roles does not mean, however, that every profit dollar, no matter how it was made, is economically justified. Nothing in that list justifies the profit dollar made illegally, or through monopoly power, or through exploitation of any other factor of production. But taken together, the points do add up to a strong case for profits as both rewards and signals in a market economy.

In the reading which follows, the president of the Aluminum Company of America (ALCOA) makes a case for deeper understanding of the profit motive. As you read, keep these questions in mind:

1. Why do you think Mr. Harper felt it necessary to try to explain the role of profits?
2. Which of the several roles of profits does Mr. Harper seem to emphasize in this speech?

The Case for Profits

JOHN HARPER

From a speech delivered May 23, 1963. Reprinted with permission of the Aluminum Company of America.

Despite apparent prosperity, the climate for economic growth in our country—and for free enterprise itself—has been showing signs of potential trouble for some time. This situation cannot go on for long if we wish to have adequate growth, high productivity, and enough jobs for a growing work force.

At the root of the problem, in my judgment, is our widespread failure to understand the nature of our economic system. I am particularly concerned about our repeated failure to [use] the power of profit incentive to [encourage] productive effort, investment, and innovation. While not a cure-all, this incentive is the key to economic growth. Through its ability to stimulate human effort, we have achieved a more abundant way of life for a greater number of people than was even dreamed of a century ago. If we want to maintain and increase our high standard of living—both in the material and cultural sense—it is essential that the importance of the profit incentive be reaffirmed and encouraged by all sectors of the economy—by individuals as well as by government.

Yet, today many of us look with suspicion on the profit motive, and—for no apparent reason—are either nibbling away at it or seem to want to do away with it entirely. Can it be that the individual effort, initiative, and discipline—which are still fundamental to our personal security now and in the future—are losing their place in our lives as we come to rely more and more on the government? Are we so comfortable and well fed that we are becoming "fat" and complacent? . . .

That profits are the key to future prosperity and fuller employment is apparent from our experience during the past five years [1958–63]. Consumers have been spending at record rates each year, and so have our national, state, and local governments. Economic growth, however, has remained sluggish, with unemployment at uncomfortably high levels. The one factor that has not increased sufficiently is gross private domestic investment, which represents, primarily, capital outlays by businessmen.

But for business investment to increase, there must be an adequate incentive to invest. . . . Yet, profits now provide a rate of return on invested capital which is only slightly above what an investor can earn on an insured, risk-free savings account and which is actually below the return on the tax-exempt security. . . .

Profit incentive is the spark plug that generates economic activity through the expectation of a return—or profit—[proportionate to] the risks involved. It is the only workable alternative to a society based on fear and compulsion. But it is more than an alternative. It not only provides a voluntary way of motivating people to take action—to take worthwhile business risks—but it also [encourages] a high level of efficiency and innovation in order to maximize the profit potential. When allowed to function properly, it also automatically provides employment for a growing work force. Today's profit provides the means—and the only lasting means—of creating new jobs; the expectation of future profit provides the incentive to do so by stimulating the required new investment.

43 The Rich and the Poor in the United States

In a free market society the *for whom* question is answered mainly by the distribution of personal income. If you earn $10,000 a year, you can buy that amount of goods and services. You will also, of course, be able to use the services provided by the government—such as public schools and highways—and you will be defended by the government-supported armed forces. This reading considers the way in which wealth is distributed in the United States. It is based upon statistics gathered by the U.S. Bureau of the Census.

Statistics cannot tell us much about the quality of life of the rich and the poor in the United States. That job is better done by novelists and reporters. But statistics can present an outline of distribution, showing how individual families fit into the general picture. As you study the following tables, keep these questions in mind:

1. The United States is often called "a middle-class society." Do the statistics support or refute that notion? How?
2. Which statistics seem to be the result of the interplay of free market forces? Which ones seem to reflect modifications of the free market?

Who Gets What

All statistics in this reading are from Herman P. Miller, Rich Man, Poor Man *(New York: Crowell, 1964). Mr. Miller is a Special Assistant in the U.S. Bureau of the Census.*

1. The Incomes of American Families

Annual family income level	*Number of families at this level in 1959*	*% of families at this level*	*% of nation's income received by families at this level*
Under $2,000	6 million	13%	2%
Between $2,000 and $4,000	8 million	18	8
Between $4,000 and $6,000	11 million	23	18
Between $6,000 and $8,000	9 million	19	20
Between $8,000 and $10,000	5 million	12	15
Between $10,000 and $15,000	5 million	11	19
Between $15,000 and $25,000	1½ million	3	10
$25,000 and over	½ million	1	8

2. Changes in Distribution

Family income level (measured in 1962 dollars)	*% of families at this level*		
	1929	*1947*	*1962*
Under $3,000	51%	30%	21%
Between $3,000 and $6,000	34	40	31
Between $6,000 and $8,000	7	14	18
Between $8,000 and $10,000	3	7	11
$10,000 and over	5	9	19

How does this table help explain the growth of suburbia?

3. Which Families Are Poorest?

Characteristic of family head	*Number of families in poorest 20% of all American families (1959)*
Farmers	1.6 million
Aged	2.6 million
Family headed by female	1.6 million
Non-white (mostly Negro)	1.0 million
All others	3.0 million

Note: All poor farmers are classified under "farmers." Thus, a farming family headed by an elderly Negro woman would be classified under "farmers." All elderly people who are not *farmers are classified under "aged." All families headed by a female who is neither a farmer nor elderly are classified under "family headed by female." Because of this, all Negro poor families are not classified under "non-white." "All Others" includes many Spanish-speaking Americans.*

Why are so many poor people elderly?
Why are so many poor people farmers?

4. Which Families Are Richest?

Occupation of family head	*% of family heads holding this occupation in the richest 5% of all American families* 1950	1960
Self-employed		
Professionals	11%	11%
Farmers	8	2
Owners of unincorporated businesses	23	13
Salaried		
Professionals	10	18
Managers	18	30
White collar	30	26

Why did the percentage of rich owners of businesses slip between 1950 and 1960?

Why has the percentage of professionals working for a salary risen between 1950 and 1960?

How is the growth of industrial research and development programs reflected in this table?

What happened to the farmers? Why?

5. Education and Lifetime Earnings

Highest grade completed	*Lifetime earnings (from ages 18 to 64) for men*
Elementary school	
Less than 8 years	$143,000
8 years	184,000
High school	
1 to 3 years	212,000
4 years	247,000
College	
1 to 3 years	293,000
4 years or more	417,000
4 years	385,000
5 years or more	455,000
Average for all education groups	229,000

According to the Horatio Alger myth, ingrained in American folklore, anyone with "stick-to-it-iveness" and the desire to succeed can become rich. What does this table say about that myth? Does it prove that myth definitely false?

6. Does High School Matter for Craftsmen and Operators?

Occupation	*Average incomes (1960)* *Elementary or junior high school graduates*	*High school graduates*
Bricklayer	$5,100	$6,300
Carpenter	4,800	5,700
Mechanic	5,000	5,900
Plumber	5,700	6,700
Bus driver	4,400	5,400
Toolmaker	6,700	7,300
Electrician	6,100	6,600
Painter	4,400	5,100
Truck driver	5,200	5,700
Fireman	5,300	6,100

Note: The above figures are for white men aged 35 to 44. The figures are based on the 1960 census report.

Why do you suppose that craftsmen and operators with more education get better jobs?

7. Income of White and Negro Men in Selected Occupations (*1960*)

Occupation	*Number of Negro workers*	*% of occupation that is Negro*	*Median earnings* *	
			White	*Negro*
Men employed	3,644,000	8.4%	$4,855	$2,703
Engineers	4,000	0.5	7,452	7,076
Medical and other health workers	12,000	3.4	7,953	4,642
Schoolteachers	28,000	6.8	5,701	4,450
Farmers and farm managers	154,000	6.5	2,324	788
Farm laborers	257,000	21.4	1,256	816
Managers, officials, and proprietors	63,000	1.4	6,719	3,869
Mail carriers	20,000	10.4	5,309	5,101
Sales workers	47,000	1.6	5,036	2,809
Construction craftsmen	120,000	5.5	4,839	2,855
Foremen	16,000	1.5	6,651	4,791
Mechanics and repairmen	117,000	5.3	4,798	3,478
Trucking	248,000	12.7	4,539	2,638
Laundry and dry cleaning	36,000	33.3	3,253	2,600
Durable goods manufacturing	147,000	9.8	4,695	3,749
Nondurable goods manufacturing	114,000	9.1	4,465	3,272
Janitors	265,000	37.2	2,833	2,543
Police and firemen	25,000	3.8	4,932	4,276
Waiters, cooks, and bartenders	81,000	15.8	3,267	2,759
Nonfarm laborers	745,000	24.9	3,210	2,394

* *To find the* median *earnings, you arrange all the individual earnings along a scale or spectrum, and find the middle figure. In other words, if the earnings of five men are $10,000, $7,000, $5,000, $2,000 and $1,500, then the median is $5,000 because there is an equal number of people with higher and lower earnings. The average income for those five men, on the other hand, would be $5,100—their total incomes divided by five.*

Name several possible causes for the differences in earnings between whites and Negroes.

Why are the differences relatively small for mail carriers, police, and firemen?

What figures help explain the continuing migration of Negroes from farms to cities?

8. Regional Differences in Incomes (*1959*)
(for selected states with 100,000 or more Negroes)

State	*Average incomes*		*Negroes' income as % of whites'*
	White	*Negro*	
United States (overall)	$4,337	$2,254	52%
Northeast			
Massachusetts	4,452	3,063	69
New Jersey	5,172	3,375	65
New York	4,812	3,372	70
Pennsylvania	4,369	3,246	74
North Central			
Illinois	5,056	3,651	72
Michigan	4,983	3,768	76
Ohio	4,903	3,492	71
South			
Kentucky	2,938	1,787	61
Mississippi	2,796	904	32
Texas	3,756	1,916	51
Virginia	3,758	1,907	51
West			
California	5,109	3,553	70

How does this table help explain the continuing migration of Negroes from the South?

44 Summary: Distribution in the United States

We have seen that in the United States, the *for whom* question is answered mainly in the marketplace. Those who sell their productive services—their labor or the use of their land or capital—for the highest prices get the most money with which to bid for the available goods and services produced by others.

Today's lesson, completing this unit, fills out the picture of distribution. While we rely heavily on the free market to determine who gets what, we have shown ourselves unwilling to rely solely on this market. More and more, the government has tried to soften some of the harshest effects of the free market. To do so, it has tried to distribute some of the economy's goods and services on a basis other than pure market competition. But it must be remembered that many governmental actions which affect the distribution of income have other purposes as well: The government has also been trying to keep employment high, prices stable, growth rapid, and institutions free. As you read keep the following questions in mind:

1. How does a minimum wage interfere with the free market?
2. How do labor unions affect the distribution of income?
3. Do you think income should be distributed more fairly in the United States? If so, how might this best be done?

Modifying the Market Mechanisms

"It may be efficient, but it's harsh and cruel." Such a judgment has often been voiced by critics of the market economy. The firmest evidence for that judgment came from some of the abuses of the past: the long, hard hours worked by women and young children in factories and mines; the "work or starve" sermons from pulpit and press; and the use of governmental force to defeat early attempts to form unions.

In reply, there are two separate arguments offered by those who defend market economies on grounds of their humaneness as well as their efficiency. First is the broad argument that market economies, far from making the lot of the average man worse and worse (as Karl Marx had predicted), have done just the opposite. The standard of living for most Americans, for example, has risen to heights that the rest of the world often finds dizzying.

But that broad argument is not enough. It still leaves the possibility that, while most people might benefit from a market economy, a few could still suffer so much that their burdens would be intolerable for any society that claims to be humane. Here the second argument enters: The market economies, such as that of the United States, have modified market mechanisms in order to redistribute goods and services in the direction of their poorest citizens. That those efforts have not wholly succeeded is only too obvious to anyone who visits the urban or rural slums in the United States. But modifications have been made, and they demand an examination so that we can see their contributions and their limitations alike.

Five devices which redistribute income toward the poor are worth particular note—and each device turns out to have its own problems built into it.

1. The direct welfare system: The oldest approach to giving the poor more of a society's goods than their labor alone could purchase for them is through direct gifts, in the form of cash or goods. In the United States, most of such aid is made through the federally assisted but state-administered programs of aid to mothers with dependent children—fatherless families. This program distributes food or money on the basis of need.

And its cost in dollars, especially in the largest cities, is still growing rapidly. Few people criticize the idea of direct welfare for those who cannot support themselves. But the present welfare system of direct aid has run into choruses of protest from several different directions.

The problems: Some complain that the welfare system is too loose and too generous. They point to the rising costs, and to the seeming inability —or even unwillingness—of some welfare recipients to become independent. But these critics are matched by others who come at the problem from another point of view. These people argue that the payments are stingy and that the investigations into poor people's eligibility for welfare is degrading to those who, through no fault of their own, cannot support themselves or their families.

2. *The public education system:* In a society where a good education is ever more important for getting high-paying jobs, public education is itself an indirect way of redistributing income. In theory, public education offers every child the chance to graduate at least from high school, at governmental expense. Most states go further and provide college education at state universities or colleges either free or for slight fees. And few Americans would deny that our system of free education for all has benefited the nation.

The problems: Yet the educational opportunities have been far from equal. Often children in wealthy communities have the added advantage of the best public schools in the area. Slum children often have received a second-rate education at best, and this early handicap has sometimes led them into poor-paying jobs or no jobs at all. Even for wealthy communities, the constantly rising costs of education are a problem. How much longer will American communities be able to provide the quality of schooling they want for their children?

3. *The income tax system:* Two features of American income taxes are worthy of special note. One is the steepness of the federal tax rates, which go as high as 70 per cent extra on income over $100,000 for single taxpayers. The second is that, unlike taxpayers in some countries, nearly all Americans do pay their taxes, with or without grumbling. The income tax indirectly redistributes incomes because the rates become higher as incomes rise. Thus wealthier Americans pay bigger *percentages* of their income in taxes as well as paying bigger *absolute* amounts. (How does this differ from sales taxes?) At the same time, many governmental services supported by taxes are provided to all citizens, whether their tax bills are big or small.

The problems: Tax laws are extremely complicated; and they include a certain number of loopholes. By taking advantage of those loopholes, few millionaires, for example, pay anywhere near 70 per cent of their extra incomes in taxes. And it is not yet clear that the poorest Americans, who pay small taxes, receive very much in the way of governmental services either. Some poor Americans seem almost to live outside of the organized society. Finally, progressive income taxes raise a puzzling question: How high can taxes be before you sap people's incentive to work hard and to earn more money?

4. *Minimum wages:* One popular device to modify the free market in order to help the lowest paid has been the minimum wage. Federal, state, and local laws have been passed saying that no employer may pay less than a certain minimum hourly rate (currently $1.60 under federal law) to his employees.

The problems: Minimum wages raise the possibility that employers will reduce the number of jobs rather than pay some of their least productive employees as much as the minimum wage. If this indeed happens, the minimum wage law would help those who kept their jobs, but would bring new hardships to those the employer dismisses. And even for those who keep their jobs, the minimum wage often fails to keep pace with the rising cost of living. In that case, the minimum wage would scarcely ensure an adequate standard of living.

5. *Social Security:* As a final example, the United States has modified the market mechanisms to ensure that retired workers have some income. Under the Social Security system, most workers and their employers contribute to the Social Security Administration, which in turn agrees to give each contributing worker a stated sum each month he or she lives after the age of 65 (62 for women). Unlike public welfare, Social Security benefits are considered to go to the aged worker as a matter of right, not of charity.

The problems: The main dispute in recent years has been over the adequacy of Social Security payment levels. If an elderly couple had no other income, their Social Security payments would leave them poor. Some critics also remind us that the system is of no help to some of those who need it most: the rural poor and the urban unemployed who have not qualified for the program.

In sum, all of these experiments combined have not been so successful as to eliminate poverty from the midst of the wealthiest society in the world. The continuing effort to do something about poverty promises to stay on the front pages for years to come.

In the search for ways to modify the distribution of goods and services, our society has aimed at two goals: We have been trying to preserve the incentives built into the market system; and we have also been trying to remove the harshest effects of reliance on those incentives. In a word, we have been trying to build a fair system of distribution. And, because a society's definition of "fair" is rarely static, our distribution system will probably change in the future as much as it has in the past.

Chapter 10

Distribution in the Modified Command Economy

STATING THE ISSUE Karl Marx long ago described the ideal distribution system as one which was based on pure cooperation. Every citizen was to work his hardest at the job he could do best—not for personal reward, but for the good of his fellow men. And the people would share the goods and services they produced by their common efforts as they needed those goods and services. Thus, a family of eight would presumably receive several times the income of a childless couple.

As we shall see in Chapter 10, the Soviet Union is still far from Marx's ideal distribution system. In trying to achieve the ideal Communist distribution system, the Soviet Union has encountered no greater problem than that of *incentive*. According to the dictionary, *incentive* means something that moves or motivates people to actions. In the market economies, the chief incentive has been profit; work harder or better, and you stand a good chance of making more money. Marx, however, believed that the profit incentive was based on greed and selfishness. In the Communist society, he declared, selfishness would vanish.

Selfishness, however, has not vanished in the Soviet Union. In fact, the Soviet leaders, in their quest for rapid growth, have often turned to the profit incentive as a way of persuading men to work harder. At the same time, the centralized controls of the command economy have sought to keep incomes from becoming too high.

So again, we find a tension—this time between the desire for a rapidly growing economy, and the desire for a purely Communist economy. Chapter 10 examines the results of this tension, and the problems and prospects of the Soviet distribution system in the second half of the twentieth century. It deals with these main questions: To what extent is the Soviet distribution system governed by command and Communist theory? To what extent is it governed by the marketplace? How does the Soviet Union answer the *for whom* question?

45 The Stated Aims of the Command Economy

One of Karl Marx's most quoted slogans is, "From each according to his ability, to each according to his needs." In that one sentence is the kernel of the distribution system for an entire economy, for it says:

How shall workers be allocated to the various jobs that need to be done in the economy? Let each man do what he is best able to do.

How shall the economy's production be divided among those who helped to produce it? Let each man have what he needs.

Today's reading looks at how Marx's slogan has been both used and modified by the Soviet Union. As you read, keep the following questions in mind:

1. Why do you suppose the Soviet Constitution of 1936 modified Marx's slogan?
2. Has the failure of Marx's slogan been due solely to selfishness?
3. How do the guidelines set forth in the Soviet economics textbook of the late 1950's differ from the guidelines set forth by Adam Smith?

Marx and the Soviet Union: Ideals and Realities

Many Americans assume that Marx must have spelled out his system of the distribution more fully than he did in the single sentence, "From each according to his ability, to each according to his needs." But the full paragraph from which that sentence is drawn sheds scarcely any more light on how fair distribution is to take place:

> In a higher phase of Communist society, after the enslaving subordination of individuals under division of labor, and thereby also the distinction between mental and physical labor, has vanished; after labor has become not merely a means to live but is in itself the first necessity of life; after the productive forces have also increased with the all-round development of the individual and all the springs of cooperative wealth are gushing more freely—then and only then can the narrow horizon of bourgeois rights be fully left behind and society inscribe on its banner: *"From each according to his ability, to each according to his needs!"*

Plainly, Marx was vague on just how and when the Communist vision of fair distribution was to be achieved. A man can make what he will of those words of Marx—and many a follower of Marx has made them mean what he wanted them to mean.

But certainly when we compare Marx's ideas about distribution with the distribution of market societies, it becomes clear that the two differ sharply over what persuades a man to work hard and well. The market society assumes that man should be rewarded according to his efforts: Let him work hard at those tasks which society values, and he will receive proportionate wages in return. The Marxist view assumes that man, in a Communist world, will *want* to work for the well-being of all: He will put forth his best effort not for greater material rewards than flow to others, but simply for the same share as anyone else whose needs are like his own.

Except for a monastery or a Polynesian island here or there, we know of no societies where men have achieved the Marxist ideal of selfless effort on behalf of all and equal sharing of all material goods. Certainly the Soviet Union has not achieved the sort of Communism Marx proposed.

For the first years after the Communist Revolution, Soviet leaders made excuses to explain why incomes were not yet equal and labor not yet voluntarily done. But bit by bit, the excuses turned into a theory to support unequal distribution, at least for the time being. Thus, the 1936 Soviet Constitution, written under Stalin's guidance, changed Marx's slogan in a small but significant way: "From each according to his ability, to each according to his *work*" (italics added). And an official Soviet economics textbook published in the late 1950's could sum up the new theory and practice of distribution in this way:

> The socialist economics system is deeply hostile to equalization of wages, [to] ignoring the differences between skilled and unskilled, heavy and light work. Skilled work, as work of much higher quality, demands training of the worker and gives greater production than unskilled work. On the strength of this, it is paid more than unskilled work. Such a system of pay stimulates increases in the qualifications of workers. For equal skill, more difficult work is paid more than less difficult. . . .
>
> In connection with the economic necessity of much greater reward for labor in leading branches of the national economy, higher wages are established for workers of such branches of heavy industry as metallurgy, coal, oil, machine construction, etc. Under otherwise equal conditions, also, more highly paid are workers . . . in districts having especially great significance in the economic life of the country, and also in distant and little populated regions. Thanks to this, wages are one of the economic instruments of the planned distribution and redistribution of skilled manpower between enterprises and branches of social production in accordance with the demands of the . . . planned development of the national economy.

But the ideal of Marx's original slogan continues to have its hold on official Soviet spokesmen. Indeed, the pressures of the Chinese Communists, who claim with increasing vigor that they and not the Russians are the real Marxists, may be pushing the Soviet Union's leaders to insist more and more that someday there will be an economy of equals.

A statement from the 1961 Congress of the Communist Party of the Soviet Union illustrates both where the leaders think the Soviet Union is today, and where they hope it will go:

> The socialist principle "From each according to his abilities, to each according to his work" has been put into effect in the Soviet Union.
>
> The building of a Communist society has become an immediate practical task for the Soviet people. . . . What is Communism? Communism is a classless social system with . . . public ownership of the means of production and full social equality of all members of society. . . . From each according to his ability, to each according to his needs will be implemented. Communism is a society in which labor for the good of society will become the prime vital requirement of everyone, a necessity recognized by all, and the ability of each person will be employed to the greatest benefit of the people. . . . Labor will no longer be a mere source of livelihood, it will be a genuinely creative process and a source of joy.
>
> By 1980 the material and technical basis of Communism will be built up ensuring an abundance of material and cultural values for the whole population. . . . Soviet society will come close to a stage where it can introduce the principle of distribution according to needs.
>
> In the process of Communist construction, economic management will make use of material and moral incentives for high production figures.

Central to this whole argument is the phrase "an abundance of material and cultural values." For a society in which each takes according to his needs but gives fully according with his ability assumes both (1) enough of all material goods to go around and (2) a strong cooperative attitude to suppress greed, laziness, and other common human traits.

According to its leaders, the Soviet Union is now in the intermediate stage between the bourgeois values of the past and the Communist values of the future. In the next few lessons, we shall see what steps the Soviet Union is now taking to motivate workers and to distribute the economy's goods.

46 Labor Markets in the Soviet Union

Labor markets in a market society, as we saw in Reading 38, are governed largely by supply and demand. The leaders of the Soviet Union, however, are not willing to let supply and demand govern their nation's economy. Their goals are planned, and so are the means they will use to achieve those goals. Thus it should come as no surprise that the use of the Soviet Union's most important resource—labor—is not left entirely to the whims of individual workers. But, as we shall also see, Soviet workers nowadays do have considerable freedom to choose what they would like to do and where they would like to do it.

One institution that you will not find mentioned in the readings for this chapter is the labor union. In the United States, labor unions strongly influence distribution. But, while there are labor unions in the Soviet Union, they have little real power. Soviet labor unions are controlled by the government, and do not bargain collectively about wages or working conditions. Their main function is to encourage higher productivity.

Today's reading presents an American labor economist's analysis of how the Soviet labor market works. As you read, keep the following questions in mind:

1. How does current Soviet practice fit Marx's slogan, "From each according to his ability"? How does it fit Adam Smith's analysis?
2. Who in the United States decides how many openings there will be in different vocational programs?
3. In which ways is the Soviet job market ruled by command? In which ways is it ruled by free market choices? How would the labor markets of the United States, the Soviet Union, and the Eskimos fit onto a spectrum showing the importance of individual workers' preferences?

Finding the Right Worker for the Right Job

EMILY CLARK BROWN

Based on material from Soviet Trade Unions and Labor Relations, *by Emily Clark Brown. Copyright © 1966 by the President and Fellows of Harvard College. Cambridge, Mass.: Harvard University Press.*

Two principles govern the workings of labor markets in the Soviet Union: Workers have a duty to work, and a right to work.

The duty to work means the duty to engage in "socially useful labor," and not to be an idler or to live off of private profit. Private profiteers are considered "parasites" in the Soviet Union—people who reap the reward of the economy's production without contributing to it. The duty to work applies to men and women alike, although women with young children are exempted when there are no day-care programs for their children. The right to work means, in theory, that there is no unemployment. In practice, the duty to work isn't always lived up to; loafers and "parasites" still have to be cracked down upon. Nor can the right to work always be exercised in practice. Some workers find themselves between jobs because of seasonal, technological, or planning problems. Still, unemployment seems to be much lower in the Soviet Union than in the United States.

Getting the right workers into the right jobs is another matter. On the one hand, since the early 1950's, workers have officially had the right to change jobs when they liked. On the other hand, Gosplan [pp. 121–122] estimates the number of workers needed in each sector of the economy, the wages those workers will receive, and their expected productivity. The plans do not proceed with uniform smoothness—shortages develop here and surpluses there. The overall aim remains that of placing workers in jobs which the economy needs to have done and which the workers themselves want to do.

One way Gosplan tries to insure that essential jobs will be filled is by planning training programs. The Soviet student may choose what kind of a school he wants to apply for. But the success of his application will depend on the number of openings in the particular kind of school he is interested in. And Gosplan decides how many students there will be in each of the secondary schools, vocational schools, and advanced institutes. Those decisions are meshed into the overall estimates of the economy's needs for skilled manpower. But for most occupations, training on the job is still the most common way of producing the number of skilled workers needed each year.

Job placement is scarcely a matter of chance in the Soviet Union. School directors, industrial executives, and government officials all play parts in seeing to it that students leaving school are steered into jobs that use their talents. Yet the system is far from perfect. There are no coordinated job information and placement services to inform job-seekers of what jobs are available and where. And many young Russians find that they do not like the job their school suggests for them. Many resign and look for other jobs, though they do run the risk of being considered grumblers.

A special problem in the Soviet Union has been luring labor into work in the most distant, least developed areas of the east and Far North. Intensive publicity campaigns have urged young people to volunteer for such pioneering. Occasionally, Communist Party discipline has been used to persuade young people that here is where they can make their biggest contribution to the nation. Hundreds of thousands have apparently responded to those appeals—or to the extra financial rewards that go with work in hardship areas. But, one way or another, volunteers appear to have taken the place of the slave labor that once was relied upon for whatever economic development there was in the remotest, coldest regions.

Wage differences, based upon rewards for more valuable work and compensations for unpleasant jobs, are being used more and more. The differences sometimes are very large between the least and the most skilled worker, and between the worker in the pleasantest parts of the country and the worst parts. Unlike the wage structure in the United States, the Soviet wage structure is not determined mainly by supply and demand. Again, wages are what the planners decide they will be. But it is also clear that Soviet planners are further than before in building a wage structure that is responsive to the state's needs for higher and better production and to the workers' desires for better lives.

Despite these recent developments, the Soviet labor market shows no signs of turning into a totally free labor market. But planning itself may well become more flexible, for when workers are pleased with their jobs, they are likely to produce more. Thus, to achieve the planned aims of its command economy, the Soviet Union may find it most practical to give workers more freedom in choosing their jobs.

47 Labor and Incomes in the Soviet Union

Today's reading focuses more closely on how workers are motivated to work in the Soviet Union's modified command economy. This discussion of rewards and punishments for workers should be set alongside the description of the Soviet executive's life given in Reading 35.

The first part of today's reading, written by an American expert on the Soviet economy, was published in 1960. Most of what it says, however, still applies today. But to bring it up to date, the author might want to give even more emphasis to the role of piece-rates and more attention to the still further relaxation of some of the rules governing the worker's ability to change jobs.

The second part of today's reading is a table, giving incomes for various jobs in the Soviet Union in 1963. As you read, think about the following questions:

1. What is a "positive incentive"? Which ones seem to be most important for Soviet workers? For American workers?
2. What is the "piece-rate system"? How does it work in the Soviet Union? Who sets the norms? Why might an American labor union object to such a system?
3. Think of several ways the ranking of American jobs according to income would differ from the ranking for Soviet jobs. What does the ranking of Soviet jobs tell us about the goals of the Soviet economy?

1. Wage-Setting: An Economic Strategy

ROBERT W. CAMPBELL

From Soviet Economic Power *(Boston, Mass.: Houghton Mifflin Company, © 1960), pp. 134–138. Reprinted by permission.*

The thousands of managers are far outnumbered by the millions of production workers who wield the tools and handle the materials and products at the factory bench, in mines, or on the construction job. Surely the productivity of any economy must depend to a considerable extent on the degree of motivation of these ordinary workers. Unless the worker brings to his job a measure of carefulness, some pride in his work, and a willingness to learn, the capacity of the economy to produce and to progress must surely suffer. . . .

Payment According to Productivity. The general approach to labor policy is not much different in principle from that regarding the managers. The regime presents highly contrasted possibilities to the Soviet workers. Those who enter certain elite occupations, those who are earnest workers and overfulfill the work norms, those who are willing to acquire new skills and move up the educational ladder will receive much higher rewards than their fellows. On the other hand, those who are unskilled, do not fulfill the work norms, and are generally unproductive will suffer low wages, loss of certain benefits, dismissal, and perhaps even criminal punishment. This general picture can be illustrated with a few details.

First of all, on the positive side, there [are great differences between] the wage rate[s] established for different jobs. At the basis of the wage system in every branch of Soviet industry is a scale which sets out a number of skill classifications corresponding to different responsibilities and degrees of skill. A basic rate of pay is established for each of these categories. Generally speaking, the [differences in] wages among the skill classifications is greater than would be true in a comparable American plant or industry. For many of these pay scales, the difference between the pay of the person in the highest skill category and that of the person in the lowest is 2.8 times, in others 3.5 times, and there are some industries in which [the] base pay rate of the highest skill category is 4.5 times as high as that of the lowest. Such great [differences] between the highest- and lowest-paid manual workers in a plant is rare in industry in the United States. In addition to this variation within industries, considerable variation between pay scales exists for different industries. Those which the government considers high-priority industries and which require special skills generally have much higher pay scales than does, say, the food industry.

[The Soviet Union also makes] extensive use of the piece-rate system. . . . To a far greater extent than in American industry, the Soviet worker is paid on the basis not of how much time he puts in, but by how many units of output he produces. In recent years, about 75 per cent of Soviet industrial workers, for instance, have been paid on a piece-rate basis. The corresponding fraction for American industry would be much smaller. Under the piece-rate system, there will be set for each job a certain hourly or daily norm of output which the worker is supposed to try to fulfill. If he fulfills the norm just 100 per cent, he gets the basic wage specified in the wage scales described above. For exceeding the output norm he will receive a wage higher than that specified in the wage scale. Moreover, in recent years about a third of Russian industrial workers have been paid on the basis of what the Russians call the "progressive piece system." That is, the rate of pay per unit of output goes up as the norm for production is exceeded. For producing more than a certain number of units per hour, the worker will be paid at a successively higher and higher rate, so that if he overfulfills the norm by 10 per cent he may get 20 per cent more income than if he just fulfilled the norm. . .

Soviet wages are further differentiated according to the unattractiveness of the work. . . . In order to get people to work in the Far North and in some of the remote eastern areas, wages almost double those in most parts of the Soviet Union are offered. In some other branches of industry there may be [wage differences] for dangerous work, for underground work, and other unattractive features of certain jobs.

Coercive Labor Discipline. Positive incentives in the form of monetary rewards for working hard, for entering elite occupations, and for improving one's skills are accompanied in the Soviet Union . . . by legal forms of labor discipline. There has traditionally been a considerable degree of compulsion in Soviet labor policy. For instance, all Soviet workers carry what are called labor books. The labor book shows the worker's name, his qualifications, the jobs he has held, the pay he has received during his whole working career. When a worker takes a job, he turns his labor book over to his employer, who keeps . . . it as long as the worker is in his employ. Since a worker cannot get a new job without presenting this labor book to his new employer, he must virtually have permission from his old employer to leave his job. . . . Moreover, during some periods of Soviet history, the law has provided severe punishments for workers who were late to work, who came to work drunk, or were absent from work. At one point a worker who was twenty minutes late to work might end up with a prison term of two to four months. . . .

The balance between these positive and negative incentives has varied over time. Emphasis on the negative incentives became particularly strong beginning in the late 'thirties and during the Second World War. . . . In recent years, however, the trend has been more and more away from the negative incentives. . . . The Russians are recognizing that a relatively free labor market, dominated by positive incentives, is more effective than one characterized by [force].

Thus far nothing has been said about the Soviet slave labor camps. During much of the history of the Soviet regime there have existed what the Russians call corrective labor camps, to which persons were sentenced for various kinds of offenses against the regime. No one knows just how many people have been in these camps, but at times prisoners have numbered in the millions. Camps were often located in remote parts of the country, such as Siberia and the Far North, and prisoners were used for various economic activities, such as lumbering, building canals, or digging coal in mines above the Arctic Circle. But these camps do not really deserve much attention in a discussion of Soviet labor policy. Their operation is more an aspect of the Soviet totalitarian political system than a considered policy of labor utilization. Such labor is extremely inefficient, and although some [production] was gotten out of the prisoners, the slave labor camps involved a costly waste of labor, even from the point of view of the regime. This was one of the most hated and feared features of the regime and after the death of Stalin, most of the prisoners were [freed].

2. The Soviet Pecking Order

ALFRED R. OXENFELDT and VSEVOLOD HOLUBNYCHY

From Economic Systems in Action, *3rd ed. (New York: Holt, Rinehart and Winston, Inc., 1965), p. 135.*

BASIC ANNUAL WAGES IN THE SOVIET UNION, 1963
(in U.S. dollars)

Legal minimum, rural areas	$ 360
Legal minimum, urban areas	400
Collective farmer (1962)	574
State farm worker	586
Office typist	588
Textile worker	679
Construction worker	746
Machine tool operator	746
High school teacher	824
Steel worker	872
Coal miner	1,092
Physician, M.D.	1,260
Lawyer	1,376
Average for all workers and employees	*1,445*
State farm manager	3,530
Technician	3,724
Engineer (oil industry)	4,238
Master foreman (machine-building)	5,028
Doctor of science, department head in a research institute	5,730
Factory director (machine-building)	6,240
University professor	7,070
Cabinet minister, republic government	9,125

Note: Except for the average wage figure, none of the other figures in the table include bonuses. If they had, the wages would have totalled about 15 per cent higher. Remember also that it is extremely difficult to compare the dollars earned by Soviet and American workers. Soviet workers receive housing and medical care free, for example, while prices for many consumer goods are high.

48 Summary: Distribution in the Soviet Union

To pull the threads of the past few readings together, we go back to the quotation from Marx with which we began this chapter: "From each according to his ability, to each according to his needs." In today's reading, Harry Schwartz, a member of the editorial board of *The New York Times* and a frequent writer on the Soviet economy, asks whether the Soviet Union today has achieved the goal that Marx set forth. Mr. Schwartz wrote the article in 1961, but it seems consistent with all that he has written about the Soviet Union in more recent years. As you read, keep the following questions in mind:

1. In what ways does the Soviet Union, as depicted by Mr. Schwartz, resemble the United States?
2. What values does Mr. Schwartz seem to bring to his description?
3. Would more production push the Soviet Union closer to or further from Marx's ideal system of distribution? Why?

Is There Communism in the Soviet Union?

HARRY SCHWARTZ

From Harry Schwartz (ed.), The Many Faces of Communism *(New York: Berkley Publishing Corporation, 1962), pp. 19–24. Copyright © 1961, by The New York Times Company. Reprinted with permission.*

Even amid all the cloudiness of current Soviet thinking about the perfect Communist future, certain points are clear and can be used as a basis for trying to judge how close the Soviet Union now is to the ultimate Communist society. Let us look at four vital points in this matter:

1. *Communist society will have to be one of great abundance so that all needs can be met.*

Soviet spokesmen have shown an awareness of the potential instability of human desires. They have stated bluntly that they do not envisage communism as a state in which everyone can have all the automobiles, houses, yachts and trips around the world he wants. Instead, they talk about the "reasonable needs" of people, implying that it is intended to set up a system of norms—so many pounds of meat, so many suits of clothes and the like—defining what people are entitled to.

But, even on such limited terms, Soviet spokesmen have admitted that it would require more production than that of the United States at present to meet the requirements for Communist "abundance."

On this score it is evident that the Soviet Union is still far from the Communist ideal. . . . [T]he Soviet Union still does not have anything like enough housing, enough food, enough clothing, enough durable goods to meet its people's needs.

Moreover, the new Communist party program concedes that even if its ambitious economic plan for the next twenty years is fulfilled, full Communist abundance will not have been reached, although by 1980 the U.S.S.R. is planning to produce more than twice as much as the United States produces now. There is, of course, no assurance that these ambitious production plans will be achieved.

Just how far behind the United States—let alone a state of Communist abundance—the Soviet Union is may be seen from a few statistical comparisons. In 1961, for example, the United States produced three times as many eggs per person as did the Soviet Union, more than twice as much meat per person, and 70 per cent more grain per person. Soviet production of automobiles in 1961 was only equal to about one week's normal production of the United States passenger-car industry. Soviet production of cotton cloth—the basic clothing material in that country—was only about half that of the United States per person.

Putting all the available material together, it seems safe to say that the standard of living in the United States is on the average almost three times as high as that in the Soviet Union.

2. *Communist society will have to be inhabited by people moved by motives different from those the West knows.*

Work in that society, the Soviet blueprint holds, will be "the prime vital requirement of everyone." Moreover, the amount and quality of work people will do in that society will apparently have no relationship to their income, so that apparently the citizens of the Communist society will not require incentives. Are the Soviet people anywhere near such a highly developed sense of social obligation and social responsibility as this requirement suggests?

For the moment, at least, the answer seems to be clearly in the negative. The Soviet wage system contains substantial inequalities of payment, aimed deliberately at rewarding those who work hard and have the most skill while giving the least payment to those who work poorly and have little or no skill. . . .

Moreover, it is clear that the Soviet Union contains an appreciable number of persons whose main object in life seems to be to get along with as little work as possible, or at least as little honest work as possible. The tightening up of Soviet law this past year testifies to this. A campaign has been waged against "idlers" and "parasites" who disdain honest factory or farm labor but make their living in the black market. Such unsavory characters can now be exiled from their places of residence. Another recent revision of Soviet law makes it possible to apply the death sentence to counterfeiters, to persons who embezzle large amounts of state property, to speculators in foreign currency and the like. Several such death sentences have already been handed down.

All in all, the picture of the ordinary Soviet citizen that is recorded daily in the Soviet press is hardly one to suggest a population of near-paragons who have almost reached the level of selflessness that perfect communism seems to assume. Rather, the picture that emerges is one of human beings just as subject to the pull of self-interest, to laziness and to the desire for easy, sometimes illicit, gain as those of other lands.

3. *Communist society is one in which there will be "full social equality of all members of society."*

How near to perfect equality is Soviet society today? Not very near at all, any candid inspection of the Soviet scene suggests. The real income of a top Soviet official, writer, or scientist is on a level with that of an average resident of Westchester County [a wealthy suburb of New York City]; at the bottom of the Soviet economic system there are millions living at a poorer level than the American who receives unemployment insurance.

Inequality of power is even more marked than economic inequality. . . .

These inequalities in contemporary Soviet life have led inevitably to sharp social inequality. A standard target for Soviet satire is the upper-class mother who is appalled when her son or daughter comes home and announces he or she plans to marry the offspring of an ordinary worker. Soviet college students, and their parents, tend to look down upon proletarians doomed to lives in the factory or on the farm, and upper-class Soviet families pull every string possible—and sometimes pay expensive bribes—to avert the awful calamity represented by the failure of a son or daughter to enter the university. . . .

4. *The Communist society is to be composed of "free" people. . . .*

Soviet society today, one must conclude, is a long way from the Communist Utopia. It is still a poor civilization inhabited by people who are moved by self-interest rather than by idealistic concern for others. Soviet society is shot through with many different kinds of inequality and its citizens are far from free.

Undoubtedly, the Soviet Union is likely to make much material progress over the next two decades, so that by 1980—if World War III is avoided—the Soviet people should be able to live much better than they do now. But anything approaching the kind of abundance genuine communism assumes seems far out of reach.

Even more out of reach, it would appear, is the kind of selflessness that the official picture of communism calls for. Whether that ideal of selflessness is ever realizable in any society is doubtful indeed.

As for the inequality rife in the Soviet Union, it is based in part upon the dictatorial character of the regime and in part simply upon natural inequalities of talent.

Finally, the lack of freedom of Soviet people is a necessity of the Communist Party dictatorship and could be ended only by removal of that dictatorship. . . .

The conclusion seems inevitable that whatever kind of society the Soviet Union will have in 1980 or later it will not be the ideal communism Marx had in mind but was careful never to spell out. But there is nothing to stop the Communist rulers of the Soviet Union—if they are still in power two decades from now—from calling whatever society they may have then "communism." After all, one of the powers a dictatorial regime enjoys is the power to decide what words mean, and that power has been exercised by the Soviet regime for many years.

SUGGESTED READINGS

Dunbar, Robert G., *The Farmer and the American Way,* pp. 69–82.
Question: What has government done to raise the income of farmers?

Federal Reserve Bank of Philadelphia, *The New Poverty,* pp. 1–10.
Question: What does the term "the new poverty" mean?

__________, *Unemployment in Prosperity: Why?*
Question: Why do we have unemployment in a time of prosperity?

Industrial Relations Center, University of Chicago, *Profits at Work,* pp. 1–23.
Question: What roles do profits play in a market economy?

Rieber, Alfred D. and Robert C. Nelson, editors, *The USSR and Communism,* pp. 182–198.
Question: How did the Soviet Union's answer to the *for whom* question change between 1921 and 1950?

Schwartz, Harry, editor, *The Many Faces of Communism,* pp. 73–82.
Question: Describe the standard of living of a typical Russian family.

__________, *The Many Faces of Communism,* pp. 217–29.
Question: How do Soviet health services help to answer the *for whom* question? Why does the Soviet Union place more emphasis on medical care than on many other consumer goods and services?

__________, *The Many Faces of Communism,* pp. 167–75.
Question: For what economic reasons are Soviet and American television programs so different?

Senesh, Lawrence and Barbara Warne Newell, *Our Labor Force,* pp. 19–51.
Question: Why does income vary from one job to another? What role have labor unions played?

Theobald, Robert, *The Rich and the Poor,* pp. 29–37.
Question: In what relative quantities are goods and services distributed among the nations of the world?

__________, *The Rich and the Poor,* pp. 37–47.
Question: What are some of the ways in which economic growth can change a society's answer to the *for whom* question? How could government modify those changes?

__________, *The Rich and the Poor,* pp. 108–17.
Question: How should we distribute the additional goods and services which additional economic growth will produce?

__________, *The Rich and the Poor,* pp. 132–46.
Question: What are the benefits of international giving described in this chapter?

Unit Six

The Pursuit of Growth and Stability

SO FAR, we have considered the internal workings of the market and command economies. We have seen how individual producers and consumers and the government help to answer the *what, how,* and *for whom* questions. In Unit Six, we shall examine the market and command economies as a whole, and see how the overall state of those economies affects the lives of their citizens.

Two of the major goals of both the United States and the Soviet Union are economic growth and stability. Both desire growth, because both desire more goods and services to provide a more satisfying answer to the problem of economic scarcity. Both desire stability, because both societies believe that everyone should have a chance to work, and everyone should have the security that he will have a job and a decent income in the future.

Unit Six presents the chief methods of measuring growth and stability, the effects of growth and stability on the average citizen, and the successes and failures of the United States and the Soviet Union in achieving growth and stability.

Chapter 11

Growth and Stability in the American Economy

STATING THE ISSUE When Congress debates a tax hike, few Americans are unaware that the federal government's economic decisions affect their own lives and pocketbooks. As we have noted, every economic decision in an economy is interrelated to all of the other economic decisions. Thus, unless you live alone on a desert island, your economic freedom is never absolute. You may think that you can do whatever you please but, in fact, the actions of others set limits on your own freedom.

Chapter 11 considers the interrelatedness of the American economy on the large scale. In effect, it is an economics lesson based on the famous sermon of John Donne, the preacher and poet: "No man is an island, entire of itself; every man is a piece of the continent, a part of the main-[land]."

The interrelatedness of the American economy works in three ways. First, the individual decisions of producers and consumers affect each other. Second, those decisions affect the government and the overall growth and stability of the economy. And third, the government and the overall growth and stability of the economy affect the individual decisions of producers and consumers.

As Reading 22 pointed out, government has played an important role in the American economy from the founding of the republic. But in recent years, the federal government has taken on a new role: By conscious, calculated actions it has tried to promote growth and stability. Thus, through their elected representatives, the American people have acted collectively to introduce an element of planning into their economy. They have done so, however, to strengthen, not to destroy, the free market economy. The United States may be moving further away from the free market end of the market-command spectrum. But the main economic decisions in the United States continue to be made by individual producers and consumers. The government would say on its own behalf that it has only been trying to help those free decisions mesh together in a way that will produce the least hardship and the most prosperity.

Chapter 11 raises the following broad questions: Why does the United States desire growth and stability? How are the various sectors of the American economy interrelated? What has the government been doing to promote growth and stability?

49 What Difference Does Stability Make?

Most critics of the market economy stress two themes: Market economies benefit the few at the expense of the many, and market economies are unstable. In Reading 43, we saw that there have indeed been some people left behind in the economic race in the United States's market economy. But we also saw that, slowly and imperfectly, the market economies seem to be dealing with the worst of their injustices.

Reading 49 looks at the second charge—that market economies are unstable. The critics claim that market economies move from boom to bust and back again. At one moment, they say, the market economies operate at too low a level, throwing millions of people out of work. At another moment, they say, market economies are trying to operate at too high a level—and rising prices result.

As you read, keep the following questions in mind:

1. What are depression, inflation, and deflation?
2. What does it mean to say that the unemployment rate is 6 per cent?
3. What is a price index? What does it mean to call the price index for a certain year "100"?

1. The Perils of Uneven Growth

Several key terms are used in any discussion of economic stability in a market economy:

Depression: a slack period in economic activity, when many workers and factories are idle. Mild depressions are called *recessions*.

Inflation: a rise in the prices of most goods and services.

Deflation: a fall in the prices of most goods and services. Deflation usually occurs during depressions.

Business cycles: the rises and falls in the level of economic activity over any period of time. There is little evidence that such cycles follow steady or predictable patterns.

The economist's favorite measuring stick for gauging the performance of an economy is the Gross National Product, which will be the subject of Reading 51. Today, we'll introduce two other measuring sticks to highlight the problem of instability: the unemployment rate and the price index.

The unemployment rate

Unemployment statistics, gathered regularly by the federal government, show the percentage of people wanting to work who have no jobs. The following graph shows the figures from 1929 to 1966.

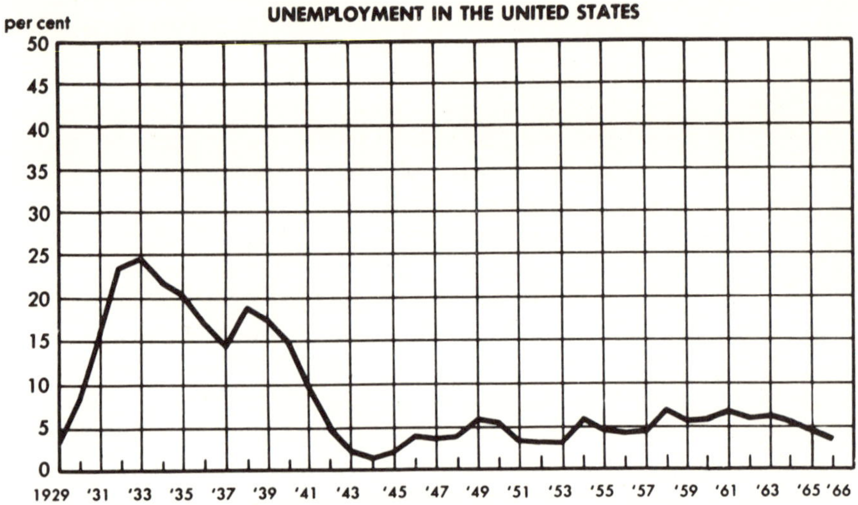

Source: *Economic Report of the President, January, 1967* (Washington, D.C., 1967), p. 236.

When did unemployment reach its peak? Why was unemployment so low in the years 1943–45?

The most dramatic story told by the data is the magnitude of the Great Depression of the 1930's. In its worst year, one out of every four persons was out of work. (The human side of that story is presented in the second part of this reading.)

The unemployment rate is an essential measure for an economy that wants to eliminate joblessness. But the unemployment rate sometimes hides as much as it reveals. In recent years, for example, the unemployment rate has been low. But certain groups have been carrying the brunt of joblessness.

A popular saying among Negroes is, "Last hired, first fired." The statistics bear out the truth of that saying. When a recession comes to an end, Negroes are usually the last to be re-hired. And when a recession begins, they're usually the first to be laid off. The same applies to Spanish-speaking Americans.

Unemployment is also particularly severe among the young. In 1966, when only 2.5 per cent of American males over the age of twenty were unemployed, 12.1 per cent of American teen-agers seeking work were jobless.

In the 1960's, many jobs go begging despite the large number of unemployed workers. To try to remedy this situation, government and business have sponsored retraining programs to teach unemployed workers skills that are in high demand.

The price index

Well before Thomas R. Marshall, Vice-President of the United States from 1913 to 1921, proclaimed that "What this country needs is a good five-cent cigar," Americans were painfully aware of inflation. Since the founding of the republic, elections have sometimes seemed to turn on the issue of rising prices.

A price index gives us a way to measure just how much inflation—or deflation—is occurring. Such an index works by measuring the change in price, over a period of time, for the same, fixed bundle of goods and services. For clarity, the price of that bundle in a given year is set at 100. Thus, if the price of the fixed bundle rose 6 per cent in three years, the price index for Year III would be 106. And if the price of the fixed bundle fell over the three year period, the price index for Year III would be 94.

The most quoted price index today is the Consumer Price Index prepared by the United States Bureau of Labor Statistics. It compares prices in different years with average prices during the years 1957–59. The following graph traces the price story since 1929, with the 1957–59 average set at 100.

CONSUMER PRICES
1957-59 = 100

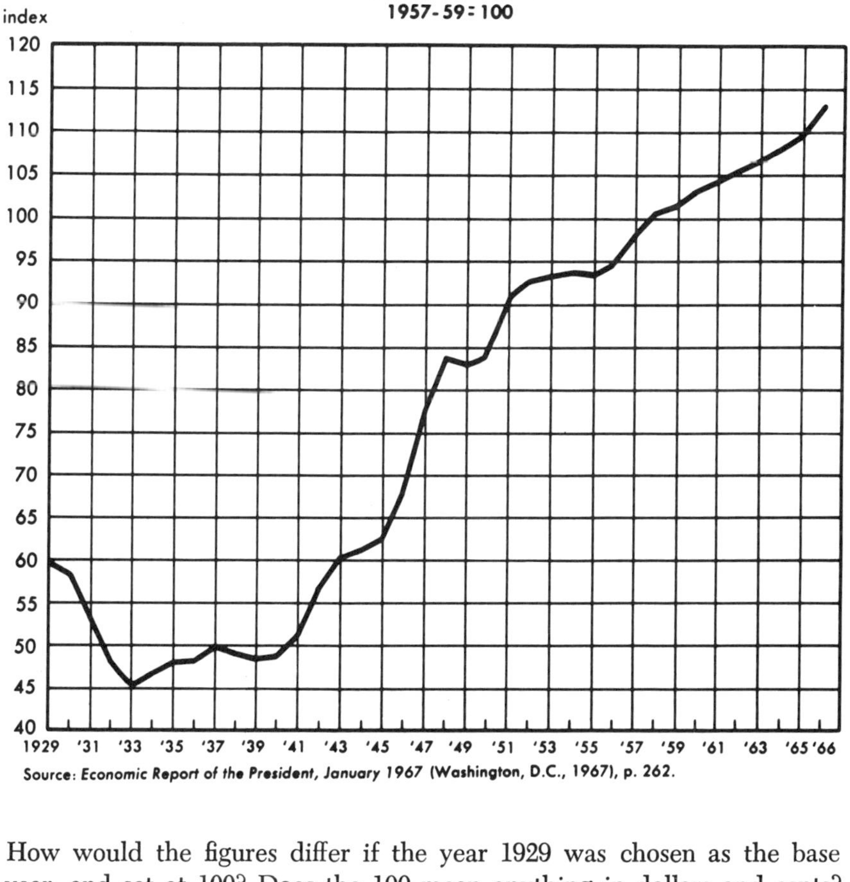

Source: *Economic Report of the President, January 1967* (Washington, D.C., 1967), p. 262.

How would the figures differ if the year 1929 was chosen as the base year, and set at 100? Does the 100 mean anything in dollars and cents?

Again, averages may conceal important stories. Not all prices rise at the same rate. The cost of medical care, for example, has been rising much faster than the cost of food and clothing. And prices rise at different rates in different parts of the country.

In recent years, the rate of inflation has been mild. For most Americans, price inflation has been more than offset by rises in income. Others, however, live on fixed incomes—incomes that do not rise steadily from year to year. These people include many white-collar workers and laborers who are not represented by labor unions, and the elderly who live on fixed pensions and Social Security payments.

For the economy as a whole, however, the mild inflation of recent years has seemed a healthy sign of the continuing growth of the economy. Still, if we try to expand our economy too quickly, severe inflation may be the result. Economists have the experience of post-World War I Germany to give them occasional nightmares. There, inflation was so severe that money lost its value overnight.

Like amateur tightrope-walkers, the American people are trying to avoid both severe unemployment and severe inflation. But unlike the American people of a few decades ago, today's tightrope-walkers have stronger nets built under them by government—as we shall later see.

We've discussed definitions and statistics. Now we'll look at what the words and numbers can mean in human terms. As you read the following excerpt from a congressional hearing held in 1932, refer back to the graphs on pages 180 and 181.

2. The Human Side of Economic Statistics

KARL DE SCHWEINITZ

From Federal Cooperation in Unemployment Relief, *Hearings before a Subcommittee of the Committee of Manufacturers, United States Senate, 72nd Congress, 1st session, on S. 4592 (Washington, 1932).*

MR. DE SCHWEINITZ: When I appeared before the Subcommittee last December [1931], I stated that there were 238,000 persons out of work in Philadelphia and that we estimated unemployment in the city in ordinary times to be between 40,000 and 50,000. There are now 298,000 persons out of work. In other words, whereas in December our employment was a little less than five times what one might call normal unemployment, today it is six times normal unemployment.

In December I told you that 43,000 families were receiving relief. Today 55,000 families are receiving relief.

In December our per family grant was $4.39 per week per family. It is now $4.23 per family. Of this $4.23 per family, about $3.93 is an allowance for food. This is about two thirds of the amount needed to provide a health-maintaining diet. . . . I want to tell you about an experience we had in

Philadelphia when our private [charity] funds were exhausted and before public [relief] funds became available. . . .

One woman said she borrowed fifty cents from a friend and bought stale bread for three-and-a-half cents per loaf, and that is all they had for eleven days except for one or two meals.

With the last food order another woman received, she bought dried vegetables and canned goods. With this she made a soup and whenever the members of the family felt hungry they just ate some of the soup. . . .

SENATOR COSTIGAN: Are the cases you are citing typical or extreme?

MR. DE SCHWEINITZ: They are typical. . . . Here is another family which for two days had nothing to eat but bread, and during most of the rest of the time they had only two meals a day. Their meals consisted of bread and coffee for breakfast, and bread and raw or cooked carrots for dinner. . . .

SENATOR COSTIGAN: What you say is not only shockingly true but Senator Copeland, of New York, has recently reported cases of known starvation this past winter.

MR. DE SCHWEINITZ: The hospitals have had definite cases of starvation. . . .

A great many people raise the question as to whether the unemployed are a good-for-nothing lot and are out of work because of their own fault. They are not. We have definite studies to show that they had had long and good work records and that they are active, earnest human beings. All they want is a job. . . .

I want to repeat that today the unemployed are upstanding, intelligent, earnest, capable people, but if we put the children in these families [through] a period of malnutrition such as they are going through today, what sort of people are we going to have twenty years from now, and what will we say at that time about them? What kind of working people will they be if we continue treating them as we are treating them now?

50 What Difference Does Growth Make?

Reading 49 dealt with the United States' search for an economy that would avoid drastic fluctuations in output from year to year. Reading 50 deals with a parallel search: the search for a steadily larger Gross National Product (GNP) each year. (GNP, which means the total output of goods and services, will be discussed more fully in Reading 51.) Thus, whereas Reading 49 suggested that we want to avoid this:

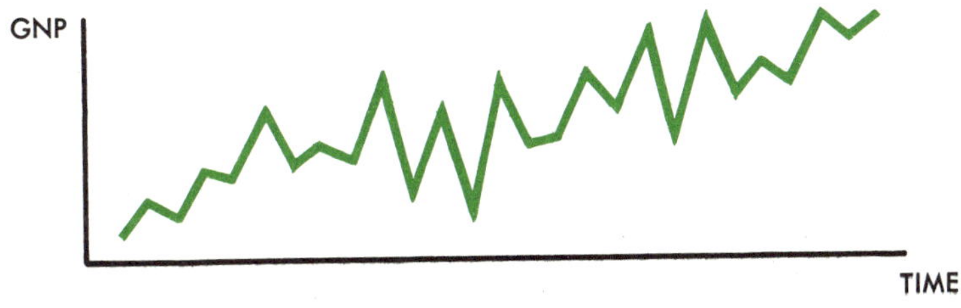

so, today's reading suggests that we want to avoid this:

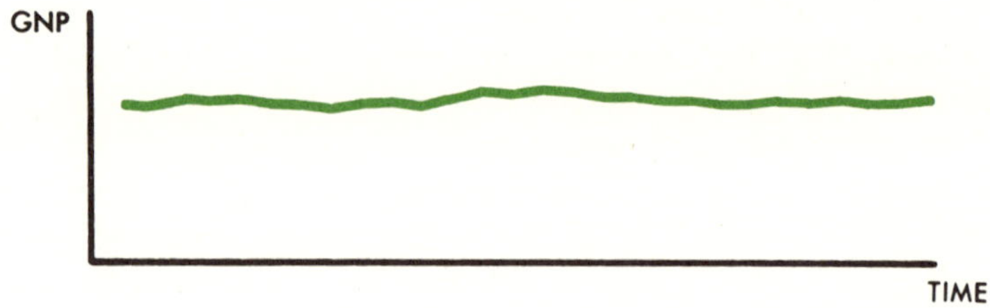

The result is that we're looking for an economy that will grow like this:

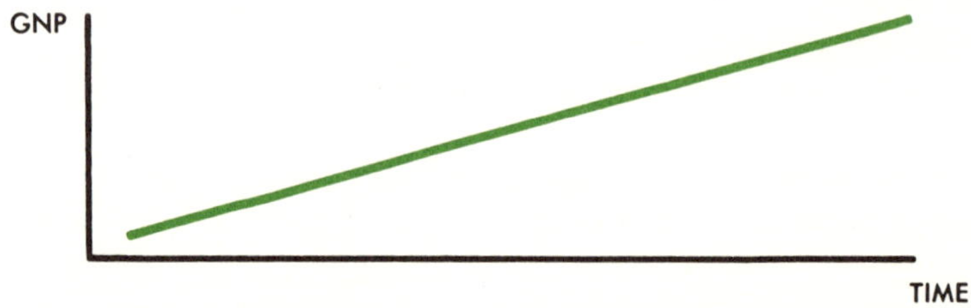

The growth of an economy is measured by the annual increases in GNP. Often, it is more useful to measure economic growth in terms of *per-capita* growth—increases in output per person. Since 1900, the GNP of the United States has been growing at an average rate of more than 3 per cent per year. During that time, the population of the United States has been growing at an average rate of a little more than 1 per cent per year. The net result? Per-capita output has been growing at a rate of over 2 per cent per year. In other words, the goods and services available for consumption by the individual household have been rising at a rate of over 2 per cent per year.

Nevertheless, the richest country in the world keeps trying to grow even more rapidly. The reason is that even the United States faces the old problem of scarcity, first mentioned in Reading 1. Americans want further growth in order to be able to devote more resources to improving cities, schools, transportation, and the very polluted air so many of us breathe. The United States needs to create enough new jobs—through an expanding economy—to absorb workers displaced by technological changes on the farms, in offices, and in factories. And Americans want further growth to lick the problem of continuing poverty for the few, even while the many become still more wealthy.

Those goals probably come as no surprise. Most Americans are aware of the many problems at home that will require money as well as intelligence for their solution. Since colonial days, Americans have felt confident that money and brains could solve nearly any problem they faced—including problems of international politics. The following reading, written by one of the chief economic writers on *The New York Times*, discusses some of the limitations of the power of American wealth.

As you read, consider the following questions:

1. How do values enter into the question of what influence the United States can have on the world's economies?
2. Why has the effectiveness of foreign aid been limited?
3. Why has the military might of the United States been relatively less costly than the military might of the Soviet Union?

What Can Economic Power Do?

EDWIN L. DALE, JR.

From The New York Times Magazine, *March 19, 1967.*

A new government statistical series has just disclosed the astonishing fact that United States manufacturing capacity has doubled since 1951. We added as much in the way of new plant and machinery in the last 15 years as we built in the first 150 years of the nation's industrial history. And we may well double capacity—and actual output—again in another 15 or 20 years.

All of this would be interesting enough by itself, but it becomes awesome when we recall that 15 years ago the United States already had far and away the world's largest economy. Now it is nearly twice as big, and simple arithmetic shows that it is widening the gap over the rest of the world all the time. Even if some other nations, such as Japan and the Soviet Union, show larger percentage growth than we in many years, the absolute margin of the United States increases. . . . (Suppose the size of the Soviet economy is put at 50 and that of the United States at 100, and suppose the Soviets grow at an unlikely 8 per cent a year and the United States at 5 per cent; after five years the United States would be about 125 and the Soviets 70, for a gap of 55 instead of 50 today.)

The world is becoming increasingly aware of the sheer giantism of the American economy—and of some of the business firms that make it up. Much of the world does not like what it sees. A Belgian is not overjoyed to learn that General Motors sales in a year are more than his nation's entire GNP; an Englishman or Frenchman, used to a long history of power and influence, is likely to be resentful at the discovery that United States economic growth in one year is equal to half the British or French GNP or the whole of Canada's. And as for the poor countries, their sense of . . . frustration can only be increased by their awareness of the wealth enjoyed by the vast majority of Americans.

In a future that is foreseeable—not so far down the road as to be beyond imagination—some other countries will get where we are now, in terms of the standard of living of their people. Nearly all German and British and Japanese families will own cars, for example, probably within a generation.

A little farther down the road, it is possible that most Russian families will own cars, too.

There is nothing unique, or unrepeatable, about our American experience. A combination of education, technology, and reasonably sophisticated government policy to avoid [severe] inflation or depression can eventually bring other industrial countries to our present level of per-capita income, and perhaps even poor countries in a distant future. . . .

In any case, it is rightly said and universally known that the United States has almost unbelievable "economic strength." But those two words . . . do not have self-evident meaning.

Just what does our wealth, our economic power—and its continuing growth—mean for the United States as a nation in the world? . . . [As an example, let's look at the] question of . . . foreign aid.

Here . . . our economic strength gives us, on paper, great [influence]. This includes, of course, the wondrous capacity of our agriculture in a hungry world. There is no doubt, too, that we can use, and have used, our money to [obtain] certain changes and decisions in foreign countries. . . . But the limits turn out to be more impressive than the strength.

The first . . . limit is that our Congress and people do not much like the idea of foreign aid. We simply do not give a great deal—the total is well under 1 per cent of our GNP, even including food give-aways.

The second is that there are great dangers and obstacles involved in bluntly using our money as a bribe to win desirable changes in policy in other countries. The great majority would simply say, "Keep your money, and we'll keep our pride—and our policy." . . . Besides, with a very few exceptions our aid is only a tiny fraction of even a poor country's total resources—hardly enough to give us great [influence] over what they do. . . .

[In fact,] even if we gave a great deal more foreign aid, we could not achieve the partially idealistic and partially selfish purpose of orderly economic development in the poor countries. After more than a decade in the great and frustrating effort to achieve economic development, the world is sadder and wiser; it has found, among other things, that outside capital, while helpful, is not nearly enough to bring about the desired result. There are grave limits to what money can accomplish. . . .

What does our economic power really mean?

It means, first and foremost, a high standard of living for our citizens. Our polluted air and crowded highways notwithstanding, this is a blessing that none of us should overlook. Our wealth has created problems and we certainly have not achieved "the good life"; but our high money incomes have opened up for the great majority of us opportunities for enjoyment and enrichment undreamed of in all history.

It means, second, a relatively painless military power of such dimensions as to make us as safe as a modern nation can be. But perhaps the key words are "relatively painless." The Soviet Union also has enormous military power with only half the economic strength; it was willing to make the sacrifice.

It means, third, a penetration of other countries by our private corporations that is viewed by both us and those nations with mixed feelings, can be cut off by others at any time, and appears to [be unconnected] to the achievement of American diplomatic and political goals.

It may mean, fourth, something in the way of "power of example." Most . . . people in the world, probably even including the Russians, can now see that modern capitalism works pretty well. . . . Many of the Communist countries are even groping toward a form of the profit motive and a more market-oriented price system.

This does not mean, however, that the Nassers, let alone the Castros, or the Indira Gandhis, all follow the example. Nor does it mean that broadly following the economic example says anything about a nation's foreign policy. Ask de Gaulle.

Beyond those four things—only the second of which has [much connection] to the pursuit of our world goals—our economic strength means astonishingly little. If our economy doubles its size again by 1980 or 1985, and further widens its lead over all the rest, this will not make us any better able than we are now to prevent revolutions and aggressions and general waywardness in the rest of the world. Nor will it [improve] our ability to achieve constructive goals such as freer world trade, monetary reform, or economic development of the poor countries.

Perhaps this should not disturb us. Ours is not a tradition of conquest, nor even one of throwing our weight around. But it is well . . . that we recognize and reflect upon the [fact] that our enormous wealth, apart from our military strength, is [little help] in the game of international politics.

We are a giant, to be sure. But the pygmies all about us will not do our bidding—even when we tell them it is for their own good.

51 Measuring Performance: The GNP

It is time now to talk more explicitly about ways of measuring the success of economic decisions. An economic system, after all, is only a means to an end. For the Kwakiutls and Eskimos, the economic goals were fairly simple. As long as enough food was produced, and as long as less basic needs such as the potlatch could be fulfilled, their economic systems were successful—in terms of their own values.

But complex industrial societies like the United States and the Soviet Union value economic growth and progress. It becomes important, therefore, for these societies to have some way of measuring their economic output. Today's lesson will introduce one of the most useful yardsticks of an industrial economy's performance: the Gross National Product (GNP). As you read, keep the following questions in mind:

1. What is the GNP?
2. If a foreign diplomat boasted that his country's GNP had risen 20 per cent in the past year, what questions could you ask him to find out how much real growth his country had achieved?
3. How would you go about calculating the annual GNP for the Island of Wisteria, described in Reading 31?

GNP: Yardstick for an Economy

Gross National Product is nothing more than the sum of all the goods and services that a country produces in a given period of time, usually a year. GNP doesn't mean a nation's stock of wealth—the railroads, buildings, and furniture produced in all the years of the past. It means everything that the nation has produced just in the past year. It includes the value of all the cabbages produced during the year, and all of the other vegetables. And the value of all the television sets and bathing suits and textbooks produced during the year. And the services, too—the value of the doctors' services and the dry cleaners' services a nation consumes. And the new buildings put up and the equipment that went into those buildings. GNP makes no value judgments: It includes whiskey and cigarettes as well as milk and medicine. It includes military armaments, too, if the nation is using its resources to produce such things. All of those things—from cabbages to missiles—become part of the GNP.

But how can we add up all these things to make a single sum? How can we add radishes and stockings and tonsil operations and airplanes? We have only one way of adding them up, and that is by using the prices at which these goods were actually sold. GNP, then, gives us a money total of all the goods and services produced.

Figuring a nation's GNP, however, is trickier than simply adding up all the sales made during a year. Nor is GNP always a perfectly accurate tool with which to measure an economy's performance during a year, or to compare its performance with that of some other economy. A few cautionary notes are in order:

1. To see whether and how an economy is growing or shrinking, it does not much matter how accurate the GNP statistics are, so long as the methods of estimating the GNP are similar from year to year. In the United States, we leave out the value of housewives' services in calculating GNP. (Is it because most of those who calculate GNP are men?) We might very well include those services some year in the future, but we should not fool ourselves into thinking that we'd had real growth in GNP just because we decide to include an item that was excluded from earlier counts. If housewives' services are included one year and excluded the next year, then comparisons between the two years will not

tell us much about the growth or shrinkage of our national economy. For that reason, it is a complicated matter comparing the GNP's of two different countries if each country has its own method of deciding what goes into and what is left out of the GNP.

2. If you use GNP to measure the growth or shrinkage of an economy, you must also take into account inflation and deflation. If the general price level rises sharply from one year to the next because of inflation, and you include all items in the GNP at those higher prices, it may look as if the GNP has gained remarkably during the year. But most of those gains are not real gains, for most do not reflect real growth in the nation's stock of goods and services. (Bread at fifty cents a loaf is not any more filling than the same loaf of bread at twenty cents.) To get a more realistic picture of economic growth, the GNP figures for different years must be adjusted for price differences. Here, the price index discussed in Reading 49 is most helpful. Then, if GNP is calculated for two successive years using figures adjusted for any change in the general level of prices, a higher GNP in Year II over Year I will represent a real advance.

3. To measure accurately what the GNP means in terms of the well-being of individuals, GNP must be seen in relation to population. Here, the use of per-capita figures, discussed in Reading 50, comes into play. For its growth to have a real effect, an economy must increase its GNP at a faster rate than the rate at which its population is increasing. (This point is particularly important for such poor countries as India and China, where the annual rises in GNP are largely offset by dramatic increases in population.)

4. Finally, GNP tells us little of the quality of an economy's products. A bad novel sold for $5.95 counts for just as much in the GNP as a good novel sold at the same price. If an economy produced little else but guns, and produced more of them every year, its GNP would indicate growth. But whether the lives of that country's people were really improving would be questionable.

Keeping those cautionary notes in mind, let's examine some GNP figures for the United States:

TABLE 1. UNITED STATES GROSS NATIONAL PRODUCT
(in billions of dollars)

Year	*Value of goods at time of production*
1929	$103.1
1939	90.5
1949	256.5
1959	483.7
1966	739.5

Source: Economic Report of the President, *January 1967* (*Washington, D.C., 1967*)

1. What do these figures indicate about stability and growth?

Table 2. United States Gross National Product
(in billions of dollars)

Year	*Value in 1958 prices*
1929	$203.6
1939	209.4
1949	324.1
1959	475.9
1966	647.7

Source: Economic Report of the President, *January 1967 (Washington, D.C., 1967)*

1. Why do the figures in Table 1 differ from the figures in Table 2?
2. What conclusions can be drawn by combining the figures in Table 1 and Table 2? How, for example, can the GNP be higher in 1939 than in 1929 in Table 2, while Table 1 showed a fall in GNP during the 1930's?

Table 3. Population of the United States

Year	*Total population*
1929	121,767,000
1939	130,880,000
1949	149,188,000
1959	177,830,000
1966	196,842,000

Source: Economic Report of the President, *January 1967 (Washington, D.C., 1967)*

1. Using 1958 prices and Table 2 figure how much the GNP increased between the years 1929 and 1939.
2. What was the per-capita GNP in 1929 in 1958 prices? What was the per-capita GNP in 1939?

52 Decision-Makers: The Consumer

This and the following two readings examine the three components of GNP and the effects each can have on GNP as a whole. Economists usually think of GNP as divided into three parts; then they tie those three parts together in the equation: GNP = C + I + G. The *C* in that formula stands for the goods and services produced for the personal consumption of all the economy's families. The *I* stands for all the goods produced for investment purposes—the buildings, machines, and tools that can be used eventually to produce other goods or services. And the *G* to the right of the "equals" sign stands for the goods and services produced for our collective consumption through federal, state, and local governments.

In a market society, goods and services are produced only when there is a demand for them. Thus, either private consumers, private businesses, or government must want a particular item and be willing to pay for it in order for it to be produced. And so it is that the separate decisions made by consumers, businessmen, and governmental leaders determine the total level of business activity and, hence, of the incomes flowing into the hands of the economy's people. These next three readings look at three separate decision-makers: the consumer, the businessman, and the governmental leader.

Unless *C*, *I*, and *G* fit together smoothly, GNP will grow too slowly, will try to grow too quickly (producing inflation), or will grow unevenly. *C*, *I*, and *G* are interrelated; a change in one of them will have profound effects on the other two and on the GNP as a whole.

Today's reading concentrates on *C*. The following two readings discuss *I* and *G*. As you read, keep these questions in mind:

1. Why does a small change in *C* produce a large change in *I*?
2. Why does a small rise in *C* tend, in time, to produce a still larger rise in *C* itself?
3. How is the consumer the kingpin?

Personal Consumption: Kingpin of the Market Economy

In the United States, spending on goods and services for personal consumption accounts for more than spending for investment and government put together. In 1966, for example, GNP totalled $740 billion. This was its distribution:

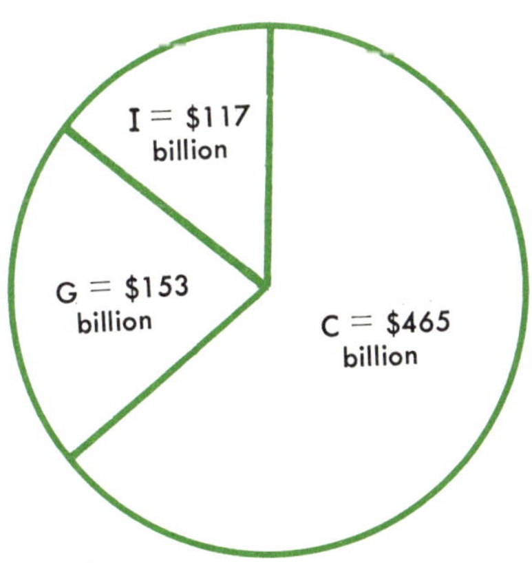

(The remaining $5 billion represented the excess value of our exports over our imports, and is not treated here.) That distribution is not surprising, for our market system operates largely in response to consumer demand. (What fraction of the Soviet Union's GNP would you expect to find in personal consumption?)

For most families, income is the chief determinant of what the family will spend in a given year for personal consumption. In fact, studies have shown that, if the average American family earns an extra $100 in a given year, it will probably spend about $92 of that extra income, and save only $8. Conversely, if a family's income falls by $100, it will probably spend about $92 less on personal consumption, and cut its savings by only $8.

As a family's income rises or falls, the amounts it spends on different personal consumption items do not all change in the same proportion. No matter what its income, a family needs a certain minimum amount of food. If a poor family's income falls $100 from one year to the next, it probably will not cut its spending on food as much as it will cut its spending on less essential items.

A family with an annual income of $50,000 probably spends more on food than a family with an income of $5,000. It may even spend two or three times as much. But it will probably not spend ten times as much, unless it takes to eating black caviar for breakfast, lunch, and dinner. Hence, the family with an income of $50,000 spends a smaller *proportion* of its income on food than the family with an income of $5,000.

Changes in income have a much larger effect on consumer spending for *durable goods*—goods that are expected to last a number of years. True, many Americans consider such durable goods as automobiles and toasters as necessities of life. Those items, however, are not necessities in the same way that food is. You need food every day because your body demands it. But you can put off buying that new convertible, or that instamatic, slide-up toaster. Thus, purchases of durable goods fluctuate more than food purchases. When families' incomes rise, or when families expect them to rise, many more durable goods will be sold than when families' incomes fall, or when families expect them to fall. This fact was borne out during the Depression of the 1930's. In those years, food purchases fell, as the average family turned to a cheaper diet. But food purchases did not fall nearly as much as purchases of automobiles, homes, and other durable goods.

Businessmen who produce durable goods, therefore, are strongly affected by even small changes in personal income. In a year of even mild recession, thousands of families may postpone buying new toasters. This can have a profound effect on spending for investment—spending by toaster manufacturers for new toaster-making machinery for example.

In a normal year, a toaster manufacturer would buy a certain number of new machines for his factory to replace machines that had worn out. But in a year of recession, with a sharp drop in sales, a toaster manufacturer would likely postpone buying new machinery, for the new machinery would only produce toasters that could not be sold. Hence, a small drop in personal income could bring investment in the toaster industry almost to a halt. What effect would this have on the companies that manufacture toaster-maker machinery? What does this say about the relationship between *C* and *I*?

Now we'll look at the other side of the coin. In a prosperous year, families that had put off buying toasters would finally buy them. How will this affect spending for investment—spending by toaster manufacturers for new toaster-making machinery? What effect will this have on the companies that manufacture toaster-making machinery? And again, what does this say about the relationship between *C* and *I*?

Now let's see what happens when the sales of the toaster-machine manufacturers change. In a recession year, as we have seen, the sales of toaster makers could drop sharply. Faced with this turn in fortunes, the toaster-machine manufacturers would be likely to lay off employees. Those employees, in turn, would spend less for personal consumption. And that would mean smaller sales for the supermarkets, home construction companies, and other businesses from which the employees ordinarily buy goods and services. Thus, a decline in spending could have a downward spiraling effect; it could lead to a further decline in spending, as the whole economy shrinks and GNP falls.

In a prosperous year, on the other hand, more toaster-making machines would be sold. Employees of the toaster-machine manufacturer would probably earn higher wages from overtime. They, in turn, would have more money to spend on food and durable goods. Thus other people's incomes would also rise. In this case, the upward spiraling effect increases GNP and expands the economy.

As we have seen, personal consumption and investment are closely linked. A small change in personal consumption can produce a great change in investment. And that change in investment can, in turn, affect personal consumption. It was because of the interrelatedness of *C* and *I* that American auto manufacturers tried to combat the 1958 recession with the slogan, "You auto buy now."

In sum, the decisions of millions of separate households govern the *C* component of the GNP in a market economy. And nothing influences those decisions as much as real or expected changes in each family's income. However big the changes in families' spending in any year, the changes are likely to be even greater in the investment spending of industry—the *I* component of GNP. Thus, a change in one part of the economy can produce reverberations that spread and spread.

53 Decision-Makers: The Business Investor

We now turn to the second major part of GNP: business investment, the *I* in the equation GNP = C + I + G. In Reading 52 we saw that a small change in C can have a large effect on I. Now we focus on I itself. Business investment can be roughly divided into three parts. First is building construction—including factories, railway lines, homes, and office buildings. Second is equipment that can be used to make other goods—such as trucks, tractors, machinery in factories, and carpenter's tools. Third is *inventory*, the stocks of goods produced and stored by producers until they are sold. Inventory is counted as investment because it represents goods that can be sold in the future.

This lesson concentrates on why businessmen decide to invest or not to invest and what effect their decisions can have on the economy as a whole. As you read, think about the following questions:

1. How can a change in I produce a change in C?
2. For what economic reason may one businessman's decision to invest influence another businessman's decision?
3. What are some of the factors that can make an investment profitable or unprofitable?

Investment: A Gamble for Profits

When economic historians try to sort out the causes of the Great Depression of the 1930's, they often look for the weak spots in the generally prosperous economy of the 1920's. Often they draw two interrelated conclusions.

First, consumer spending—the C in the GNP equation—was in a dangerous state in the late 1920's. Most families that could afford such new and expensive items as homes and automobiles had already bought them. Millions of other families, however, had such small incomes that they could not hope to buy those items. It is clear—at least with the advantage of hindsight—that producers of expensive, durable goods were in for trouble. Soon they would be producing more than they could sell; the prospects for new investment spending for machinery to produce such goods were far from hopeful.

This brings us to the second point economic historians often make about the economy of the 1920's. In the late 1920's, they agree, GNP was still rising, and businesses were making handsome profits. All businesses, however, were not sharing evenly in those profits. In fact, investment in building construction was dropping off. This, economists now realize, may be a sign of a threatening recession or depression for, in the United States, millions of jobs depend on the building-construction industry.

The 1920's and the subsequent Great Depression may have been one of the most dramatic examples of the impact of investment decisions on the economy. But the same basic process—businessmen deciding, on the basis of their estimates of the economic outlook, how much to spend on new plant and equipment—works in every year.

Business investment in the 1960's, as well as in the 1920's, is the result of independent decisions made by millions of businessmen. We cannot, of course, explain the causes behind all of those millions of decisions. But it is clear that the most important factor affecting investment is the way in which businessmen see their prospects. Suppose a businessman is considering building a new plant. He will do so only if he thinks he can make a profit. And he must estimate whether the profit from the new plant will be greater or less than the profit he could make by otherwise using the money needed to build a new plant—or by just letting the money gather interest in a bank.

Any investment, of course, is a gamble. A businessman cannot be absolutely sure that his investment will pay off in the future. But few businessmen plan their investments blindfolded. They try to make educated guesses about the future. And because their future profits and livelihood may depend on the accuracy of those guesses, businessmen are sensitive to many trends in their own field and in the economy as a whole.

New technical improvements, for example, can make businessmen hopeful—or discouraged—about future profits from further investment. The invention of an automobile that needed no gasoline might spur investment in new automobile plants, but it would probably discourage construction of new oil wells. Businessmen are also sensitive to federal, state, and local governments. If businessmen feel that the government is unsympathetic to business, and likely to raise business taxes, new investment could well be postponed. Businessmen react to thousands of other developments as well—from their own current profit pictures to the weather.

In fact, businessmen's feelings are like some of the old-fashioned childhood diseases. Although their origin is hard to pin down, they are very contagious. Depressions and times of prosperity can be read in part as a barometer of businessmen's educated guesses about the future. Good times are periods when most businessmen are hopeful about future prospects. Thus, they invest more, and thereby create more jobs and more income for consumers—which, in turn, spurs still more investment. Bad times are periods when businessmen are reluctant to invest because they fear that they will lose from their investments. When this happens, there are fewer jobs and less income for consumers—and this, in turn, reduces business investment still further.

The following excerpt illustrates the importance of businessmen's educated guesses about future profits. It is taken from a *New York Times* article on the effects of the 1964 tax cut:

> Perhaps the [healthiest] development was the confirmation by the General Motors Corporation of reports that it was undertaking a record two-year $2 billion capital-spending plan that would result in the creation of some 50,000 new jobs.
>
> This was the latest and one of the most dramatic instances of corporate confidence. American industry is embarked on record capital investment that is linked both to the present high level of consumer spending and to

the expectation that such spending will be nudged higher once the benefits of the new tax law fan out into the economic stream.

While the General Motors spending announcement provided stocks with a new stimulus, it was not an isolated corporate development.

On a more modest scale, thousands of other corporations are shaping plans for higher capital spending. These represent one of the strongest props under the economy at the moment.*

Why did the tax cut make General Motors hopeful about the profitability of new investments? What effect do you think General Motors' announcement had on steel and rubber corporations?

54 Decision-Makers: The Government

Today's reading looks at government spending, the third major part of GNP. Although Americans often think of federal, state, and local government spending as separate from the rest of the economy, they are in fact as interrelated with *C* and *I* as *C* and *I* are with each other. The effects on *C* and *I* of changes in government spending will be discussed in Reading 56. Today we will concentrate on government spending itself—what it is and what it represents.

As you read, think about the following questions:

1. What are the main sources of government income? What are the largest government expenditures?
2. Why is it often convenient for Americans to have some of their resources spent by governments, instead of by private consumers and businessmen?

1. Patterns of Government Spending

In the nineteenth century, the American economy could be almost completely described by the equation, GNP = C + I. While governments had a considerable influence on the economy in those years (see pp. 77–78), government spending was relatively small.

The federal government maintained a small army and navy, and paid the salaries of officials; but the cost was so low that an income tax was unnecessary. The federal government, in fact, was run mainly on revenues from tariffs and from taxes on liquor and tobacco. With World War I and the Depression of the 1930's, however, federal government spending finally rose above the $5 billion mark. Then came World War II. To supply its own huge armed forces, and to help supply those of its allies, the United States increased its federal government spending enormously, to a high of $96 billion in 1944.

* From *The New York Times,* March 22, 1964.

Since World War II, the Cold War and the huge expense of modern weapons have pushed federal spending further upward. In the year that started July 1, 1965, and ended June 30, 1966, the federal government spent $107 billion. Of that total, the biggest part went for defense—$55 billion. Another $5 billion was spent on programs for veterans, an expenditure resulting from past wars. Interest owed people who had bought government bonds, also sold largely in past wars, came to $12 billion. In other words, $72 billion of the total federal expenditure of $107 billion went for past, present, and future wars. And $6 billion more was spent on the space program, which has contributed to weapons development. The remaining $29 billion was used mostly for education, housing, the War on Poverty, transportation, and the salaries and office expenses of all federal employees.

Federal government revenues in that same year came mostly from individual income taxes and corporate income taxes. Smaller amounts came from excise taxes on such items as liquor and cigarettes, and from tariffs.

In the 1920's, state and local government spending still surpassed federal government spending. Today, state and local governments spend just about as much as the federal government. While the federal government bought $77 billion worth of goods and services,* all state and local governments bought $76 billion worth. About 40 per cent of that $76 billion went for education. Smaller amounts were spent on welfare and highways. Most of the revenues of states, counties, cities, and towns came from sales taxes, property taxes, grants from the federal government, and state and local income taxes.

2. Automobiles or Highways?

Consumption and investment spending, as we have seen, are determined mainly by the individual decisions of millions of consumers and businessmen. Government spending is determined by those same consumers and businessmen, when they act as citizens in a democracy. Thus, government spending can be seen as the result of a decision by the citizenry to let its government spend some part of the nation's resources to satisfy wants that could not be satisfied by free enterprise alone.

National defense, for example, could not be practically conducted by millions of businessmen and consumers in the free marketplace. Instead, the citizenry as a whole has decided that it is to its advantage to have armed forces, and that those armed forces can best be recruited, trained, equipped, and commanded by a central government.

Cities and towns have public police and fire departments for the same reason. Leaving those important services to the free marketplace would

* Total federal spending was higher than this because each year the federal government transfers certain amounts of money by Social Security payments, for example. However, no direct purchase of goods or services is involved.

be risky. A private fire department might well lose money: Fire-fighting equipment is expensive, and those who needed the fire department's services might not always be able to pay for them. Moreover, private owners of fire-fighting companies might push their charges to excessive levels once they found a customer who, with a fire blazing in his attic, was in no position to argue over prices. For these reasons, the community has usually decided that it is to the community's advantage to pay taxes to support a public fire department.

When a legislature considers a tax bill, then, it is deciding whether that money would be better spent by the community as a whole, or by individual producers and consumers. Because of the fact of economic scarcity, when a government spends money for goods and services, that same purchasing power cannot be used by individual consumers and producers.

Americans place a high value on letting individuals decide how they want to spend their incomes. But Americans also value the many services governments can perform. Hence, the United States has had to strike a balance between private and public spending—a balance between spending for consumer goods like automobiles and public services like highways. Ideally, that balance should represent the best possible use of the nation's resources.

As an example, let us look at that question of automobiles and highways. Individually, most American families have decided that they want to spend part of their income on at least one automobile apiece. More automobiles, however, create a need for related goods and services.

Some of these related goods and services can best be provided by private businesses. Thus, because of the growing number of automobiles, thousands of gas stations and motels are flourishing. More automobiles also require related public services. If we decide to buy more automobiles, we may need to accept higher taxes to pay for better highways, traffic policemen, municipal hospitals, and protection against air pollution caused by automobiles. Thus private spending for automobiles and government spending for services required by automobiles are interrelated.

The problem, as we mentioned before, is to find the ideal balance. Because their resources are limited, Americans must make hard choices. They must decide how much personal income they are willing to surrender in taxes for the governmental services required by automobiles. They may even have to decide whether they would like a greater number of automobiles, or a good highway system for a smaller number of automobiles.

The problem of the balance between private and public spending—between spending on automobiles and highways, for example—is only one of the lively issues centering on government spending. At least as important is the question of how much government spending will best stabilize the economy at a point where employment is highest and inflation the least. Reading 56 will return to that question.

55 Money Matters Too

Money may be the root of all evil; but it is not the root of all economics. The subject of money is mysterious and complex—and it is not central in understanding the basic elements of an economic system. It is for that reason that we have postponed a discussion of money until late in the course.

Today's reading is divided into two parts. The first part discusses what money is. The second part discusses how money can affect the economic activity of a society. As you read, keep the following questions in mind:

1. What is money? How are you discharging a debt when you buy a pair of shoes?
2. Why do interest rates behave like prices?
3. How can the Federal Reserve System try to prevent inflation? How can it try to prevent depression?

1. Money: What It Is

Few words in the English language are the focus of more emotion than *money*. And few words are more poorly understood. The source of most of the confusion is the common failure to see one central point: Money *is* what money *does*. Money doesn't have to have any value in itself; cows and gold and wampum beads and scraps of paper have all been used as money. And only the cows and, for some purposes, the gold have much value in themselves. What makes those things useful as money is the fact that other men were willing to accept them in payment of debts.

As we have noted, all societies do not use minted metals and printed paper for money. But all societies do find that money must have certain properties before it will be widely used and accepted as a way of discharging debts. To be generally accepted in an advanced society where trading is heavy, money must have these properties:

1. It must be difficult to reproduce, so that the total quantity in circulation is under control. Otherwise, each unit would lose its worth, for someone could flood the market with his own version of the money.
2. It must be easy to transfer from one place to another, even in very large sums.
3. It must be relatively stable in form, so that it doesn't quickly change in appearance.
4. It must be capable of being broken easily and precisely into units of different sizes.

Test the importance of each of these properties by asking whether ice cubes would make satisfactory money in this country.

In the United States when most people think of money, they think first of a stock of bills and coins in various denominations. In the United States, there was about $38 billion circulating in coins and bills at the end of 1966. But in truth, the money supply at the end of 1966 was much larger, for the total money supply also included the $132 billion in checking accounts in banks. These bank deposits are money just as much as the coins and bills circulating from hand to hand. Why? *Because they meet the simple test that they could be used to settle debts nearly as easily as the coins or bills could be used.* (Unless you looked like a highly suspicious character, a shoe store would accept a $10 check or money order drawn on your personal banking account as readily as a $10 bill in exchange for a $10 pair of shoes.)

With $132 billion in bank accounts, and only $38 billion in what Americans like to call "hard cash," it is obvious that there would not be nearly enough coins and bills to go around if everyone at once tried to have his bank deposit changed into coins and bills. Yet panics are rare. One did occur in March 1933, in the midst of the Depression. People then feared that their bank deposits might be lost—and some banks were indeed going bankrupt. But unfortunately, thousands of people did the one thing they should not have done. They rushed to their banks and demanded that their bank deposits be turned into bills and coins at once. The banks found themselves short-handed, and many went bankrupt.

Fortunately, there is usually a more even balance between the number of people putting their coins and bills into bank deposits, and the number of people withdrawing their bank deposits in the form of coins and bills. In fact, it takes fewer and fewer bills, in proportion to the GNP, to transact the nation's growing business. Today, about 80 per cent of the money that changes hands in the United States is in the form of checks.

There is another reason why your money is safer in a bank today than it was in 1933. Today, most banks belong to the Federal Deposit Insurance Corporation (FDIC), a government agency which insures every bank account smaller than $15,000. Thus, so long as your bank belongs to the FDIC, your bank account is safe, even if the chief teller cleans out the vaults and flees to the French Riviera.

2. Money: What It Can Do

The primary purpose of money, of course, is to carry on trade. If you're a secretary, a shoe store does not have to demand four hours of stenography in exchange for the $10 pair of shoes you want to buy. It can simply accept $10 of the money you earned taking dictation for someone else.

Money has another important function as well, a function directly related to the stability and growth of the economy. By lending out money, banks and similar institutions can make it possible for business to expand production or construct new plants before increased sales dollars start coming in. Lending also makes it possible for consumers to buy automobiles, homes, or appliances before they have saved enough money to buy those items outright.

Thus, if there isn't much money around for lending purposes, the economy will be slowed down, for both consumption spending for large items and business investment will be reduced. If the supply of money is relatively scarce in relation to the demand, fewer businesses and individuals will be able to get loans, and those who do get loans will have to pay more in interest for the privilege of borrowing. (The interest rate, which is the price of using money, usually behaves just like the prices for any other item. Small supply and large demand for money drives the interest rate up, and large supply and small demand drives it down.) Conversely, plentiful money and low interest rates will lure more businesses into expanding, and more customers into buying large items.

The supply of money, unlike the supply of most other goods and services, is determined mainly by the federal government. Coins and bills are, of course, issued only by the federal government. And the federal government decides how much to mint and print according to estimates of the need for coins or bills for business transactions in which checks are either a nuisance (to buy a newspaper, for example) or unacceptable (for people who have no bank accounts).

The volume of bank-deposit money is a more complicated matter. The key decisions are again made by the government. Suppose that the federal government feared that a recession was about to begin, or that the economy should grow faster. For these purposes, it would want to make money more plentiful and interest rates lower—for that would encourage investment, and thus expand the economy.

To achieve those goals, the federal government would use the Federal Reserve System, a system of banks that serve the government and private banks. (The Federal Reserve System is a government agency but, like the Supreme Court, it is largely independent of the President and Congress.) To stimulate the economy, the Federal Reserve banks would buy back government bonds from banks and private citizens. The sellers of those bonds would then most likely deposit in bank accounts the money received from selling their bonds. Then the private banks, in turn, finding themselves with more money in their accounts, would be willing to make more loans.

The same mechanism works in reverse. Suppose that the government wants to slow down the economy to prevent wild inflation. Then the Federal Reserve banks can sell government bonds to banks and private citizens. The Federal Reserve banks would keep the money received from selling those bonds out of circulation. The result? Banks would find themselves with less money in their accounts and would make fewer loans.

Using the Federal Reserve System to control the supply of money is but one way in which the federal government can promote stability in the economy. The mechanisms are neither precise nor foolproof. But they have given us a more stable economy than we might otherwise have had.

56 America's Quest for Stability and Growth: The New Pattern

"The power to tax," Chief Justice John Marshall wrote in one of his most famous decisions, "is the power to destroy." As we shall see in Reading 56, the power to tax is also the power to build. In Reading 55, we saw how the federal government can help promote economic stability by controlling the supply of money. Today we shall see how the federal government can promote stability by tinkering with the equation: GNP = C + I + G. The views expressed in the following reading are not held by all economists, let alone all Americans. Some believe that the government should play a less active role in the economy. But nearly all economists now agree that the government cannot help but have some influence on the economy. Whatever happens to *G* will have an effect on the equation GNP = C + I + G.

As you read, keep the following questions in mind:

1. What did Keynes recommend that a government do to head off depression? Why?
2. What did Keynes recommend that a government do to head off inflation? Why?
3. Does the adoption of Keynes's theories make the United States more or less of a market economy? Why?

An Economic Theory in Action

When the Depression of the 1930's hit most of North America and Europe, governments found their incomes dwindling as tax receipts fell and their expenses rising as emergency relief needs became more pressing. Most governments thought they had but one possible course to follow: They must raise tax rates to increase revenues, and cut non-relief expenditures to lessen total government spending.

When those actions seemed to do no good, most governments were at a loss for new ideas. Some citizens began listening to the Communists, who proclaimed that if the entire capitalist system were replaced with Communism, there would be no unemployment and no depressions. But an English economist named John Maynard Keynes (*canes*) did not believe that the world had to choose between Communism and depression. He saw another way out, a way that could make the market economies more stable, while preserving their freedom.

Keynes first attacked the market economies' traditional answers to depressions. Raising taxes, he pointed out, simply leaves households with less income. And, since personal consumption depends mainly on income, still lower personal-consumption spending would result. As earlier readings in this chapter pointed out, lower consumption spending would discourage businessmen from investing in new plants or modernizing their equipment. Instead, they would be forced to lay off still more workers—and the depression would become worse than ever. Cuts in government spending would have the same effects, for the government would be forced to fire some of its employees.

Instead, Keynes proposed, governments should decrease taxes and increase spending during a depression. The idea seemed ridiculous, for most politicians, most economics professors, and most economics textbooks still proclaimed that the government would suffer just as much from an unbalanced budget as a family would. The "conventional wisdom" of the day decreed that, as government's revenues fell and its expenses grew in a depression, taxes must be raised and all non-essential spending curtailed.

Using historical examples, let us see what Keynes's theories meant for this "conventional wisdom." We start with the equation developed in Reading 52: GNP = C + I + G. That formula was unfamiliar to both President Herbert C. Hoover and Governor Franklin D. Roosevelt of New York, the two candidates for the Presidency in 1932. But both pledged to try and end the Depression by sharply raising GNP:

Goal

↑

GNP = C + I + G

So far, Keynes could not have agreed more. But Hoover and Roosevelt proposed using the old methods—raising taxes and cutting government expenditures—to achieve the goal of higher GNP. They both declared that a balanced federal budget was the only way to end the Depression.

With the advantage of hindsight, we can now say that the methods proposed by Hoover and Roosevelt would have been disastrous. Higher taxes and lower government spending would have cut personal consumption and investment spending even further. This, then, would have been the picture:

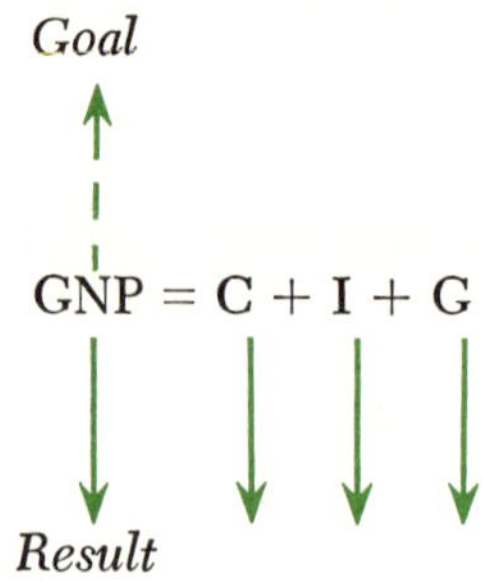

The *C* would have dropped as people's after-tax income fell. (Recall that income is the biggest determinant of *C*.) And *I* would have dropped as businessmen saw that they could keep less of the profits they made.

As it turned out, President Roosevelt fulfilled his pledge to raise taxes—and the economy suffered as a result. But at the same time, he increased government spending, and thereby helped the economy recover. Roosevelt increased government spending because he saw the need for federal government programs to put unemployed Americans back to work, not because he read Keynes's writings. But the effects were the same as if he had.

Now let's skip over thirty intervening years to 1963–64. President John F. Kennedy and, after Kennedy's assassination, President Lyndon B. Johnson faced a sluggish economy. No severe depression seemed to be threatening, but there was less growth and more unemployment than the government thought was necessary. The federal government was already spending more than it was taking in. What should be done?

The wisdom of the 1920's would have said, "Increase taxes and cut spending!" But the ideas of Keynes and other economists influenced by Keynes were gaining acceptance by the early 1960's. Neither Kennedy nor Johnson proposed higher government spending to enliven the economy, perhaps because each feared congressional opposition to such a proposal. But each in turn became a vigorous advocate of lower taxes.

Lower taxes? When the budget was already unbalanced, and the government already had an enormous debt? That was what Keynes would have proposed, and that is what Congress approved in 1964. And the tax cuts of 1964 had just the effects Keynes would have predicted. Lower taxes meant higher take-home pay; and Americans spent most of those extra dollars on consumer goods and services, prompting businessmen to expand production. In sum:

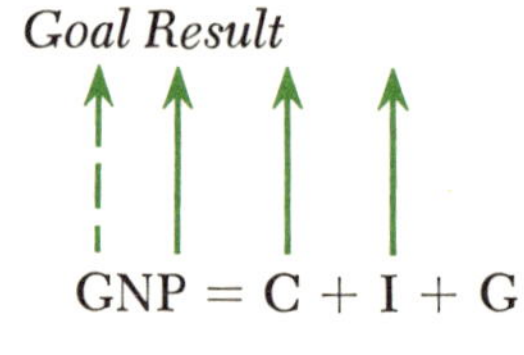

Keynes's theory finally had a clear-cut test—and proved itself. The American economy began the longest single period of uninterrupted growth that it had ever seen except in wartime.

But economics still remains an inexact science. Economists still do not know just how much to change either tax rates or government spending to achieve the stability and growth we desire. Moreover, economics and politics are thickly intertwined. Even if we could calculate the exact size of a tax rate or a government spending level needed to achieve greater stability and growth, those prescriptions would have to be translated into actions by the President and the Congress. Tax increases are rarely popular—yet the same logic which says that tax cuts may head off depressions says that tax hikes may head off inflation. And once a government program has begun, it is difficult to cut it back—yet if government continues its high level of spending even when there are no idle resources lying around to be employed, the effect may be to drive up prices.

Those who are optimistic about the future of the American economy assert flatly that we'll never again have a depression comparable to the Great Depression of the 1930's. They are confident that both major political parties will use the ideas of Keynes and the powers of government to head off any threatening depression. But even the most optimistic defenders of our economic policies of today have some gnawing doubts. They wonder if we'll prove both wise and courageous enough to restrain the economy when it becomes overheated—and to act fast enough when it becomes sluggish. None of this means that Americans are abandoning their heavy reliance on free markets and private decisions to achieve our economic goals. It only means that we have decided to use the powers of government to help the market system work better.

And what would Keynes himself, who died in 1946, have thought? He'd have been surprised neither by the slowness with which his ideas took hold, nor by the power of those ideas once they did take hold. As Keynes himself wrote at the end of his classic work, *The General Theory of Employment, Interest, and Money:*

> [T]he ideas of economists and political philosophers, both when they are right and when they are wrong, are more powerful than is commonly understood. Indeed the world is ruled by little else. Practical men, who believe themselves to be quite exempt from any intellectual influences, are usually the slaves of some defunct economist. Madmen in authority, who hear voices in the air, are distilling their frenzy from some academic scribbler of a few years back. I am sure that the power of vested interests is vastly exaggerated compared with the gradual encroachment of ideas. . . . [S]oon or late, it is ideas, not vested interests, which are dangerous for good or evil.*

* From John Maynard Keynes, *The General Theory of Employment, Interest, and Money* (New York: Harcourt, Brace & World, Inc., 1936).

Chapter 12

Growth and Stability in the Soviet Economy

STATING THE ISSUE The workings of the Soviet economy, like the workings of the American economy, can be described by the equation GNP = C + I + G. But there is one important difference: In the Soviet Union, the size of *C* and *I*, as well as *G*, are determined mainly by the government. Consumer expenditures in the Soviet Union are regulated by the salaries which the government pays and the consumption goods which the government offers for sale. Through most of its history, the Soviet Union has tried to keep consumer expenditures low. Hence it has paid small salaries in relation to the total GNP. And it has offered only relatively limited quantities of consumer goods for sale.

Keeping consumer expenditures low has an economic purpose. It can help produce a large investment for capital goods—a large *I*. That large investment is achieved in two ways. First, by paying small salaries in relation to total GNP, the Soviet government has more money left over to invest in capital goods. Second, by controlling the quantity of consumer goods available, the government encourages saving in state banks. That money, too, can be used for capital expenditures by the government. Thus in the Soviet Union, *I* takes up a larger slice of the economic pie than in the United States.

The goal of the Soviet Union's emphasis on capital investment is economic growth—a rising GNP. Eventually, the Soviet leaders promise, the Russian people will share the fruits of their labor in the form of a vastly improved standard of living. But until that time, the Soviet people are asked to sacrifice their current standard of living in favor of building a stock of capital goods that will raise their standard of living in the future. And, barring massive foreign aid, a relatively low *C* does seem to be the only way to produce a rapidly growing *I* and a rapidly growing GNP.

Chapter 12 describes the achievements and failures of the Soviet Union in its pursuit of a rising GNP. It raises these central questions: How do the United States and the Soviet Union differ in their approach to economic growth? Where has the Soviet Union had its greatest successes in promoting economic growth? Where has it had its greatest failures?

57 The Soviet Record to Date

In the Soviet Union, economic growth receives far more attention than economic stability. The official Soviet line is that there is no such thing as unemployment in the planned economy. Western experts on the Soviet economy are not so sure; in any event, they insist that there is considerable *under*employment—that is, less than fully efficient use of labor, particularly in agriculture. But, except for the frequent crises in agriculture, it does seem true that the Soviet Union has not seen as big rises and falls in employment as the market economies of the West have seen.

The next two readings, therefore, focus on the problem to which the Russians address themselves so often: the problem of rapid growth in the economy. Today's reading looks at the economic policies and achievements of the regimes of Joseph Stalin and Nikita Khrushchev. (For historical background, refer to Reading 32.)

As you read, keep these questions in mind:

1. How does the drive for economic growth in the Soviet Union resemble the drive for economic growth in the United States? How is it different?
2. Why are Soviet consumer goods often made impractically?
3. How has the poor performance of Soviet agriculture retarded the overall growth of the Soviet economy?

Stalin's Legacy and Khrushchev's Quest

During his twenty-five year reign, one thought dominated Stalin's approach to economic issues: industrialization. Both for domestic development and for protection against what he saw as a hostile world, Stalin used all of his great power to industrialize the Soviet Union as rapidly as its resources would permit. The current standard of living was neglected in favor of electric power and petroleum, iron and steel production, heavy machinery and armaments.

In pushing for economic growth, Stalin used both the carrot and the stick. Those who helped achieve his targets for heavy industry's growth were well rewarded. Those who lagged behind or pushed for other goals, such as an increase in consumer goods, were punished, often brutally. Stalin used the full force of a totalitarian state to build the base for a strong industrial future.

In the terms that mattered most to Stalin, his reign was a success: The economy produced 1 million metric tons of steel a year when he came into power, and 34 million metric tons when he died; its production of electricity rose from less than 2 billion kilowatt hours to over 119 billion kilowatt hours in the same period. Moreover, Stalin's emphasis on armaments and practical science built the foundation on which the Soviet Union's dramatic space and weapons triumphs of the late 1950's were based.

But the cost was high. Life for the consumer improved very little in those years. Most Russians lived in constant fear of the cruelty of the government. And in at least one sector, agriculture, there was near chaos throughout the Stalin regime.

By 1955, two years after Stalin's death, Nikita Khrushchev had emerged as the leader of the Soviet Union. The new Premier wasted little time in harshly attacking Stalin's policies. "The cult of [Stalin's] personality has caused the employment of faulty principles in party work and in economic activity," he told the Twentieth Congress of the Communist Party of the Soviet Union in February 1956. New economic signals began to flow from the Kremlin. There was still the same bold talk about overcoming the West's industrial leadership—"We will bury you," Khrushchev asserted. But with that talk there also came a slackening of some of the tightest controls, a new emphasis on consumer goods, and a new concern about agriculture.

Under Khrushchev, industrial production continued to forge ahead. It may not have risen the full threefold that Khrushchev claimed; but it at least doubled. On the other hand, for all of Khrushchev's concern and his interest in trying new methods, he was considerably less successful in agriculture, where production failed even to approach the goals set by Gosplan.

Khrushchev's economic policies were more successful in the late 1950's than the early 1960's. By the early 1960's it was becoming increasingly evident that the Soviet economy was trying to do too many things at once. The space and armaments exploits were continuing; the production of consumer goods was sharply on the rise; and the growth of heavy industry was continuing. Perhaps it was the continuing drive for more heavy industry that was creating the biggest difficulties. With a GNP less than half that of the United States, the Soviet economy was devoting almost as many resources to investment goods as the United States was. The military and space expenditures were also close to those in the United States.

Points of strain began to show up. In 1959, agricultural production leveled off, while population kept rising. The Russian people, while consuming about the same number of calories as Americans, were still heavily dependent upon potatoes and grains. About 70 per cent of their diet consisted of those low-quality foods, as compared with about 28 per cent for Americans.

The production of consumer goods, while rising in quantity, was scarcely satisfactory. Khrushchev himself put his finger on the problem in 1959:

> It has become the tradition to produce not beautiful chandeliers to adorn homes, but the heaviest chandeliers possible. This is because the heavier the chandeliers produced, the more a factory gets since its output is calculated in tons. So the factories make chandeliers weighing hundreds of kilograms and fulfill the plan. But who needs such a plan? . . .
>
> Many consumers often don't want to purchase our Soviet-made furniture. They look for foreign furniture because it is more [sensible]. The plan for furniture factories is stated in rubles. Consequently the factories find it more advantageous to make a massive armchair since the heavier the chair the more expensive it is. [On paper,] the plan is thus fulfilled since the furniture makers add this and that to the armchair and make it cost more money. But who needs such armchairs? If they were to manufacture ordinary chairs, do you realize how many would have to be made to fulfill the plan? The factories ponder: armchairs or ordinary chairs? The weight of the armchairs finally decides the issue in their favor. Everybody knows this. Everybody talks a good deal about this, but still the armchairs win.*

Khrushchev recognized the problems in agriculture and the production of consumer goods; but his remedies failed to solve them. Whether the problems resulted from poor planning, or the clumsiness of overall planning itself, is not clear. The Communist Party, however, blamed Khrushchev. In 1964, he was ousted, partly because of his failures in economic policy.

Premier Aleksei Kosygin, who together with Leonid Brezhnev succeeded Khrushchev, brings a deeper knowledge of formal economics to his job than did any of his predecessors. Nevertheless, Kosygin appears to share Stalin's and Khrushchev's zeal for growth. Like them, he will have to balance the interrelated needs of heavy industry, armaments and space industries, agriculture, and all the consumer goods industries. Whether Kosygin's knowledge of economics will make him more successful than was Khrushchev remains to be seen. He may see ways in which less overall planning and more use of incentives will hasten growth. But an economy long used to sweeping plans for growth, and proud of many of the accomplishments already made, is not likely to try totally new approaches to growth. As far as can now be seen, the Soviet Union, despite greater use of incentives, will probably continue to have an economy run basically by command—just as the United States, despite the growth of government, will likely continue to have an economy run basically by the market.

* *Pravda,* July 2, 1959. Quoted, in English translation, in Harry Schwartz, *The Soviet Economy Since Stalin* (Philadelphia: J. B. Lippincott Company, 1965), p. 141.

58 The Soviet Path to Growth

Karl Marx was primarily an historian, not an economist. Like many historians before and since, he tried to do the impossible: He tried to predict the future. Communism, in fact, is a philosophy of history. It can prove itself fully accurate only if the pure communism which was Marx's ideal comes to pass in the future. Partly for that reason, the Soviet Union's leaders are deeply concerned about the future.

This final reading on the Soviet economy looks at the Soviet Union's future as seen by an American expert on the Soviet economy. The article was written shortly after Premier Nikita Khrushchev was overthrown and replaced by the team of Leonid Brezhnev and Aleksei Kosygin. News stories since that date suggest that the conclusions of the article are still accurate. The hopes and prospects for the Soviet Union's future have changed little since 1965.

As you read, keep the following questions in mind:

1. Judging from the readings in this unit, how do you think the attitudes toward economic growth differ in the United States and the Soviet Union?
2. Why do you suppose the Soviet leaders make so many predictions about their own economy that turn out to be wrong? Could American leaders do better in predicting the economic future of the United States? Why or why not?
3. How do the main economic goals of the Soviet Union seem to be changing? If they are achieved, in what ways will the Soviet Union resemble the United States? In what ways will it remain different?

Planning for a Communist Future

HARRY SCHWARTZ

As the 1960's neared their mid-point, it was clear that the Soviet economy had lost much of its former capacity to impress and inspire awe in other nations. The alarm about the higher rate of Soviet economic growth that had marked the 1960 American Presidential race was . . . absent in the 1964 contest. The leaders of Communist China, a country still recovering from its own economic [failures] of 1959–1962, addressed the leaders of the Soviet Communist party with these mocking words in February 1964: "We would like to say in passing that . . . we are very much concerned about the present economic situation in the Soviet Union. If you should feel the need for the help of Chinese experts in certain fields, we would be glad to send them."

Even Premier Khrushchev, the [confident] propagandist who had so often earlier predicted capitalism's economic defeat by superior Soviet performance, reflected the changed situation by warning, before his ouster: "If the socialist system gives a person fewer economic and spiritual goods than the capitalist system, certain people are going to think it over and say: 'Why the devil did we substitute one for the other?' " His subsequent removal from power resulted in part, as we have seen, from the unsatisfactory results of his economic policy as compared with the extravagant predictions he had made.

Here is the way the positive aspects of the first full post-Stalin decade, 1954–1963, were summarized by an outstanding Soviet economist:

> About 60 per cent of the industrial production of the entire [forty-six years] of the Soviet state's existence was produced in these ten years; capital investments during that time accounted for more than two thirds of the total invested during the forty-six years. Both power plant capacity and the amount of electricity generated more than tripled during the decade. The metallurgical industry turned out more than 450 million tons of pig iron and over 630 million tons of steel, amounts considerably exceeding the output of these metals during the [previous hundred years]. Petroleum production was more than 1 billion tons, [also surpassing production of the preceding century].

Academician Arzumanyan, who wrote these words, might have made other claims as well. Between 1953 and 1964 a vast technological revolution took place in Soviet industry with resulting great increases in productivity. In these years the Soviet Union . . . became a fully modern military power with all of the modern weapons created by science at its command. . . . [It also] partially built and partially bought abroad a merchant fleet, making it one of the world's great marine powers, as well as acquiring a jet-powered civil avaiation system fully comparable to that of any major nation. For the long run, the most important accomplishment of the first post-Stalin decade may have been its vast expansion of Soviet higher education and the rapid rise in trained personnel—particularly of scientists and technicians. . . .

Agriculture proved the [weak link in] the Soviet economy in these years. . . . All of Khrushchev's 1957 hopes for quickly providing his people with a . . . diet abundant in meat and other protein foods were dashed. Instead, in early 1964 much of the average Soviet citizen's daily bread was made from grain bought at great cost from the United States, Canada, and elsewhere. . . .

One clear thread runs through the entire complex economic record of the period we are considering. It is the consistency with which great plans have been announced with much publicity and boasting and then abandoned a few years later. This pattern began with the . . . program to raise the standard of living, a program announced in 1953 and already doomed to failure before . . . 1955. . . . The pattern continued with the Sixth Five Year Plan that was announced in early 1956, and [largely] abandoned by the end of that year. . . . Khrushchev's programs for equaling American meat production in 1960 . . . met a similar fate. And so too did the Seven Year Plan for 1959–1965. . . .

This . . . inability of Soviet leaders to see ahead perfectly even for . . . periods [of] five or seven years [raises] serious doubts about the twenty year program for economic development during 1961–1980 embodied in the Third Program of the Soviet Communist Party. That Program, adopted in October 1961, claims to provide a blueprint for putting the Soviet Union on the very threshold of the ideal Communist society by 1980, declaring in its last words: "The Party solemnly proclaims: The present generation of Soviet people will live under Communism!" In the wake of Khrushchev's removal, it might have been supposed that his successors would scrap [that program] as a prime example of [Khrushchev's] "harebrained scheming." But in their first pronouncements, at least, the Brezhnev-Kosygin team indicated their continued [reliance on] this Program. This attitude was rather obviously open to change, however.

[As for] Soviet consumers, per-capita real income is to be more than 250 per cent higher in 1980 than in 1960. The average real income per employed worker is promised to be almost double the 1960 level by 1970. What these promises mean concretely is spelled out this way [in the Third Program]:

> The entire population will be able to satisfy amply its wants for high quality and varied food products. The role of livestock products (meat, fats, eggs, dairy products) and of fruit and high-grade vegetables in the people's diet will rise substantially in the near future. The demand of all parts of the population for high quality consumer goods . . . will be generously satisfied. The output of automobiles for the public will be considerably expanded.

But this is not all that is promised. By 1970 the housing shortage is to be ended and all families living in overcrowded and poor housing are promised new apartments. By 1980 "every family, including newlyweds, will have a well-appointed apartment satisfying the needs for healthy and cultured living." . . . By 1970 the standard work week will be 35–36 hours, while minimum vacations will be increased first to three weeks and then to a month annually. By 1980, the Program promises, "The Soviet state will present to the world a model of really full and all-embracing satisfaction of the growing material and cultural requirements of mankind." . . .

The first point to be made about this ambitious set of plans is that the Soviet Union has stumbled badly in the first years following the adoption of this Program. The reduction in housing construction in the mid-1960's, the bad 1963 grain harvest, the 1962 increase in meat and butter prices —these are changes [that clash with the hopes] encouraged by the Program. Even by Soviet calculation, the country's national income increased an average of only somewhat more than 5 per cent annually during 1961–1963. But this is only about half the growth rate required to reach the 1970 goal of a national income 250 per cent that of 1960. Similarly the rate of industrial production growth during 1961–1964 has been less than that required to meet either the 1970 or 1980 goal, while agricultural output in 1963 was, as we have seen, actually less than that in 1960. That fact hardly augurs well for the goal of 150 per cent more farm production in 1970 than in 1960, despite the improved 1964 harvest.

In the light of the evidence now available, it is difficult to doubt that the relatively poor performance of the Soviet economy since 1960 has already caused the Moscow leaders quietly to abandon the Program's production goals, at least for 1970 and perhaps even for 1980. . . .

[It thus seems doubtful] that this generation of Soviet citizens will ever live in a state of Communist abundance resembling in any way the glittering [predictions made] by Karl Marx a century ago. . . . [T]he Soviet boasts that by 1970 the Soviet Union will have the world's highest standard of living and a greater industrial production than the United States [already seem hollow]. Those claims could only become reality if the United States in 1970 were in the throes of a major depression. The entire history of the years since World War II testifies eloquently to the determination of most influential political elements of the United States that such a catastrophe must be averted. As and when needed, the instruments available to assure continued economic growth and near full employment in the United States will be employed actively by the government to supplement the natural forces operating within the private economy. The Soviet Union is most unlikely to win that fervently desired economic victory over the United States during this decade.

But to state these conclusions is not to deny the likelihood that the Soviet Union will make substantial economic progress in the years ahead, including [a] rise in the standard of living of its people.

SUGGESTED READINGS

Daugherty, Marion, *Understanding Economic Growth,* pp. 24–39.
Question: What are the keys to economic growth?

____________, *Understanding Economic Growth,* pp. 40–56.
Question: What are the stages of economic growth described in this chapter?

____________, *Understanding Economic Growth,* pp. 57–110.
Question: What have been the key factors which account for rapid economic growth in the United States?

FEDERAL RESERVE BANK OF NEW YORK, *Money: Master or Servant?* pp. 1–43.
Question: What role does the Federal Reserve System play in the economy?

———, *The Story of Checks,* pp. 1–20.
Question: What role do checks play in the American economy?

FEDERAL RESERVE BANK OF PHILADELPHIA, *Inflation and/or Unemployment,* pp. 1–13.
Question: How are inflation and unemployment related to each other?

———, *The Mystery of Economic Growth,* pp. 1–10.
Question: How can an economy grow?

———, *The National Debt,* pp. 1–10.
Question: In what ways is the national debt useful? In what ways can it be dangerous?

HEILBRONER, ROBERT, *The Worldly Philosophers,* Chapter 9.
Question: What was the major contribution of John Maynard Keynes to economic theory? In what ways did he disagree with Adam Smith?

SENESH, LAWRENCE and BARBARA WARNE NEWELL, *Our Labor Force,* pp. 52–74.
Question: How does automation affect stability and growth?

THEOBALD, ROBERT, *The Rich and the Poor,* pp. 57–74.
Question: How can economic growth bring about inflation in a developing country? What are some of the ways in which such inflation could be controlled?

Unit Seven

In Conclusion

FAR FROM TRYING to teach you all that is known about economics, this course has mainly tried to teach the language of economists, a few of their key principles, and, above all, something about their way of thinking. By now, you should know the problems that concern economists, the concepts with which economists try to understand those problems, and some of the ways economists try to solve those problems. In part, economics is an abstract science—a mathematical equation like $GNP = C + I + G$, for example, can be applied to any economy in the world. But economics is also a behavorial science—a study of human behavior as men and women go about trying to solve the problem of scarcity. For that reason, this course has presented factual material about existing economies, both to teach you something about the economies of the world, and to give you facts to which you can apply the concepts which economists use. But it has also shown how one's values shape the way he sees those facts.

This final unit draws together some of the chief facts and concepts with which we have been concerned—and applies them to the question of values, which was introduced in Chapter 1.

59 Which Economy Is Best?

We conclude as we began, with the matter of values. But now, having studied the three types of economic systems, we should have more facts and concepts on which to base our conclusions. As you read the following imaginary interview, keep the following questions in mind:

1. What are the explicit and the implicit values of the three speakers?
2. On what issues do the three speakers agree? On what issues do they disagree? Why?
3. How might an Eskimo disagree with Miss Ishwar? How might he disagree with Messrs. Anderson and Rozanov?

A Short Discussion of an Eternal Question

MODERATOR: Good evening. *House of Wisdom* is pleased to welcome Mr. C. B. Anderson, an Iowa newspaper editor; Mr. Z. K. Rozanov, an economist in Gosplan; and Miss V. S. Ishwar, a member of the Parliament of India. Our topic this week is, "What Is a Good Society?" Mr. Rozanov, will you begin?

ROZANOV: Certainly. Clearly, the good society must be one that is good for the masses of the people and not just for the favored few. This means that there can be no exploitation of labor by private ownership of capital. Capitalist owners have no interest in using the nation's resources in ways that are best for the nation. They seek only profits. And the good society must put people above profits.

ANDERSON: Now wait a minute—you're assuming that——

ROZANOV: You wait. You'll have your chance. My American friend is stung, evidently because he senses that in spite of its wealth, his own society still has millions of poor people. And its annual rate of growth is so slow as to recall to my mind an old Russian proverb——

ANDERSON: I object! Mr. Rozanov isn't describing my country as it really is; he's describing it as the Communist Party tells him to. Let him come and see for himself. He'll see that the average American lives far better than the average Russian. No society has ever produced so much for so many.

ROZANOV: I have seen pictures of your "good society"—with its automobile graveyards and its neon signs and its disgusting rock-and-rolling dances. You spend much of your resources on wasteful and frivolous junk. You don't produce what the people really need.

ANDERSON: How do you figure that? If you ask me, a good society is a society that gives the individual consumer the freedom to choose what *he* thinks is best for himself. That's the strength of our society. The consumers decide what's going to be produced—they don't leave it up to you and your fellow planners.

ROZANOV: I suggest that you might not want to dismiss planning so cavalierly. A good society needs rapid growth. And we're growing faster through planning than your tired economy is growing without planning.
ANDERSON: Ten years ago, I might have been forced to agree with you, Mr. Rozanov. But we're matching you in the 1960's. So let's wait and see whether your reported long-run growth rate is real and not just a trick with statistics. Let's see whether you keep on growing so fast in the next fifty years. And let's see whether your growth really means anything for the average consumer.
ISHWAR: I've been listening to both of you gentlemen, and I get the impression that you think the good society is the wealthiest and the fastest growing one. Is that all there is to it?
ROZANOV: Of course not. We said that you also have to ask how the wealth is shared——
ANDERSON: And we asked what the growth is used for—is it for the consumers or merely for the state?
ISHWAR: I see. Then I will have to assume that you both think my society is not good. Everybody knows that Indians are poor. And yet, despite our great problems, I think of our society as being a good one—and on the way to becoming still better.
MODERATOR: Well, do you think that India will follow either the Russian or the American paths to improvement?
ISHWAR: The best answer to that question came from our beloved Mahatma Gandhi. He said, "I want the winds of all nations to blow through my house, but I don't want to be swept off my feet by any of them." We want material things, of course. We want an end to starvation and homelessness. And we are learning from the experiences of both the United States and the Soviet Union. But we have our own values. We will insist that the good society has to have more than material wealth.
ROZANOV: Ah, but we agree! We have never said that man lives by bread alone.
ANDERSON: We agree too. We're concerned about the quality of American life. Why we have more symphony orchestras than——
ISHWAR: You both say you agree. But so much that you do reflects an all-consuming race for economic goods. You quarrel with each other not about who is doing the most for man's spirit but about who is doing the most for man's stomach.
ANDERSON: We don't just quarrel about stomachs. We're also in conflict about freedom—economic freedom.
ROZANOV: Freedom! I would be pleased to hear from Mr. Anderson what use a good society can make of the freedom to be unemployed.
ANDERSON: And I will be pleased to tell you that a good society can make a lot of use of the freedom to work where you want, the freedom to go into a business and make a profit—or suffer a loss, and the freedom to be able to spend your income on the goods you want to have—not on what the state thinks you ought to have.

ISHWAR: But all of this is materialism again.

ANDERSON: Not so. An American can choose to spend his money on fine books or paintings or just in going to an uncrowded ocean beach to sit and think. Material wealth can broaden us. It doesn't have to interfere with spiritual values.

MODERATOR: Miss Ishwar, what does economic freedom mean to you as an Indian?

ISHWAR: That is not an easy question. Only twenty-five years ago, we were fighting for our political freedom. And now we're fighting for economic freedom—freedom from hunger. And I'm not sure if we have any right to talk about other kinds of economic freedom so long as men's stomachs are empty.

ROZANOV: We agree. And that is why Communism is the best system for poor nations that have cut the fetters of colonialism.

ISHWAR: Your rapid progress is well known to us, Mr. Rozanov. But even while we are hungry, we want to conquer hunger through politically democratic ways. And we want to grow in a way that never permits material wealth to destroy spiritual values. We don't want India turning into a copy of the United States *or* the Soviet Union. We want to preserve our traditions and our own Indian way of life.

MODERATOR: You seem both to want growth and to fear it.

ISHWAR: That may well be true. Economic growth has never been a part of our hopes until very recently. Today's average Indian doesn't live much better than the average Indian of 4,000 years ago. And many of the factories we've seen in our country have made a few men rich while exploiting the workers. Gandhi taught us that industrialization, at least on the mass scale of the West, is evil because it makes one man rich at the expense of others.

ANDERSON: But our society disproves it. No one denies that the early days of industrialism were no county fair. But workingmen formed unions, and now more than half of them live in suburbs and are doing very well indeed. Some people get more than others—but that's been true of every society in history—including yours, Mr. Rozanov.

ROZANOV: In our country, no one starves and everybody has a job, while your capitalism has never defeated unemployment.

ANDERSON: I'll admit it's a problem for us. But in the last few years, we've been doing something about it. Another characteristic of a good society is that it knows its problems and admits them. We want full employment in the United States, but we also want as little government interference as possible. Those goals sometimes clash. We could probably maintain full employment if we had complete central planning, but I doubt if we'd want to pay that price. We're trying to stabilize our growing economy, but we also want to keep it free.

ISHWAR: You gentlemen have brought up one area in which India seeks its own path. To the Russians, government is the central organizer and the chief agency for building a good society. In America, government seems to be viewed as a necessary evil—something to turn to only when there is no other choice. The Indians seek a middle path—a combination of the free economy and the planned economy.

MODERATOR: Mankind has been arguing these issues for hundreds of years, so it's no surprise to me that we've reached no final answers. "What is the good society?" seems to be one of those questions that can never be answered by a dictionary or a textbook, because there is no single right answer. But I would like to thank the three of you for joining us, because you have attacked the question with intelligence and knowledge—and nothing is so dull as a discussion of an eternal question in which no one knows what he is talking about. Good night.

60 The Road Ahead

Having examined the three types of economies in the past and in the present, we will take a brief look at the future. As we noted before, economics is not an exact science. An economist cannot predict the future of an economy with the same confidence that a physicist can predict that a heavy object will fall toward the center of the earth. What follows, then, are only the author's educated guesses. Their purpose is not to tell you what is going to happen to the economies of the world, but rather to stimulate you to make your own estimates—based on the fifty-nine earlier readings—about what lies ahead of us.

As you read, keep the following questions in mind:

1. What are the author's explicit and implicit values? How do they differ from your own?
2. How do you think the economy of the United States will change in the next fifty years? How would you like to see it change?
3. How do you think the economy of the Soviet Union will change in the next fifty years? How would you like to see it change?

One Economist's Opinions

No one economic system seems likely to sweep the whole world.

Men differ too much, their resources vary too widely, and times are changing too rapidly for any one economic system to become universally acceptable or pratical. No one has yet identified any single clear "wave of the future" for all mankind.

No one system will appear to be "best" to all men.

There are values held in common by many peoples around the world—but there are also significant differences in the values men and women attach to such ideas as political freedom, economic progress, and the just distribution of goods and services. Given these differences, people will see their own economic system very differently from the way in which outsiders will see that same system.

All of the rapidly growing economies have emphasized individual incentives to some degree.

The United States is far from being alone in emphasizing individual incentives in guiding its economy. The United Kingdom, most Western European nations, Canada, Israel, Australia, and Japan have all pursued somewhat similar policies. And the Soviet Union, after years of denouncing individual materialism, is introducing incentives into some parts of its economic life.

All of the strong industrial nations have shown themselves ready to reshape economic institutions in order to redistribute some part of their wealth towards the poorest of their citizens.

The contagious idea of the last decades of this century appears to be that of equality of opportunity for all citizens. The record to date is blurred, but the grip of the idea upon men's imaginations seems solid. It shows up in the civil rights struggles and the War on Poverty in the United States, in the Soviet Union's modified policies towards distribution, and in the aid which industrial powers have begun to extend to the least developed parts of the world.

No economic system has yet licked the problem of scarcity.

Even in the wealthiest of nations, man's capacity to want more goods and services outruns the capacity of the system to produce more goods and services. Economic activity, in all types of economic systems, continues to involve the age-old game of allocating relatively scarce resources among relatively unlimited ends or desires.

All of the world's economies face a common concern: rapidly rising world population.

Historians of the future may sadly note that in the last half of the twentieth century, man finally developed the know-how to eliminate poverty, only to find that the effects of that achievement were all but canceled by rapidly rising population. A struggle for resources seems inescapable in the future.

No economic system can any longer stand in isolation from the others.

World events, from the peaceful opening of more trade relations to the development of intercontinental missiles with nuclear warheads, have thrown all nations into closer touch with one another. Economic systems are likely to keep competing with one another, but there will also have to be patterns of cooperation lest the competition lead to mutual destruction.

No economic system can afford to stand still.

Events and circumstances change so rapidly from year to year that every economy interested in progress has had to reshape its economic institutions time and time again in response to new needs and new opportunities. That pattern of unending change seems inevitable for the future. The economies of tomorrow may resemble those of today only in that they will still face the problem of scarcity and the questions of what, how, and for whom to produce.

Index

Italicized page numbers preceded by *c* refer to a chart.
Boldface page numbers refer to definitions of economic terms.